M000043104

THE NATURE OF CALIFORNIA

THE NATURE *of* CALIFORNIA

RACE, CITIZENSHIP,
AND FARMING SINCE
THE DUST BOWL

Sarah D. Wald

University of Washington Press
Seattle and London

© 2016 by the University of Washington Press
Printed and bound in the United States of America
Composed in Chaparral, a typeface designed by Carol Twombly
20 19 18 17 16   5 4 3 2 1

All rights reserved. No part of this publication may be reproduced or transmit-
ted in any form or by any means, electronic or mechanical, including photocopy,
recording, or any information storage or retrieval system, without permission in
writing from the publisher.

UNIVERSITY OF WASHINGTON PRESS
www.washington.edu/uwpress

Library of Congress Cataloging-in-Publication Data
Names: Wald, Sarah D., author.
Title: The nature of California : race, citizenship, and farming since the Dust
    Bowl / Sarah D. Wald.
Description: Seattle : University of Washington Press, 2016. | Includes biblio-
    graphical references and index.
Identifiers: LCCN 2015042762 | ISBN 9780295995663 (hardcover : acid-free pa-
    per) | ISBN 9780295995670 (pbk. : acid-free paper)
Subjects: LCSH: American literature—20th century—History and criticism. |
    Agriculture in literature. | National characteristics, American, in literature.
    | Citizenship in literature. | Race in literature. | Nature in literature. |
    Ecocriticism. | American literature—21st century—History and criticism. |
    California—In literature.
Classification: LCC PS228.A52 W35 2016 | DDC 810.9/35879405—dc23
LC record available at http://lccn.loc.gov/2015042762

The paper used in this publication is acid-free and meets the minimum requirements of American National Standard for Information Sciences—Permanence of
Paper for Printed Library Materials, ANSI Z39.48–1984.∞

To Celia Wald (1946–1992) and Alan Wald

Yes, I will be a writer and make all of you live again in my words.

—Carlos Bulosan, *America Is in the Heart: A Personal History*

Contents

Acknowledgments

I am fortunate to have participated in a number of intellectual communities marked by overwhelming generosity. Appropriate acknowledgment of everyone who assisted me with this project seems impossible.

This project would not have been possible without support, insight, and guidance from Ralph E. Rodriguez and Arlene Keizer. My scholarship is stronger because of advice and encouragement from Matthew Garcia and Karl Jacoby. Thank you to Mireya Loza, Aiko Takeuchi-Demirci, Janet Fiskio, Sarah Jaquette Ray, Joni Adamson, Susanna Bohme, Tara Fickle, Sara Fingal, Gillian Frank, Margaret Konkol, Eric D. Larson, Heather Lee, Stephanie LeMenager, David Vázquez, and Jeannie Shinozuka for reading and commenting on manuscript drafts, sometimes more than once, and sometimes with little turnaround time. Marcia Chatelain, Elise Dubord, Gabriel Mendes, Julie Weise, and Susanne Wiedemann offered invaluable professional guidance about the writing and publishing process. Conversations with Mike Amezcua, Senia Barragan, Mark Bray, Thomas Chen, Joseph Clark, Erin Curtis, Lori Flores, Caroline Frank, Elizabeth Hoover, Karen Inouye, Melanie Kohnen, Wendy Lee, Monica Martinez, Julie Avril Minich, Salma Monani, Gabriela Nuñez, Malgorzata Rymsza-Pawlowska, Felicia Salinas-Moniz, Sarah Seidman, Mario Sifuentez, Priscilla Solis Ybarra, and Brett Werner mark my work as well. This book was written because of the support of multiple writing groups, including a writing accountability group organized by Michelle LaFrance and a summer writing group organized by Laura Arnold Leibman. I will always cherish the members of this book's first writing group: Angela Mazaris, Jessica Johnson, and Liza Burbank-Glib.

I have presented portions of this manuscript at numerous conferences, and the feedback I received from fellow panelists and audience members was invaluable. I am grateful to Paula Moya, Matthew Garcia, and Bill Johnson González for invitations to the Interdisciplinary Working Group in Critical Theory at Stanford, Guest Workers: Western Origins, Global Futures at the Huntington Library, and Opening the Archive: Bracero Program Symposium at DePaul University, respectfully. I especially appreciate the insightful response David Stentiford wrote to my work. Thank you to Priscilla Wald and Sean X. Goudie for organizing the First Book Institute, where I received valuable feedback from Bartholomew Brinkman, Natalia Cecire, Joy A. J. Howard, Carrie Hyde, Molly Pulda, Jillian Sayre, Grant Wythoff, and Michelle Huang. I have also learned a great deal from conversations with the graduate and undergraduate students I have taught over the years.

Archivists and librarians at Stanford University, UCLA, the University of Washington, and the Walter P. Reuther Library at Wayne State University have treated me with incredible generosity. Bill Johnson González, Don Mitchell, and Mireya Loza charitably shared with me archival materials they collected. The Historical Society of Southern California supported my research on chapters 3 and 4. This volume's publication was supported in part by grants from the Association for the Study of Literature and Environment (ASLE) and from the University of Oregon's Oregon Humanities Center and College of Arts and Sciences. I am grateful for their support. Christina Ocampo spent a summer acquiring Galarza-related documents for me and organizing my messy archival files, which saved me much time in the revision process. Thank you to Marc Grossman and Mary Mecartney of the United Farm Workers, Estelle Carole, Favianna Rodriguez, Culture Strike, and Marilyn Sanders for graciously allowing me to reprint artwork and photographs. Thank you to Kathleen Emery Schmeling for facilitating my use of the UFW artwork, and to Jeanne Brewster for facilitating the use of my articles by Routledge and Brill. I am grateful to Brill, Routledge, and *Food, Culture, and Society* for allowing me to reprint portions of my manuscript that appeared first in their publications.

I cannot thank enough colleagues from Brown University, Wheaton College, Drew University, the University of Louisville, and the University of Oregon for fostering collegial and intellectually vibrant spaces in which I thrived. I especially want to thank Tom Byers, Fred Curtis, Alan Dickman, Karen Ford, Susan Griffin, Sandra Jamieson, Laurel Kearns, Wendy Kolmar, Amy Koritz, Lisa Lebduska, Bob Lee, Glynis Ridley, Peggy Samuels, Susan Smulyan, and Sara Webb. Administrative staffs at Drew University, the University of Louisville, and the University of Oregon have been my personal heroes, including Kate Eggleston, RaDonna Koble, Alison Mildrexler, Marilyn Reid, Caroline Stephens, Gayla Wardwell, and Taylor West. The guidance that Anne Baker, Jackie Dirks, Laura Arnold Leibman, and Pancho Savery provided to me as a Reed undergraduate molded my interdisciplinary approach to intellectual and political projects.

Thank you to Ranjit Arab. I could not have asked for a better editor. His advice has expanded this project's scope and improved its readability. I am grateful for all of the hard work of the University of Washington Press staff in bringing this book to fruition, especially that of my copy editor, Kerrie Maynes. Thank you to the anonymous reviewers of this manuscript and of the articles that fed into chapters of this manuscript. My scholarship benefited tremendously from the time and effort they put into reviewing my work.

Friends inside and outside of my academic circles provided me with emotional and intellectual support. Thank you to Teeb Al-Samarrai, Corine Ball, Andrew Baron, Marc Boglioli, Angie Calder, Joslyn Cassady, Carol Chang, Amy Clukey, Julian Dautremont-Smith, Allan Dawson, Lauren Donovan, Greg and Mary Dyson, Megan Fischer, Brian Frank, Zac Ginsberg, Mindy Goorchenko, Amy Harwood, Marie Knapp, Sue Ellen Kroll, Jisun Lee, Jeannette Lee-Parikh, Ben Levy, Kim Marks, Carley McNeice, Ryan Mickels, Kyung Park, Katie Prevost, Melissa Quintela, Erica Rand, Missy Rohs, Luke Schram, Gina Shedid, Erin Snyder, Tarra Wong, Amie Wright, Kyla Zaret, and Audrey and Jon Zunkel-DeCoursey for conversations, encouragement, and enjoyable distractions. Thank you to Chris and Barney Connolly and Terry and Cayenne Yarnell, who allowed me to huddle in a corner with a laptop working during more holidays than I can count. Thank you also to everyone at Bark for their work protecting the forests, waters, and wildlife of Mount Hood National Forest.

Thank you to my family, especially Hannah Wald, Angela Dillard, Debbie Tribett, Mike Wald, Sharon Krauss, and Cindy and Ovide Pomerleau, and to family no longer with us, my mother Celia Wald and grandparents Dorothy and Quentin Stodola and Ruth and Haskell Wald. I offer special acknowledgment to my father Alan, who fueled my interest in ecocriticism by sending me Lawrence Buell's *The Environmental Imagination* when I was a high school junior, suggested I might consider American Studies as an undergraduate degree, and provided support and feedback as I navigated the world of academia.

Caleb Connolly patiently listened to me read chapter after chapter out loud. The readability of this book is testament to his perseverance. Whenever deadlines began looming on the horizon, he took over additional household duties, freeing up more time for my writing. Never have the words "Don't worry about it. I'll take care of it. Just work on your book," been more romantic. Thank you to Akya Sackos-Connolly, a tiger who adds joy to each day and impresses me with her capacity for empathy and the determination and creativity she brings to every task.

THE NATURE OF CALIFORNIA

"To the Farmer in All of Us"

Agricultural Citizenship as Racial Gatekeeping

L ONESOME BATTERED FARMHOUSES STAND AMONG THE FLAT
fields of the plains. White men with calloused hands and weathered
skin stare off into the distance, expressions of resignation on their
hardy faces. A US flag hangs behind a dirty window in a wood house, farm
equipment visible in the background. A picture of a pickup truck appears
behind the dedication "To the farmer in all of us." Dodge Ram aired this
Super Bowl commercial in 2013. In it, radio broadcaster Paul Harvey's 1978
"God Made a Farmer" speech overlays a montage of photographs of farmers
and US agricultural landscapes. This advertisement is one of many contemporary texts that draw on a long-standing cultural investment in the
white male farmer as the quintessential and ideal US citizen. It suggests
that the United States still strives to be a nation filled with independent
farmers whose hard labor in the earth earns the nation God's blessings. The
commercial conveys a nostalgia for the rugged individualism of America's
past that it suggests we can regain if we just buy the right truck. The Dodge
Ram, the ad implies, is the proper truck to restore the "farmer in all of us."
As this popular commercial exemplifies, the white male farmer remains a
paragon of US citizenship and national integrity even as the actual number
of US citizens who work in agriculture has steeply declined over the course
of the twentieth century.[1] In the twenty-first-century United States, access
to agrarian virtue does not require actual agrarian labor. The Dodge Ram ad
transfers the prestige of farming to consumer purchasing practices.

Around the same time that this commercial aired, the United Farm
Workers (UFW) initiated a social media campaign titled "Take Our Jobs."
This campaign sought to counter the widespread belief that undocumented

3

workers were responsible for the high unemployment rates among residents with US legal status, including citizens. The UFW's campaign points out that the US food supply chain depends on undocumented workers completing agricultural labor that US citizens refuse to do. Its website offers to help any US legal resident or citizen seeking employment as a farm laborer gain the skills they need to take these jobs.[2] Comedian Stephen Colbert participated in the campaign in a two-part segment of *The Colbert Report*. In his attempt to "prove I've got the right stuff to take back farm working jobs for Americans," Colbert unsuccessfully endeavors to build boxes, pack corn, and pick beans alongside skilled Latina/o workers. The audience laughs at Colbert's follies, and ultimately Colbert retreats to playing Farmville (an online game) in the fields while around him Latinas/os continue to labor.[3]

The UFW's campaign upends a logic that blames undocumented and nonwhite laborers for the economic precariousness of the white middle and working classes. By exposing the disdain white people hold for actual stoop labor, as opposed to the idea of farming, the UFW writes undocumented individuals into the nation. Their campaign reclassifies the labor of unauthorized migrants as necessary for the nation. White peoples' unwillingness to complete essential but difficult work establishes the national need for nonwhite workers as laborers. The usefulness of Latinas/os as sources of exploitable labor is the primary rationale the campaign provides for US immigration reform. Through his performance of expected incompetence, Colbert fulfills the script that the UFW social media campaign set out to prove: undocumented farmworkers do work that it is unthinkable and even laughable to imagine white US citizens undertaking.

At the same moment that Dodge Ram urged US viewers to identify with the farmer inside themselves, Stephen Colbert and the UFW point out the ludicrousness of the white American male stooping to pick US crops. How do two such representations of agricultural labor exist simultaneously? How can the idea of farming being a sacred calling, the occupation that establishes the virtuous character of the true American citizen, continue to resonate in a culture that also perceives actual agrarian labor as beneath white US citizens and as the natural domain of undocumented laborers? How can the imagined ideal American citizen be both a farmer and someone who eschews the physical demands of actual agricultural work? And why is farming and farm labor still one of the primary places to which we turn to sort out who is and who should be an American?

This book is the story of the paradoxical ways farmers and farmworkers in California from the Great Depression to the start of the twenty-first century have been represented. It examines the ways that textual depictions of farming and farm labor have never been only about those who labor in the earth but have also presented a place to think through questions of national belonging. To look at representations of farm labor is to read the story of the nation, national belonging, and national exclusion. Farm labor helps us understand who is allowed to belong to the nation and in what ways.

A shared cultural logic produces both sentimentalized depictions of the white farmer as the iconic US citizen and representations of Asian and Latina/o farmworkers as "abject aliens," individuals whose labor is necessary for the nation while their humanity is rendered alien and excluded.[4] The white citizen farmer and the abject alien farm laborer are subject constructions that rely on a common set of beliefs about land ownership and racialized labor hierarchies originating in the United States' legacy of slavery and settler colonialism.[5] The white landowning farmer persists as the ideal US citizen only in relation to representations of the nonwhite farm laborer as abject alien.[6]

Throughout the twentieth century, Anglo Americans, Japanese Americans, Mexican Americans, and Filipinos, among others, have navigated these broader racialized constructions of agricultural labor and land ownership in their narrative depictions of farm labor. In doing so, they have often used figurative language from nature to depict farmers or farm laborers as "naturally" being part of the nation. In such texts, depictions of nature and landscape sometimes serve to contest the exclusionary racial gate keeping of the nation by suggesting the natural belonging of excluded groups. At other times, they consolidate the nation's racial gate keeping, as when a racialized group claims the status of farm owner through an affirmation of others as abject aliens. Occasionally, such narratives deploy representations of nature to contest the naturalness of the nation itself and its legitimacy as a gatekeeper for legal, economic, and cultural belonging. Studying agrarian narratives helps identify the cultural logic through which various groups are written into and out of the nation, as well as the roles nature and land ownership play in the way we envision national be-longing. *The Nature of California* deepens our historical and contemporary understandings of racialized citizenship and alienage by helping explain the continuing cultural power of agriculture as a primary marker of one's relation to the nation. It draws from ethnic studies scholars' knowledge of immigration and citizenship and from environmental humanities schol-ars' work on race and nature.

CULTURAL CONTEXTS FOR CULTIVATION

Farming has long been linked with national identity. In the United States, this association goes back at least as far as the writings of Thomas Jeffer-son and J. Hector St. John Crévecoeur. Contemporary ideas about race in agriculture have their origin at least partly in the words of these two early American authors. Placing Jefferson's and Crévecoeur's ideas in the context of changing US immigration and citizenship law helps explain the ways agricultural labor has become weighted with a shifting complex of ideas about racialized national belonging.

The virtue bestowed upon the American farmer draws its strength from the legacy of Jefferson. Jefferson's Query XIX in *Notes on the State of Virginia* (1785) envisions a nation of small farmers. Just as Dodge Ram claimed "God Made a Farmer," so too Jefferson felt that "those who labor in the earth are the chosen people of God."[7] Jefferson depicts such cultivators as embodying a particular type of virtue, explaining, "Corruption of morals in the mass of cultivators is a phenomenon of which no age nor nation has furnished an example."[8] It is farmers' freedom from dependence that creates their virtue. Farmers, Jefferson contends, are economically independent. Their economic independence allows for political independence, since they are self-reliant, owing no debts. Farmers thus provide the bedrock of US de-mocracy, a notion known as Jeffersonian agrarianism.

Jefferson imbued his agrarian vision with implicit, and often unrecog-nized, ideas about race that remain at work in representations of farm labor today.[9] The plantation slave is an unwritten subject that haunts Jefferson's vision of the free and independent farmer in Query XIX. The slave lacks the independence of Jefferson's small farmer, and thus also lacks the ability to participate as a full citizen of the nation. While the query does not explicitly mention slavery, it enforces a logic that places slaves outside of citizenship and incapable of participating in democracy. The slave, in Jeffersonian agrarianism, lacks the inherent virtue of the farmer and is not one of the chosen people of God. The virtue of the ideal American in Jefferson's vision, a virtue upon which democracy depends, requires an understanding of citizens as white, free, and landowning. It is in the contrast between the slave and the farmer that the category of white citizenship gains its meaning. The opposition between free white citizen land owners and unfree nonwhite noncitizen laborers persists in depictions of farmers and farmworkers today. Today, Jefferson's racial scripts built around black slavery have been reactivated in relationship to undocumented Latina/o laborers.[10] The black plantation slave and the undocumented Latina/o stoop laborer perform a similar cultural function in the way they invest the white farmer with a complex of racial privilege, moral virtue, and citizenship rights.

Scholars who study citizenship provide a set of terms and ideas through which we can better conceptualize these recurring racial figures of the farmer and the farmworker. The American farmer stands in for what scholars have termed the abstract person or universal citizen. The abstract person or universal citizen is an ideal. It is the disembodied abstraction of citizenship that renders the presumed whiteness and maleness of the citizen invisible. This invisibility allows the position of the citizen to appear to be universal. The abstract person as universal citizen receives the promises of equality before the law. Yet because society's construction of race renders whiteness and masculinity as invisible, the nonwhite nonmale subject becomes embodied and marked as different. The nonwhite nonmale subject exists outside of, or on the margins of, universality. An embodied subject is denied the equality promised to the universal citizen or abstract person.[11] The abstract person is universal; the gender, race, and citizenship status of the abstract person are presumed and not seen. For example, a particular farmer may be white, male, and propertied, but society, in seeing such markers as normal and universal, renders them invisible. The farmer, in US culture, exists as a stand-in for the universal citizen and abstract person. Yet farmworkers, like slaves, are inherently embodied. Their race, gender, class, and citizenship status are marked. Thus, they cannot access easily or universally the abstract quality of US democracy.

Consequently, it matters a great deal whether someone is allowed to be a farmer. Who can access the privileges of universal citizenship and for whom is such privilege a legal and cultural impossibility? Can a farmworker ever become a farmer? Under what circumstances might that happen? This access to universal citizenship and full participation in the nation is what is at stake in many of the stories about farmers and farm labor I consider in this book. Can the racialized subject, the abject alien, ever gain access to the promises of universal citizenship and abstract personhood? If so, how?

US literature has long depicted farming as a transformative act, hence its appeal as a trope for immigrant and nonwhite authors. Crévecoeur, in *Letters from an American Farmer* (1782), uses farming to explain the possibility of the immigrant becoming American. Crévecoeur postulates that in the United States, "individuals of all nations are melted into a new race of men."[12] He continues, "Men are like plants; the goodness and flavour of the fruit proceeds from the peculiar soil and exposition in which they grow."[13] In Crévecoeur's vision, immigrants leave behind the characteristics of their many nations of origin to gain a shared American character as they are shaped by both the material land and the cultural milieu of the colonies. This simile provides a cultural counterpart for the legal concept of naturalization, the process by which a noncitizen becomes a citizen.[14] Men become part of a nation in their character and culture as they are planted in a new soil, take root, and grow. Despite being born outside of the United States, their roots have been firmly replanted, taking hold in the new land. Priscilla Wald has defined naturalization as "the conversion of something foreign— words and phrases, beliefs and practices—into something familiar or native."[15] In Crévecoeur's description, nature offers the figurative explanation for how that conversion takes place.

Through Crévecoeur's figurative language, the legal process of naturalization merges with a strategy environmental cultural studies scholar Noël Sturgeon terms "the politics of the natural."[16] We engage the politics of the natural when we deploy images of nature to claim particular behaviors or identities (race, class, gender, sexuality) as natural or unnatural. Claims that homosexuality is natural because penguins are thought to exhibit homosexual behaviors, for example, rely on the politics of the natural. Politicians readily draw on such forms of cultural logic. When they do so, they turn simultaneously to the biological and the divine. Nature, whether ruled by evolutionary logic or God's authority, is given moral legitimacy outside of the human. Identities or behaviors that are historically constituted, socially constructed, and generally in flux become seen as absolute, universal, and always already existing. The politics of the natural suggests that whatever is natural is the way that things should be and that to deviate from them is to violate the will of God or the laws of science.[17] Claiming to belong (at least figuratively) to the natural environment of the United States is one way to claim national belonging.

In the case of Crévecoeur, the figurative language of nature, describing men as plants, explains how the process of naturalization works. One gains Americanness by becoming part of the social, political, and environmental fabric of the nation. By planting roots deep in the American soil, the immigrant becomes part of the nation, shaped by the earth in which he is now rooted. Crévecoeur, writing at a moment in which the United States had not been accepted as a separate sovereignty, uses the language of nature to create a possibility for new immigrants, a move that retains ideological resonance today. Through transplantation, in Crévecoeur's view, immigrants can be naturalized. They can become native to the continent and to the country. Crévecoeur's vision recurs in the writing of many twentieth- and twenty-first-century immigrant advocates. *The Nature of California* points out the frequency with which authors, advocates, and other cultural workers throughout the twentieth century deploy the politics of the natural to establish the national belonging of groups denied legal naturalization or whose legal citizenship the state or civil society fail to fully recognize.

Starting in the late nineteenth century, the state and civil society denied many immigrants the power of legal or cultural naturalization. They considered some immigrants as inassimilable, perpetual foreigners racially unable to adapt to the requirements of US citizenship. Restrictive US immigration laws were formed in the cauldron of eugenicist thought in which lawmakers understood race as a stable biological category and races as existing in relational hierarchies. As historian Mae Ngai has argued, these "restrictive immigration laws produced new categories of racial differences."[18] In the century following the Civil War, ideas about US citizenship were remade in relation to concerns about Asian and Mexican immigration.

Understanding the barriers to legal and cultural naturalization that Asians and Latinas/os in the United States faced helps explain how and why such groups and their advocates turned to the ideas of Jefferson and Crévecoeur as they deployed the politics of the natural in their textual representations of farm labor. Much of the country's immigration apparatus was established because of the perceived impossibility of Asian assimilation. The United States' first immigration laws targeted the Chinese. In 1882, the Chinese Exclusion Act barred most Chinese immigration and prohibited Chinese naturalization. As Erika Lee says, "The Exclusion Act marks the first time in American history that the United States barred a group of immigrants because of its race and class."[19] This legislation codified the federal government's racial gate keeping. The Chinese Exclusion Act and later legislation that extended and strengthened it created the system of immigration restriction and border regulations with which we are familiar today, including the formation of the US Immigration and Naturalization Service (now Immigrations and Customs Enforcement), the creation of passports, and the development of a deportation apparatus. With the passage of the Chinese Exclusion Act, the Chinese became, in effect, the United States' very first "illegal immigrants."[20] Chinese exclusion, the result of anti-Chinese agitation in the US West, set the pattern for exclusion and antinaturalization efforts targeting other Asian groups, especially Japanese immigrants.[21] A series of court cases in the early twentieth century maintained Asian immigrants' racial ineligibility to become naturalized US citizens.[22]

In 1924, the Johnson-Reed Immigration Act became the law of the land, reasserting Asians' legal inability to naturalize as well as severely limiting the entry of Southern and Eastern Europeans, many of whom were Jewish. The 1924 Immigration Act did not just exclude groups of individuals deemed undesirable. The way it conceived of citizenship and race expanded and consolidated the category of whiteness in the United States. The act wrote previously denigrated European ethnic groups into the nation's racial fabric. Even as it created a hierarchy of national desirability for Europeans, the law affirmed the legal whiteness of all European groups.[23] It defined these European groups against the perceived inassimilability of Asian immigrants and against changing understandings of Mexicans as "illegal" entrants to the United States. Whereas the law and its implementation collapsed the categories of race and national origins for Asians and Mexicans, averring the inability of Japanese Americans, Chinese Americans, and Mexican Americans to be seen as truly American, it reduced the marks of ethnic hierarchy within the United States, considering Italian Americans and German Americans, for example, as equally white.[24]

Whereas historians of Asian immigration read the 1924 Immigration Act as the culmination of anti-Asian sentiment, historians of the Mexican experience in the United States perceive the act as the start of a period in which Mexican racialization was transformed. While the act placed no numerical limits on Mexican immigration, the act's enforcement provisions, such as visa requirements, rendered previously legal Mexican immigration an illegal act. By the end of the 1920s, Mexicans had become the largest group of unauthorized entrants in the United States. Starting in this period, US immigration law produced the status of Mexicans and Mexican Americans as an "illegal" people.[25] Mexicans and Mexican Americans became seen as permanent strangers in what was once their native land.[26]

The creation of "illegal" Mexican immigration to the United States responded to a long-standing contradiction between capitalism's need for cheap labor and nationalist desires for racial homogeneity. Mexicans during this period were classified legally as white, but they were not treated as white. They could become US citizens, but they rarely opted to do so. Prior to the 1924 Immigration Act, Mexicans were perceived as being less threatening to the nation than either Asian or Jewish immigrants because they were perceived as transitory. The state, media, and businesses did not represent Mexicans as trying to make the United States their home and instead presented them as a controllable, docile labor force, even as their actual history of strikes, unionization efforts, and protests belied this widespread belief.[27] The 1924 Immigration Act effectively encouraged Mexican immigration, while rendering Mexicans as easily deportable and thus disposable. This addressed concerns about the racial makeup of the nation as well as provided agribusiness and other industries with a strategy for labor control.[28] The racial script in which undocumented Latina/o labor is deemed necessary to the nation but at the same time unwanted and excluded was forged in this period.

According to immigration historians such as Natalia Molina and Mae Ngai, ideas about race, citizenship, and immigration were remade between 1924 and 1965, with Asian Americans and Latinas/os taking center stage in the national discourse.[29] *The Nature of California* encompasses much of this time period and focuses on a relational reading of Asian American and Latina/o racial formation. Turning to literary representations of farm labor allows us to see the ways the transformation in the two racial projects occurred side by side as well as some of the ways Japanese Americans, Filipinos, and Mexican Americans challenged these changing racial formations. It helps explain the continuing appeal of Jeffersonian and Crévecoeurian narratives in twentieth-century Asian American and Latina/o literary and cultural production by examining the roles ideologies of land and nature played in these racial projects.

RACE AND NATURE

Throughout the twentieth century, anxieties about racial purity coexisted with concerns about preserving the "pure" state of nature. The economic, political, and cultural contexts that shaped immigration policy in the United States also molded federal approaches to land and nature. As environmentally oriented scholars have shown, discourses about wilderness reinforced popular perceptions that nonwhite and foreign populations threatened the nation. By bringing this ecocritical analysis of race and wilderness to agriculture, *The Nature of California* reveals the ways ideas about race and immigration structured beliefs about farmland as much as they did wilderness. This approach contributes to immigration history and citizenship studies by emphasizing the centrality of land and nature to the racial formation of the citizen and the alien. It reveals the role of nature in the nation's racial gatekeeping.

The Nature of California is part of an emerging nexus of environmental cultural scholarship concerned with the relationship between the social construction of race and the social construction of nature. In the past, activists and academics criticized environmental literary studies for its bias toward both whiteness and wilderness.[30] Early works of ecocriticism focused disproportionately on nonfictional prose in which a white man encounters nature, such as Henry David Thoreau's *Walden* or Edward Abbey's *Desert Sol-*

itaire. Lawrence Buell has termed this older iteration of ecocriticism as part of "the first wave," and the field has developed substantially since then.[31] Second-wave ecocriticism foregrounded the concerns and critiques of the environmental justice movement in its literary and cultural analysis. The environmental justice movement focuses not on untouched landscapes but on the places where people "work, play, and live."[32] It demands equal access to environmental benefits and equal exposure to environmental ills. Drawing from a long history of civil rights, anticolonialist, and labor rights activism, environmental justice advocates highlight the unequal environmental risks that poor communities and communities of color face due to the intertwined nature of social and environmental justice.[33] Inspired by this movement, environmental literary and cultural critics increasingly examine a wider range of texts, especially depictions of urban environments, and consider representations of race, labor, and human health as more central to the field.[34] Following the turn to environmental justice, literary critics Joni Adamson and Scott Slovic have identified what they term a "third wave" of ecocriticism, "which recognizes ethnic and national particularities and yet transcends ethnic and national boundaries."[35] This third wave has included substantial scholarship investigating the role of race in constructions of nature as well as scholarship that infuses ecocriticism with the insights of postcolonial theory, queer theory, and contemporary feminist theory, including the turn toward material feminism.[36] *The Nature of California* draws from and is situated among such work, especially recent research focused on race and nature.

Scholarship by historians, anthropologists, literary critics, and sociologists has established that US ideas about wilderness rely on mutually constitutive ideas of race, gender, and empire.[37] Understanding the racial history of wilderness illuminates the way ideologies of nature shape agricultural discourse. As historian William Cronon points out, ideas about wilderness in the United States are historically constituted and socially constructed. Wilderness had to be de-peopled before it could serve as a marker of place unaltered by humans. It had to be divested from its own material history to become central to the United States' myth of national origin and national greatness.[38] Re-creating the wilderness as a peopleless landscape obscures the history of genocide upon which the United States was founded and contributes to the erasure of native claims to federal lands. It allows US residents to imagine a different and less troubling history for the nation's past and avoid Native Americans' contemporary demands for sovereignty and land rights.

Ideas about the wilderness being pure and untouched have been actively constructed against urban spaces as being environmentally and racially polluted.[39] As environmental cultural studies scholar Sarah Jaquette Ray has argued, environmentalist disgust with "polluted" or "impure" nature works in concert with environmentalist disgust with certain kinds of bodies, including non-white, queer, and differently-abled corporealities.[40] Disgust at environmental pollution cannot be easily disentangled from disgust of perceived racial pollution, leading literary critic John Gamber to suggest that ecocritics replace the concept of pollution with that of toxicity if they wish to discuss environmental poisons without conjuring up racialized discourses of polluting bodies.[41]

Progressive Era anxieties about the pollution of wilderness areas developed in concert with anxieties about immigration that threatened the racial makeup of the nation, as scholars Jake Kosek, Alexandra Minna Stern, and Peter Coates have shown.[42] The National Park System was formalized and expanded in the same fog of nativist and eugenicist thought that compelled the 1924 Johnson-Reed Immigration Act. National parks offered, in part, a proving ground for white American masculinity threatened by the feminizing qualities of urbanization and civilization, and were one of the sites where white men could live what Theodore Roosevelt called "the strenuous life." Preserving the nation's white manhood by protecting pristine nature became one front in Roosevelt's war against "race suicide."[43] Not all conservationists were so explicitly concerned with wilderness as white preservation. Some, like Robert Marshall, linked social and conservation issues in other ways, viewing both urban poverty and wilderness destruction as the consequence of unregulated industrial capitalism.[44] Yet even as Marshall saw wilderness as being for everyone, rather than just an elite, he drew from the same problematic binary of unpopulated pristine nature and polluted crowded cities that shaped eugenicist thought, and he worked alongside those with explicitly racist views on wilderness. In both versions of conservation, immigrant and impoverished city dwellers retained their association with dirt, disgust, and pollution, whether the problem was the city polluting its residents or the residents polluting the city.

Midcentury environmentalism reactivated the earlier script of racially polluting immigrants through global overpopulation. According to advocates such as Paul Ehrlich, wilderness needed to be protected from the teeming masses of the world and from suburban sprawl as much as from urban density.[45] The neo-Malthusian anxiety that Ehrlich's *The Population Bomb* spawned led some conservation advocates to urge the protection of American resources and American open spaces from groups Ray terms "ecological others." Such ecological others included racial minorities within the United States as well as people of color outside of the nation who were made increasingly visible to the United States through their anticolonialist and Third World liberation movements.[46] US advocates against overpopulation considered Mexican immigration to be as much a problem as global fertility rates. By the 1970s, "population control" was tantamount to border control.[47] The 1978 formation of the Federation of American Immigration Reform (FAIR) contributed to the reemergence of a well-funded and well-organized environmentally attuned nativist movement. Sociologists Lisa Park and David Naigub Pellow have described FAIR as "the largest and most influential immigration control organization in the United States."[48] In many ways, FAIR was born out of 1960s and 1970s environmentalism. FAIR's founders included the influential environmental leaders John Tanton, past president of both the Sierra Club and Zero Population Growth; Richard Lamm, another past president of Zero Population Growth; and Garret Hardin, whose "Tragedy of the Commons" is a mainstay of the undergraduate environmental studies curriculum.[49]

Not only have US anxieties about immigration and racial purity fed into movements for wilderness; concerns about national purity have also contributed to fears about invasive foreign flora and fauna. As historians Peter Coates and Jeannie Shinozuka contend, import bans and quarantines against nonnative species emerged historically alongside the immigration apparatus aimed at processing, detaining, and denying entry to Asian migrants.[50] Debates over the biotic citizenship of species such as the English sparrow not only borrowed figurative language from disputes over new immigrant groups but also emerged from shared concerns about dwindling native populations. Observers worried that immigrant fecundity would overwhelm native populations of humans and nonhumans alike.[51] They perceived American people, plants, and animals as proper and more productive citizens than their "alien" brethren. One participant in the debates contrasted the English sparrow, a "songless immigrant," with native birds who were "songsters, insect destroyers, [and] weed-seed eaters."[52] Although some leading advocates for native species actively participated in immigration restriction groups in the early twentieth century, Coates believes that in the twenty-first century, the "ties between conservation and prejudice, between the desire to preserve an 'American' nature and to defend old-stock America, once substantial, have largely dissolved."[53]

Although ecologists today vehemently reject ideologies of human racial purity, some organizations continue to perceive environmentalism and anti-immigrant ideologies as being intertwined. Print, media, and radio advertisements distributed by Californians for Population Stabilization are legible only when immigrants are considered racial others imperiling America's biotic environments, cultural purity, and family survival.[54] One such advertisement published in the *New York Times* and the *Nation* in 2008 erroneously claims that immigrant populations overwhelm public infrastructure such as schools and emergency rooms and drive up property taxes. In a non sequitur, the advertisement suggests that immigrants' use of social services results in forest destruction. The connection between immigrants' use of social services and the proclamation that "the bulldozers keep on coming" assumes immigrants, who also "keep on coming," imperil the cultural and natural legacy of the nation. Another more recent commercial blames immigrants for California's drought. In a commercial produced in 2014, a child asks, "If Californians are having fewer children, why isn't there enough water?" The narrator responds, "Virtually all of California's population growth is from immigration," implying that immigrants, rather than drought or industry water usage, are the primary driver of California's water shortage.[55] In displacing blame onto immigrants, the commercial naturalizes the consumption patterns of current and future generations of (white) Americans and neglects the uneven distribution and use of water in California. It also ignores the fact that California's farmworkers, many of whom are unauthorized migrants, are among those most severely affected.[56]

Californians for Population Stabilization's commercials rely on perceptions of immigrants as racial others who threaten the nation's natural and cultural purity.

As a consequence of this complex of racist and nativist ideologies historically fueling the American love of wild places, traditional wilderness narratives have not always held appeal for Asian Americans, blacks, Latinas/os, or Native Americans. Yet environmental ethics exist, and have long existed, in black, Native American, Latina/o, and Asian American literatures and cultural productions, as scholarship by Joni Adamson, Priscilla Ybarra, Robert T. Hayashi, Kimberly K. Smith, Carolyn Finney, Devon Peña, Paul Outka, Jeffrey Myers, Lee Schweninger, Kimberly N. Ruffin, Ian Frederick Finseth, David Vázquez, and others clearly establishes.[57] The lack of traditional wilderness motifs does not signal the absence of the more-than-human world in US ethnic literatures, but rather reveals the different ways "nature" often operates in these texts, suggesting the ways environmental ethics in such literature cannot be disentangled from issues of social justice, including US imperialism. Much of this literature and cultural production offers its own environmental ethic and critiques dominant ideologies of both race and nature. Rather than existing in a vacuum, literature about nature by people of color often engages with and transforms popular white understandings of "the wild."

The Nature of California brings such scholarly revelations about wilderness to representations of American agrarianism. It reveals the centrality of the racial construction of the white citizen and the abject alien to US farm narratives, similar to the ways scholars have revealed race's varied operations and uses in wilderness narratives. With a few notable exceptions, contemporary environmental humanities scholarship has neglected to foreground racial meaning as central to either American pastoral or georgic literatures. Those scholars who do analyze racial meanings in American pastoral and georgic literature, such as Jeffrey Myers and Kimberly K. Smith, generally prioritize Anglo American and African American literatures and typically focus on the US South.[58] *The Nature of California* suggests the ways in which the context of California's colonial history, land ownership, and immigration patterns shifted the articulation of racial scripts.

Whereas the wilderness plot relies on a narrative of nature in which labor does not exist, the category of work is central to American agrarianism. Studying farm literature requires confronting the fiction in which the category of labor is imagined as intrinsically opposed to the category of nature. As historian Richard White suggests, it is this assumption that all work is environmentally destructive that allows the bumper sticker "Are you an environmentalist or do you work for a living?" to make sense.[59] Pastoral narratives of agriculture have often romanticized the labor that goes into farming and rendered nonwhite workers in US agriculture invisible. In *Lie of the Land*, Don Mitchell shows how California's Edenic image requires farmworkers' invisibility, suggesting that the abundant luscious fruit of the Central Valley comes from God's hand, not from the many brown, black, and yellow hands that maintain the landscape that produces the fruit.[60] More insidiously, the popularity of locally produced food allows consumers to imagine they are buying food that is grown in a preindustrial fashion and without relying on racial labor hierarchies, a lie that Margaret Gray's *Labor and the Locavore* debunks. Gray's ethnographic research reveals that buying local is no more an assurance of fair labor treatment than buying organic is an assurance that one is supporting a small family farm, a case Julie Guthman so convincingly made.[61] *The Nature of California* reveals the role of narratives in supporting these popular fictions underlying the food movement today. Better understanding the role of nonwhite laborers in constructing the idealized relationship between the American farmer and the US agricultural landscape is a key step in creating more just narratives about race, labor, and national belonging. For *The Nature of California* aims not only to probe the relationship among race, labor, and land ownership in hegemonic narratives about agriculture, but also to understand how marginalized ethnic and racial groups who labor in California's fields have deployed and altered agricultural discourse in making their own claims on the nation.

A TIME AND A PLACE

The Nature of California examines processes of racialization and naturalization by focusing in on a particular story of US agricultural labor. It limits its consideration to depictions of farmers and farmworkers in California from the Great Depression to the present. It focuses on California because, as historian Douglas Cazaux Sackman notes, the state maintains a particular ideological significance in the national agrarian fantasy. Its bounty and wealth justified Manifest Destiny, appearing to bestow a divine blessing on US endeavors. Great Depression depictions of California agriculture as a place of deprivation where white US citizen-farmers, like John Steinbeck's Joads, were diminished into exploited farmworkers threatened a discourse central to the production of imagined US identity.[62] Representations of California as transformed from agricultural Eden into industrialized hell derailed narratives of America's national progress. If California has long suggested God's blessing on the United States, injustice in California's fields belies this divine promise of national greatness. As geographer Don Mitchell eloquently says, "Like tales in the Bible, [depictions of California's landscapes] are metonymic representations of huge stories, the trajectories of which become morality plays for America (and perhaps the rest of the world) as a whole."[63]

California also provides an ideal site for analyzing multiple articulations of racialized citizenship. Native Americans, Chinese Americans, Japanese Americans, Indian Americans, Filipinos, Mexicans, and Mexican Americans all labored in significant numbers to produce California's agricultural bounty.[64] The multiethnic literary history produced out of California agricultural experiences provides access to a rich and diverse archive of textual sources, from Hisaye Yamamoto's short stories to Helena María Viramontes's novel *Under the Feet of Jesus*. Access to a multiethnic archive deepens my discussion of racial formation in the discourse of agricultural labor and land ownership.

Asian American and Latina/o textual sources are particularly salient for comparison because members of both groups were racialized as abject aliens and alien citizens. Mae Ngai defines alien citizens as those subjects who have legal citizenship but lack substantive citizenship. They are treated as perpetual foreigners, outside of the nation, regardless of their place of birth or documentation. This is equally true of Mexican Americans deported to Mexico during the repatriation campaigns of the Great Depression and of Japanese Americans interned during World War II. In both cases people with legal citizenship were denied its protections and treated as if they were foreigners of a different nationality. The United States encouraged Asian and Latina/o immigration yet treated both groups as unwanted and as outside of the nation-state. The subject emerging from such treatment is the abject alien, a person whose labor is desired by the nation while their humanity and subjectivity are rejected. Examples include Mexican guest workers, Japanese immigrant farmers and farmworkers, and Filipino migrant workers. These groups of immigrants and migrants did not arrive in the United States by chance or by choice. These groups' arrival has much to do with the United States' role in the world, including its economic and military interventions. Prioritizing Asian American and Latina/o textual sources reveals California agriculture as a neglected site of US imperialism and US empire.

Attending to Asian American and Latina/o farmers and farmworkers side by side creates a more nuanced and relational understanding of the formation and negotiation of racialized identities in a multiethnic society. As Natalia Molina writes, "A relational treatment recognizes that race is a mutually constitutive process and thus attends to how, when, where, and to what extent groups intersect. It recognizes that there are limits to examining racialized groups in isolation."[65] Ideas about race are constructed and negotiated in relationship to one another. The racial scripts that Mexican Americans farmers and farmworkers negotiated were produced in relation to the racial scripts Japanese American farmers and farmworkers negotiated.[66]

The Nature of California progresses chronologically, from the start of the Great Depression (1929) through the present (2014). I start with the Great Depression because it was particularly formative for the popular understanding of the relationship among race, citizenship, and nature in California agriculture. The images created during this era, especially those of John Steinbeck's Joads, have served since their production as a touchstone for understanding California farms and farm labor.[67] When the Consumers Society of New York put out a pamphlet about local farmworker conditions in 1948, they titled it "The Joads in New York." Edward Murrow's documentary *The Harvest of Shame* (1960) claims to reveal "the 1960s Grapes of Wrath," while both T. C. Boyle's 1995 novel *The Tortilla Curtain*, with its opening epigraph from Steinbeck's classic, and Bruce Springsteen's 1995 song "The

Ghost of Tom Joad" reveal the significance of Great Depression images of California's Dust Bowl migrants in contemporary discussions of migration, race, and citizenship on the California-Mexico border.[68]

The reason the Great Depression was such a powerful moment in the production of popular understandings of farm labor was because the influx of white Dust Bowl refugees into California's fields blurred the categories of white US propertied farmer and nonwhite propertyless alien farmworker. In 1936, white workers became the dominant population in California's fields. This demographic shift resulted not only from the Dust Bowl migration but also from repatriation campaigns aimed at deporting Mexicans and Mexican Americans and the continuation of Asian exclusion with the 1924 Johnson-Reed Immigration Act. Many white progressives believed, erroneously, that white workers would not allow themselves to be exploited to the same extent that Native American, Chinese, Indian, Japanese, Filipino, and Mexican workers were. They believed that if they publicized the plight of these workers as displaced white farmers, the broader public would demand change.[69]

Consequently, the first two chapters of *The Nature of California* examine the conceptions of citizenship and land ownership that shaped US agricultural discourse during the Great Depression. Chapter 1 considers the depiction of land ownership and farm labor from opposing sides of California's polarized political spectrum, as I read radical journalist Carey McWilliams's exposé *Factories in the Field* (1939) against the novel *Of Human Kindness* (1940), written by one of McWilliams's powerful adversaries, Ruth Comfort Mitchell. Despite the vast distance between Mitchell's explicit racism and McWilliams's devoted antiracism, both texts embrace, to varying degrees, the possibility of land ownership for white Dust Bowl migrants in a way they do not for Filipino, Japanese, or Mexican workers. Making sense of the problematic portions of *Factories in the Field* in relation to McWilliams's demonstrated commitment to civil rights and to the rights of noncitizen workers is a significant focus of the chapter. Chapter 2 further probes the Dust Bowl migration by comparing Steinbeck's *The Grapes of Wrath* (1939) to Sanora Babb's *Whose Names Are Unknown* (written in 1939, published in 1996). Both Babb and Steinbeck address the ways white Dust Bowl migrants call into question the ideological system that positions white citizens as farm owners and nonwhite citizens as farmworkers. To read McWilliams, Steinbeck, Mitchell, and Babb alongside one another is to expose the discourse of racialized citizenship that Asian American and Latina/o authors navigated.

The second part of *The Nature of California* considers the ways Japanese American textual production from the Great Depression through the early Cold War resisted hegemonic constructions of whites as inherently being farmers and Asians as inherently being foreigners. The popular rhetoric around white Dust Bowl refugees as exploited farm laborers drew on Yellow Peril fears, responding specifically to the presence of Japanese Americans in agriculture. Apprehension about Japanese American land ownership shaped anti-Japanese sentiment in ways distinct from that faced by Chinese farmworkers, resulting in a series of Alien Land Laws enacted across the United States. "The specter of the Japanese farmer" ultimately became central to the ideological justification for Japanese American internment during World War II.[70] Japanese American texts of this period frequently turned to farming in depicting their strained relationship to national belonging. In chapters 3 and 4, I take up articles from the Los Angeles–area ethnic newspapers *Rafu Shimpo* (Los Angeles Japanese Daily News) and *Kashu Mainichi* (Japanese California Daily News), Hiroshi Nakamura's little-known novel *Treadmill*, and the well-known short stories of Hisaye Yamamoto. These texts all mobilize Japanese American agrarian citizenship as a response to the broader anti-Asian discourse operating in California throughout this period.

California agriculture is a transnational endeavor, embedded in a series of unequal relationships between nations on territory that the United States, Mexico, Spain, and California's indigenous peoples have all claimed. Chapter 5 situates the racial construction of farmers, farmworkers, and land ownership in the context of colonialism and economic imperialism. It emphasizes the shared economic, historical, and ideological conditions that shaped Mexican braceros' and Filipino laborers' migration.[71] By 1929, fifty-six thousand Filipinos resided on the West Coast, mostly young, single men working as migrant agricultural laborers. They were "US nationals," but not US citizens. Following the Supreme Court's Insular Cases, the Philippines was considered an "unincorporated territory," under US control but ineligible for statehood. The 1934 Tydings-McDuffie Act rendered the status of Filipinos already in the mainland United States more vulnerable, as they became legal aliens subject to deportation for a variety of offenses. The government also began (largely unsuccessful) programs to encourage Filipino repatriation. The Bracero Program (1942–64) likewise brought many men to labor in California fields. This guest worker program issued around 4.5 million contracts, with California receiving the highest number of braceros.[72] While the Bracero Program promised workers many protections, it was marked more by its gross violations and abuses.[73] Both Mexican braceros and Filipino laborers were desired as workers but denied full recognition of their rights within the nation-state.

Reading Mexican American labor organizer Ernesto Galarza's report on the Bracero Program, *Strangers in Our Fields* (1956), alongside Filipino labor organizer Carlos Bulosan's fictional autobiography, *America Is in the Heart* (1946), emphasizes the centrality of agricultural discourse to the anti-imperial narratives that Galarza and Bulosan generated. Both men produced texts that refuse to participate in traditional agricultural discourses. Instead, they sought to restore California's agricultural workers' full humanity by depicting such workers reclaiming a relationship to land, family, and nation rooted in their countries of origin rather than in the United States.

The histories of imperialism that mold both Mexican and Filipino experiences in the United States are likewise pivotal to the UFW, the first successful large-scale effort to unionize agricultural laborers. Today, the US pubic often understands farm union history as beginning with Cesar Chavez and the Chicano movement. Yet in 1967, it was Filipino workers, part of the Agricultural Workers Organizing Committee (AWOC), who first walked out on Delano's grape fields. Two weeks later, the National Farm Workers Association (NFWA), to which Chavez and Dolores Huerta belonged, voted to join the fight. The predominantly Filipino AWOC and the largely Mexican NFWA joined together to form the UFW. While Chavez served as the UFW's president, Filipino leader Larry Itliong served as vice president.[74]

It is to this history that chapter 6 turns, attending to often-overlooked points of intersection between the UFW and environmentalism. The UFW gained national popularity as the mid-twentieth-century environmental movement emerged. Chavez and Huerta founded the NFWA in the same year that Rachel Carson published her famous exposé of pesticides, *Silent Spring* (1962). Through a discussion of nature writer Peter Matthiessen's *Sal Si Puedes (Escape if You Can)* (1968) and Carson's *Silent Spring* (1962) alongside Chavez's speeches, El Teatro Campesino's plays *La Quinta Temporada* (1966) and *Vietnam Campesino* (1970), and UFW movement documents, this chapter examines the ways in which environmentalists thought about the struggle for farmworker rights and how the UFW engaged with ideas of nature in their movement rhetoric. The chapter also reveals how emerging environmentalists and UFW activists negotiated and reproduced racialized narratives about nature in relation to one another.

The racialized relationship between consumer and producer that emerged in 1960s and 1970s farm labor activism and environmentalism influenced the consumer politics at play in the early twenty-first-century US alternative food movement. Some public intellectuals and alternative food movement organizations adopted the rhetoric of the antiobesity movement to position the fit, healthy, and ethical consumer as the ideal neoliberal citizen. This neoliberal citizen's identity manifests in responsible consumption habits and is visibly confirmed through body size. In linking ethical consumption to nostalgic visions of agricultural land ownership, alternative food movement participants naturalize the consumer citizen as part of the American landscape. The power of the alternative food movement's adoption of antiobesity language lies in its ability to transfer the naturalizing power of farm ownership to neoliberal forms of consumer citizenship. Some food justice narratives write back against this process by addressing the burdens placed on farmworker bodies resulting from economic insecurity and labor conditions, including pesticide use. Such narratives contest the racialized ways that the alternative food movement's consumer citizenship reinforces the racial script of abject alienage and assert alternative means of political belonging.

The epilogue examines these alternative means of political belonging through consideration of the monarch butterfly's popularity in the migrant rights and climate justice movements today. It moves beyond agricultural discourse and outside California to suggest the ways that contemporary social justice movements in the United States continue to evoke nature to claim belonging to the nation. In migrant rights artwork, butterflies' align-ment with human migrants suggests a model of transnational belonging that does not depend on a single nation-state or national identity. Migrant rights butterfly art, moreover, revises the relation between humans and nature, rewriting the politics of the natural that grounds such assertions. In examining these cultural texts, I consider the possibility for twenty-first-century movements that detach human rights from legal citizenship by promoting forms of ecological citizenship that transcend borders rather than reinforce them.

There are over three million migrant and seasonal farmworkers in the United States today.[75] The average farmworker earns between $10,000 and $12,499 per year. A third of all farmworkers are in households in which the combined income falls below federal poverty lines.[76] Many farmworkers lack access to adequate housing, and recent studies have placed farmworker food insecurity rates between 45 and 55 percent.[77] It is estimated that three hun-dred thousand farmworkers suffer from pesticide poisoning annually.[78] Yet less than 10 percent of farmworkers have health insurance.[79] Farmworkers continue to lack regular access to restrooms or drinking water on the job, and women workers routinely face sexual harassment and assault.[80] Chil-dren are legally allowed to work in the fields at the age of twelve.[81] The vast majority of farmworkers were not born in the United States, and around half do not have legal documentation to work in the United States.[82] This lack of documentation, coupled with a regime of deportation, contributes to farmworker vulnerability.[83]

The ideas about nature, land ownership, citizenship, and alienage that *The Nature of California* traces shape the labor conditions that farmworkers in the US experience. Yet the stories told about farmers and farmworkers do not affect only agricultural workers. Because of the ways race, citizenship, and nature have circulated in American agrarian narratives, ideas about farming and farm labor have played an outsized role in constructing popu-lar understandings of both national belonging and immigrant illegality. Depictions of farming and farm work in the United States have emerged as one of the key sites to negotiate the racial stakes of citizenship. Examining representations of farmers and farmworkers from the Great Depression through the present helps explain the ideologies that structure contemporary immigration debates. It also reveals the power and possibility of the contemporary migrant rights movement's alternative politics of place and political belonging.

CHAPTER 1

"Settlers Galore, but No Free Land"

White Citizenship and the Right to Land Ownership in
Factories in the Field and *Of Human Kindness*

D URING THE GREAT DEPRESSION, CALIFORNIA'S FARM-
workers went on strike in unprecedented numbers. Nineteen
thirty-three was a banner year, with thirty-seven agricultural
strikes, including one in which twelve thousand cotton pickers, 95 percent
of them Mexican, walked off the job in the San Joaquin Valley in what
was the largest agricultural strike in US history to date.[1] Farm owners and
California conservatives viewed these strikes as evidence of a communist
conspiracy, ignoring the low wages and poor working conditions that fo-
mented the workers' discontent. They perceived communism as a threat to
the American garden that upended the racial logic of land ownership and
the natural racial hierarchies of farm labor. They founded organizations
such as the Associated Farmers (1934) to fight back. At the same time, communists, socialists, and New Deal liberals joined together in the Popular
Front. Many Popular Front participants perceived the vigilante violence
that labor organizers faced and the strategies the Associated Farmers implemented as evidence of fascist organizing.[2]

Despite the political gulf between the Popular Front and the Associated
Farmers, advocates for both sides often turned to land ownership as the
crux of California's "farm labor problem." Right-wing authors such as Ruth
Comfort Mitchell and M. V. Hartranft believed white citizens deserved to
own land in California and considered white Dust Bowl migrants to blame
for their landlessness. In contrast, farmworker advocates such as John
Steinbeck, Paul Taylor, and Carey McWilliams believed large land owners
were bringing fascism to the United States by undercutting white domestic

workers with "imported" nonwhite foreigners. They promoted collective land ownership by Dust Bowl migrants as one possible solution.

Unfortunately, rising concern for white Dust Bowl migrants often subsumed the agency and labor activism of Mexican, Filipino, Japanese, and Chinese workers. In focusing on white Dust Bowl migrants' right to settle in California, some Popular Front advocates obfuscated nonwhite and noncitizen workers' claims to property and civil rights. Surprisingly, Carey McWilliams's *Factories in the Field* (1939) participated in this trend. Scholars have rightfully acknowledged McWilliams as one of the leading antiracist voices of the twentieth century and as a stalwart advocate for noncitizen workers' rights.[3] Thus is it particularly telling that while *Factories* affirms white Dust Bowl migrants as the legitimate owners of California's lands, it portrays nonwhite and noncitizen farmworkers as pawns of fascist owners, a depiction that historian Sucheng Chan has refuted.[4] The structure of McWilliams's nonfiction narrative relies on the opposition between the fascist reality of capitalist land monopolization and the democratic potential of citizens' collective ownership efforts, which McWilliams terms "colonization." McWilliams envisions white workers as collective owners of California's farmlands, but does not depict the same possibility for nonwhite or noncitizen workers.[5] In this way, *Factories* directly contradicts the activism in which McWilliams engaged and the other articles he published in this period. How do we make sense of the problematic racial politics of land ownership that emerge in *Factories*?

Factories' engagement with the desirability of white Dust Bowl migrants' land ownership allowed McWilliams to refute the logic around citizenship and land ownership deployed by the Associated Farmers. Conservative novelist Ruth Comfort Mitchell's *Of Human Kindness* (originally published in 1940) captures the Associated Farmers' approach to farm ownership. It reaffirms the myths of the frontier, Manifest Destiny, and Jeffersonian democracy by rendering California as a domestic garden in which hierarchies of race and class are naturalized and threats posed by nonwhite workers are neutralized. The novel implies that when properly contained, nonwhite, noncitizen workers do not threaten the ability of white citizens, including Dust Bowl migrants, to attain the American dream by climbing the agricultural ladder to profitable land ownership.

What is at stake for both McWilliams and Mitchell is the legitimacy of California's current landholding class. Both leverage the assumed validity of white farmer-citizens as land owners to make their points. Mitchell depicts California's agricultural owners as farmer-citizens who will allow other properly trained white citizens to join their ranks. McWilliams depicts them as fascist un-Americans, and does so by revealing the ways they keep other white citizens from climbing the agricultural ladder. White citizens' right to own land operates as the assumed truth that both *Factories* and *Of Human Kindness* stake their larger claims around. Consequently, both works, intentionally or unintentionally, reify the relationship between white citizenship and agricultural land ownership.

In other venues, McWilliams actively agitated for nonwhite and noncitizen workers' full inclusion. Yet in *Factories* the popular presumption of white citizens as farm owners and nonwhite noncitizens as alien farmworkers played too great a role in shaping the cultural logic in which the monograph intervenes. Land ownership's centrality to the overarching structure of *Factories* ultimately prevents the work from endorsing the full humanity of nonwhite and noncitizen workers in the ways that McWilliams's other writings do. In this context, *Factories* appears less representative of McWilliams's personal politics and more indicative of the problematic racial politics circulating around land ownership in California during the Great Depression.

"AGRICULTURAL PEST NO. 1"

While John Steinbeck and Dorothea Lange may be among the best remembered of California's agrarian partisans today, in 1939, the Associated Farmers singled out Carey McWilliams as "Agricultural Pest No. 1."[6] After the near-simultaneous publication of *Factories*, Steinbeck's *Grapes of Wrath*, and Lange and Paul Taylor's *American Exodus: A Record of Human Erosion* in 1939, McWilliams took to the airwaves and lecture circuits. He chaired the Steinbeck Committee to Aid Agricultural Workers while Steinbeck, who McWilliams never met, remained conspicuously absent from the public debate.[7] McWilliams's writings and activities on behalf of migrant farmworkers led to his appointment as commissioner of Housing and Immigration (1939–42) by New Deal governor Culbert Olson. It also led to Republican governor

Earl Warren's campaign promise to fire McWilliams from his government post. Political writer Mike Davis called McWilliams "the California left's one-man think tank during the New Deal era," while cultural historian Michael Denning referred to McWilliams's writings as "one of the major intellectual accomplishments of the cultural front."[8] Yet significant analysis of McWilliams's contributions has been undertaken only recently, and literary interpretation of his works is nearly nonexistent.[9]

The ideological disjuncture that emerges in *Factories* is most apparent in the context of McWilliams's personal history. McWilliams began his professional career as a lawyer who socialized in California's bohemian circles. During the 1930s his practice moved to the left through his involvement with the American Civil Liberties Union and labor law. The subjects of his writing shifted from artists and literature to social injustice.[10] In 1939, he published *Factories in the Field*, which exposed the "hidden history" of California's agriculture, followed by *Ill Fares the Land* (1941), which considered the causes and consequences of agricultural industrialization on a national scale.[11]

Factories was written during a transformative period for McWilliams's political perspectives, from what McWilliams viewed as his political awakening in the 1930s to his growing comprehension of a "racial revolution" during the 1940s.[12] McWilliams credits his post as California's chief of the Immigration and Housing Commission and the national scope of his research for *Ill Fares the Land* for his growing awareness of racial injustice. His deepened attention to race appears in works published after *Factories*, including *Brothers Under the Skin* (1943), *Prejudice: Japanese Americans, Symbols of Racial Intolerance* (1944), and *North from Mexico: The Spanish Speaking People of the United States* (1948). McWilliams participated actively in the campaigns he wrote about, including chairing the Sleepy Lagoon Defense Committee (1942–44).[13] Consequently, it is important to read *Factories* not as representative of McWilliams's politics as whole but as capturing a particular moment in his political transformation.[14] Moreover, the racial politics embedded in *Factories* departs from the racial politics in McWilliams's other writings and activism of the period. The narrative structure and racial logic in *Factories* contrast with McWilliams's dedicated antiracism and antinativism. *Factories* reflects the depth of American agrarianism's racial assumptions about who should own land rather than McWilliams's personal beliefs. Its focus on land ownership overdetermines its racial politics.

As scholars have long recognized, *Factories* positions land ownership at the root of California's ills.[15] According to McWilliams, California skipped the stages of development from frontier to Jeffersonian democracy that typified US expansion. Instead, the Spanish colonial system and Mexican rule created large land holdings.[16] As he summarized it, "The ownership changed from Mexican grantee to American capitalist; the grant, as such remained."[17] Consequently, no place remained in the newly American California for ordinary white US citizens to find open land to conquer and settle, preventing the emergence of small farms. McWilliams writes, "There were at all times settlers galore, but no free land."[18] Only corrupt capitalists and corporations who manipulated the system to gain control over and expand existing monopolies benefited from the US conquest of California. Thus, McWilliams criticizes the "robber barons" that benefited from the Mexican-American War without problematizing Manifest Destiny or the United States' landgrab from Mexico.[19] *Factories* emphasizes that California's agricultural industry developed its exploitative conditions because of this oligarchic ownership of land. As McWilliams writes, "The character of farm ownership, established at the outset, is at the root of the problem of farm labor in California."[20]

McWilliams contends that a new system of land ownership is necessary to improve farmworkers' lives. He introduces this claim in the second chapter of *Factories*, "Empire and Utopia." This chapter contrasts two economic models: monopolization and colonization (McWilliams's term for collective ownership). As he tells it, "The two stories represent a conflict between two types of development, between land development under capitalism and land development under socialism."[21] According to McWilliams, land development under socialism (utopia) leads to US settlers' successful settlement of land, while land development under capitalism (empire) leads to the importation and exploitation of migrant laborers.

In McWilliams's view, land monopolization requires robbing settlers of their land, a process in which the indigenous peoples of California are notably not mentioned. McWilliams's "empire" belongs to Lux and Miller, a corporation formed by Charles Lux and Henry Miller.[22] McWilliams as-

serts that Lux and Miller consolidated their land by "brush[ing] [small set-
tlers] aside like flies" (McWilliams, *Factories*, 32). Settlers' dispossession was
crucial for the corporation's expansion. We are told, "It is apparent that if
Miller had used a shotgun instead of the courts, his methods [of land acqui-
sition] could not have been more ruthless, or essentially more illegal, than
they were" (37). The government facilitated this land fraud, as "Miller and
Lux never had the slightest difficulty in getting special acts passed by the
Legislature validating their countless thefts" (32). The state and the capitalists colluded to steal California's lands, and "the early settlers had been
squeezed out" (36). Without settlers, vast holdings of California land were
without laborers, necessitating an exploited migrant labor stream. Capitalists such as Lux and Miller recruited "tramps" and "hobos," or landless men
(36). In McWilliams's view, Miller and Lux's "empire" exemplified the way
in which monopolistic land ownership prevented settlers from claiming
land in California and generated the pattern of migrant labor exploitation.

In contrast, McWilliams's "utopia" is the socialist-inspired Kaweah Cooperative Colony. McWilliams reclaims Kaweah as an alternative model in
which settlers were actually allowed to settle land in California. Kaweah
establishes that socialism allows technological achievement, artistic expression, and a stable society without economic collapse. According to *Factories*,
Kaweah colonists committed no crimes, published a weekly magazine with
an international readership, and constructed a model road all while the
colony remained economically stable (43). McWilliams decries Kaweah's
failure as being the result of state repression. As he writes, "The creation of
the Miller and Lux empire was furthered at every step in its development
by the State and the agencies of the State; the Kaweah experiment was
consistently opposed, and finally, stabbed in the back by the State" (39). It
is murderous government corruption, rather than the failure of socialism,
that prevents utopia from developing in the Golden State.

Starting with the Kaweah experiment, *Factories* makes clear that the solution to California's farm labor ills is collective rather than individual land
ownership. McWilliams devotes significant sections of *Factories* to describing technological changes in agriculture that require capital investments
prohibitive of a Jeffersonian model. The road construction and irrigation
projects undertaken at Kaweah would be unattainable for individuals. A

functional agricultural infrastructure requires government cooperation and community collaboration. Thus the industrialization of agriculture leaves open only two achievable possibilities for California land ownership: monopoly and collectivism. Each contains its own consequences for the state's social relations. Land monopolization requires exploited farm laborers. Collectivism requires settlers. It is in the contrast between these two models of agricultural land ownership that McWilliams's problematic representation of Asian and Latina/o farmworkers as fundamentally different from white settlers emerges.

It is important to acknowledge that *Factories* presents race in ways quite progressive for its period. Echoing the ideas of anthropologists such as Franz Boas, it contends that ethnic differences result from learned cultural behaviors and social circumstance rather than from biologically determined racial difference.[23] Moreover, *Factories* celebrates cultural pluralism. It highlights each ethnic group's contribution to California agriculture. Of the Chinese, McWilliams writes, "It is correct to state that, in many particulars, the Chinese actually taught their overlords how to plant, cultivate, and harvest orchard and garden crops."[24] The Japanese receive even greater thanks: "It is impossible even to approximate the enormous contribution which the Japanese made, in the course of a quarter of a century, to California agriculture."[25] Historian Richard Weiss contends that the federal government in this period emphasized ethnic diversity to convey America's difference from the racial hatred increasingly synonymous with Nazi fascism and to inspire national unity as the threat of war loomed. The diversity education the government sponsored generally focused on white ethnics in contrast to the racial minorities that *Factories* prioritizes.[26] McWilliams's text picked up where liberal propaganda left off, supporting a more radical racial agenda that celebrated Chinese, Japanese, and other nonwhite groups as enhancing the nation's ethnic tapestry.[27]

Despite *Factories'* promotion of a progressive racial agenda, McWilliams presents white agricultural workers as entirely distinct from nonwhite workers. In chapters such as "The Pattern Is Cut" and "Our Oriental Agriculture," he emphasizes the similarity of Japanese, Chinese, Filipino, Indian, and Mexican workers. As McWilliams writes, "The history of farm labor in California has revolved around the cleverly manipulated exploitation, by the large growers, of a number of suppressed racial minority groups which were imported to work in the fields."[28] In highlighting non-white workers' parallel experiences, *Factories* renders the position of white agricultural workers in California as unique. He writes, "The influx of the dust-bowl refugees differs qualitatively and quantitatively from previous migrations."[29] This difference is a product of race. McWilliams repeatedly reminds readers of the Dust Bowl migrants' whiteness, even embedding a quote from economist Paul Taylor: "Long lanky Oklahomans with small heads, blue eyes, and surrounded by tow-headed children; bronzed Texans with a drawl, clean-cut features and an aggressive spirit; men and women from Arizona, Arkansas, New Mexico, Missouri, and Kansas."[30] In the chapter "The End of a Cycle," McWilliams predicts that white workers will break the pattern of exploitation set by nonwhite workers. We are told, "With the arrival of the dust-bowl refugees a day of reckoning approaches for the California farm industrialists."[31] McWilliams imbues white workers with a power denied Asian and Latina/o workers.

The political clout that McWilliams grants Dust Bowl migrants rests on *Factories'* collapse of race and citizenship, a move not present in McWilliams's later works. In contrast to the whiteness and citizenship that McWilliams grants Dust Bowl migrants, *Factories* depicts nonwhite workers as noncitizens and as foreigners. The depiction of nonwhite agricultural workers as foreigners was in many cases simply untrue. Although first-generation Japanese immigrants were not allowed to naturalize, their US-born children were citizens by birth. McWilliams acknowledges this, explaining that Japanese immigrants sometimes evaded measures preventing land ownership by putting leases in their children's names. Additionally, *Factories* recognizes that many Mexican Americans were US citizens when discussing their illegal "repatriation" during the Great Depression: "Beginning in February, 1931, thousands of Mexicans, many of whom were citizens of the United States, were herded together by the authorities and shipped back to Mexico, to get them off the relief rolls."[32] Between four hundred thousand and one million Mexicans and Mexican Americans were "repatriated" during the 1930s; at least two hundred thousand of them were US citizens.[33] Peculiarly, *Factories* employs this repatriation as evidence of foreign workers' susceptibility to deportation, part of a pattern preventing unionization.

He describes US-born citizens as being "shipped *back* to Mexico" (emphasis mine). Despite their citizenship, McWilliams presents such workers as foreigners first. This is particularly striking given McWilliams's active objection to the repatriation campaign; prior to penning *Factories in the Field*, he published an exposé on the illegal deportations in *American Mercury*.[34] Even when nonwhite workers lacked citizenship status, repeatedly referring to them as "foreigners" is misleading. Filipinos, Chinese, and Japanese workers could not legally become citizens, no matter how long they lived in the United States. Some noncitizens should be considered Americans, regardless of their legal status. Yet McWilliams allows race to determine which workers rhetorically remained foreign and which he considers citizens.

Factories repeatedly describes nonwhite workers as lacking not only citizenship status but also the qualities of US citizenry, chiefly the intention to settle in California. McWilliams emphasizes the supposed transience of Chinese, Japanese, Filipino, Mexican, and Indian workers.[35] They do not, in his view, intend to remain in the United States. Of the Japanese, McWilliams writes, "Being mostly men of middle age with no settled homes, or families, they were highly mobile."[36] Without families or homes, nothing suggests that such workers intend to stay in California or that they fit into popular patterns of assimilation. During the Great Depression, family was important to citizenship, both legally and culturally. As historians such as Nancy Cott have argued, being the head of family was deemed a qualifying characteristic for citizenship. This was reinforced through the distribution of New Deal federal relief, where relief was tied to the relationship of an individual to his or her family.[37] The men's lack of family illustrates a lack of roots, or "family ties," connecting them to California, and signals that they will not be reproducing members of society.

In contrast, McWilliams emphasizes that white workers intend to settle in California. Rather than being "imported" like "peons and coolies," the text describes Dust Bowl workers as being "not altogether solicited . . . they came like grasshoppers driven before a storm."[38] McWilliams reminds readers that Dust Bowl refugees migrated as families. They came "bringing their possessions with them, and they are in search of homes. Most of them are in California to stay. They are, in general, white Americans."[39] This statement makes explicit the link between families, homes, and permanence, using those descriptors to distinguish the "white Americans" from nonwhite transient workers. Dust Bowl refugees, unlike other migrant farm laborers, intend to settle in California *because* they are "white Americans."

Factories could have illustrated the citizenship characteristics of nonciti-zen workers or further emphasized the deprivation of nonwhite workers' civil rights, facts underscoring many of the legal cases and political advocacy in which McWilliams engaged. Indeed, by the mid-1940s, the elision of race and citizenship found in *Factories* is absent from McWilliams's other writ-ings.[40] Instead, *Factories* relies on a rhetorical strategy that links race to citizenship, even when it contradicted the details of his study.

By ignoring this denial of civil rights, McWilliams's text inadvertently contributed to popular understandings in this period of Asian and Latina/o workers as perpetual foreigners. The presumption of Asian and Latina/o foreignness by US civil society and the state resulted in part from the imple-mentation of the 1924 Johnson-Reed Immigration Act. As immigration his-torian Mae Ngai asserts, the 1924 Immigration Act, which was not fully im-plemented until the Great Depression, helped solidify whiteness by deem-ing Europeans white.[41] This act prevented Asian immigration and affirmed Asians as "racially ineligible for citizenship." While it did not numerically restrict Mexican immigration, increased documentation requirements and border regulation resulted in the classification of an increasing number of Mexicans and Mexican Americans as "illegal." Even though Mexican Ameri-cans, unlike Asian Americans, were not legally banned from naturalization, their status as perpetual foreigners by virtue of their perceived racial dif-ference solidified during the 1930s, as demonstrated by the repatriation campaigns and the addition of the federal census category of "Mexican" in 1930.[42] During the 1930s, aliens (both "illegal aliens" and "alien citizens") were increasingly defined as those who were neither white nor black.

This legal context helps explain the absence of black workers in *Facto-ries*. White Dust Bowl workers were not California's only migrants. Black workers also migrated west, and a significant number labored in California's fields.[43] *Factories* only briefly mentions the presence of black workers in Cali-fornia cotton fields.[44] This is striking given the extensive treatment McWil-liams paid to Mexican, Filipino, Japanese, Indian, and Armenian workers in *Factories*. McWilliams may have, intentionally or unintentionally, left black workers out of his study of California agriculture because they would disrupt the text's rhetorical opposition between white citizen labor and foreign nonwhite labor. The United States' history of slavery unsettles an easy racial dichotomy in twentieth-century depictions of citizenship. The presence of African American workers, who are treated as second-class citizens *and* are undeniably American, belies the conflation of nationality and whiteness.[45] That is, McWilliams's focus on the difference between white citizens and nonwhite foreign workers overlooks the citizenship status of nonwhite workers, which requires ignoring the presence of black workers.[46]

If one problematic racial construction in *Factories* is the portrayal of nonwhite workers as foreigners, a second significant misrepresentation is McWilliams's insistence that nonwhite workers prevented unionization. McWilliams suggests, "The extent to which the Japanese had monopolized field labor in the years from 1900 to 1913 made organization difficult, if not impossible. . . . This barrier had to be broken down, and the position of the Japanese shaken, before genuine organization could make any headway."[47] The use of the word "monopolized" links McWilliams's description of Japanese immigrants to Japan's supposed threat as a competing economy, as well as to the antimonopoly rhetoric of the white labor movement active in the anti-Chinese and anti-Japanese agitations.[48] McWilliams repeatedly details scenarios in which unionization or collectivism fails because of nonwhite workers. In contrast, *Factories* links the rise of unionization to the increase in white farm laborers. McWilliams writes that the arrival of white workers signifies that farm labor conditions will improve; "the jig, in other words, is about up."[49]

The contention that nonwhite workers prevented unionization is simply untrue. McWilliams provides the very evidence of his own rhetorical inaccuracy. He quotes the California Fruit Growers Convention of 1907 that the Japanese "are not organized into unions but their clannishness seems to operate as a union would. One trick is to contract work at a certain price and then in the rush of the harvest threaten to strike unless wages are raised."[50] McWilliams earlier interprets this indication that Japanese workers were organized into unions of a different form as evidence of their lack of interest in American unions.[51] *Factories* also provides evidence of organization for other minority groups discussed. On strikes and organized labor in 1927 and 1928, we are told, "While organized on a nationalistic basis, the Mexican unions showed I.W.W. and syndicalist influences in their methods of organization."[52] Additionally, "Filipinos no longer scab on their fellow workers, and they no longer underbid for work."[53] This is another moment in *Factories* where the details that McWilliams carefully includes belie the text's broader insistence that unionization was not possible with nonwhite workers in the fields.[54]

Factories offers citizenship as the explanation for white workers' and nonwhite workers' differently perceived tendencies to unionize. Foreign nonwhite workers, McWilliams asserts, had no control over their entry or departure from California and even less control over their working conditions. The state of industrial agriculture in California necessitated a weak labor force fully under capital's control. McWilliams says, "Here the practice has been to use a race for a purpose and then to kick it out, in preference for some weaker racial unit."[55] The text characterizes nonwhite workers as being vulnerable to deportation because they lack citizenship. Moreover, these workers were unable to vote, which McWilliams equates with political power in *Factories in the Field*. Consider the following passage: "The Filipinos have been, by and large, powerless to protect themselves. Most of the 30,000 or so Filipinos in California are ineligible to citizenship. They cannot vote or hold public office. As 'aliens' they are subject to a maze of discriminatory legislation; and, when they run foul of the law, as frequently happens, they are usually asked to accept 'deportation' as a condition of receiving a suspended sentence or being placed on probation. Local officials do not need to respect them, because they do not vote."[56]

"Alienness" is equated with powerlessness because McWilliams attributes significant power to voting. The road to success, as he sees it, is not wildcat strikes but civil rights and electoral politics.

In contrast to this description of Filipino workers, McWilliams claims white workers will use their political power as citizens to develop unions and otherwise protect themselves. *Factories* tells us that "most" Dust Bowl migrants "are determined to acquire legal residence in California."[57] Because they are US citizens, McWilliams expected Dust Bowl refugees to stay put, gain residency, and build political power. He writes, "These despised 'Okies' and 'Texicans' were not another minority alien racial group (although they were treated as such) but American citizens familiar with the usages of democracy."[58] It is new migrants' familiarity with democracy and ability to vote that would ultimately allow them to triumph over the fascist farm system in California, or so McWilliams believed.[59]

This move is part of a broader analysis McWilliams offers about the opposition between fascism and democracy, or empire and utopia. McWilliams found fascist tendencies in the land monopolization typical of capitalist development in California. He wrote of California, "Here the mechanism of fascist control has been carried to further lengths than elsewhere in America."[60] In the chapter "Farm Fascism," McWilliams explicitly compares the Associated Farmers, a probusiness organization of agricultural interests, to German Nazis.[61] He fears the rise of vigilantism that enforces mob rule over federal protections. Moreover, he finds the collusion between local and state governments and the statewide agricultural industry indicative of fascism. He connects rising fascism to the presence of foreign labor through land monopolies.[62] McWilliams writes, "The existence of larger ownership units made possible the exploitation of cheap, coolie labor; while the availability of great reserves of cheap labor delayed the subdivision of the land and prevented land settlement by small individual owners."[63] The text implies that if small settlers had created a Jeffersonian democracy on a California frontier, or if a socialist colonization project had succeeded, nonwhite workers would never have been "imported." The causation *Factories* presents is significant: Capitalist development leads to foreign labor, which leads to mechanisms of fascist control. In contrast, white citizen labor leads to unionization, which leads to socialist land colonization projects and democratic rule. McWilliams's oppositional logic denies nonwhite workers agency, depicting Chinese, Japanese, Filipino, and Mexican workers primarily as pawns in a repressive system. The potential for societal change remains in white workers' hands.

Disturbingly, *Factories* insinuates that white US citizens ought to collectively own California's farms while leaving nonwhite and foreign workers out of the picture. This is apparent in McWilliams's account of the failure of frontier conditions and Jeffersonian agriculture to develop in California. In this discussion, McWilliams repeatedly references "settlers."[64] In every reference, the settlers are unable to settle. For example, the land grant system is "but one of the means by which ownership was centralized and the settler excluded."[65] Later, McWilliams writes, "In the whole sickening story of land fraud in the United States there is no more sordid chapter than the methods by which, in less than a decade, California and its settlers were robbed of millions of acres of valuable land, land intended for individual settlement, for homes and farms."[66] White Dust Bowl migrants' inability to settle shows the continuation of this pattern of injustice. *Factories* predicts that democracy will return to California when white Dust Bowl migrants are able to "settle" California in socialist colonization projects. When fascism has left California, there will no longer be a need (or a place) for nonwhite "foreign" labor. Migratory labor will be a trend of the past, and settled white citizens will preside over the state. The rhetorical strategies that *Factories* employs end with the disturbing implication of US socialist democracy as white utopia.

Undoubtedly, McWilliams never intended to construct a text that rhetorically excluded nonwhite citizens from a future in California. Yet his choice of words reveals the racial politics often at play in American agrarianism. McWilliams's language relies on the reader's desire to see land owned and controlled by white US citizens. He references the brutal exploitation of Native American labor, but never mentions the injustice of their lost land. Nor does the loss of land owned by Spanish colonizers and Mexican residents seem to compare to the injustice of white US "settlers'" exclusion from land ownership. In erasing the validity of indigenous and Mexican claims to California land, McWilliams reinforces US appropriation of the land. By erasing the historical contest over California's national status, he naturalizes land ownership by US citizens, a category he constructs as white.

The exclusion of nonwhite labor from California that *Factories* envisions is not seen in McWilliams's other writings during this period. In contrast to the description of Filipino labor given above, consider McWilliams's 1935 article "Exit the Filipino":

> The Filipino, militantly race-conscious, began to protest against his exploitation in California at an early date, and has grown increasingly rebellious. . . . The Filipino is a real fighter and his strikes have been dangerous. . . . On September 3 a union of white workers employed in the

packing sheds returned to work under an agreement to arbitrate. In fact, they were told to return to work by Joseph Casey, A. F. of L. official. But the Filipino field workers refused to call off the strike. Today, after his brief but strenuous period of service to American capital, the Filipino faces deportation, as a fitting reward for his efforts.[67]

Here McWilliams refuses to represent Filipino workers as passive victims. He contrasts Filipinos' militant union activity with the corruptness of an "American" union. Moreover, in sarcastically referencing deportation as a fitting repayment for hard labor, the passage asserts that Filipino workers belong in the United States. Along with other immigrants, they have contributed to the nation and should be rewarded.

How can we understand such an intellectual rupture in McWilliams's published writings? Historian Daniel Geary points out that "while anti-fascism gave McWilliams a clear sense of what he opposed, it led him to divide the world into two opposing camps—fascist and antifascist."[68] McWilliams's desire to divide the story of California agriculture into these two opposing camps contributed to the problematic conflation of race and citizenship within *Factories*. Binary logic overly determined the rhetorical structure of the text.

However, *Factories'* questionable racial politics also results from the limitations of larger ideologies surrounding US agricultural landscapes and property ownership. *Factories* narrates the relationship between race and citizenship through land. Farm ownership carries cultural weight as the right of white citizens. McWilliams invokes this relationship between white citizenship and agricultural land ownership in order to characterize "farm fascism" as un-American. It is the weight of the American agrarianism mythos that leads McWilliams to unintentionally write nonwhite workers out of the United States.[69] If we borrow philosopher and gender theorist Judith Butler's definition of discourse as the limits of acceptable speech, McWilliams's text exposes those limitations for American agrarianism precisely because of *Factories'* contrast with McWilliams's careful analysis of race and citizenship in other forums.

As problematic as I find *Factories'* rhetorical structure to be, Japanese Americans, Mexican Americans, and Filipinos reacted favorably to the book.

These communities' civic organizations sponsored speeches and lectures following its publication. Complimentary reviews were published in the left-wing Japanese American paper *Doho* (which regularly published letters and guest columns by McWilliams). Even the more conservative *Kashu Mainichi* promoted McWilliams's analysis of Japanese agricultural contributions. *Kashu Mainichi* condemned and red-baited agricultural strikers yet celebrated McWilliams by employing his public lectures to support the Issei pioneer narrative the paper endorsed—a narrative that, in part, celebrated Japanese American contributions to the nation (see chapter 3).[70] McWilliams believed that with a higher level of political organization, communities of color could have found even more opportunity for political advancement through the publicity his work accrued. In spite of ethnic communities' ability to employ the work positively and regardless of McWilliams's antiracist intentions, *Factories* suggests the problematic consequences of the assumed relationship between US citizenship and US land ownership for alien citizens and noncitizens alike.

CALIFORNIA'S ELITE RESPONDS

According to McWilliams, Republican novelist Ruth Comfort Mitchell was livid about *Factories*. She used her political connections to force the cancellation of McWilliams's column in *Westways*. She also responded with a novel, *Of Human Kindness* (1940), arguably the most artistic of the conservative responses to *The Grapes of Wrath* and *Factories* (the two were published nearly simultaneously).[71] Prior to penning *Of Human Kindness*, Mitchell was already a significant regionalist author with several published poetry collections, sixteen novels, and numerous articles in *Women's Home Companion*, *Good Housekeeping*, and *McCall's*. She was also the wife of California senator and Associated Farmer Sanford Young.[72] Her novel focuses on a landowning California family, the Banners, including husband Ed (who runs for Senate), wife Mary, and their two children, daughter Sally and son Ashley. Through the Banner family, Mitchell defends California's agricultural system, repudiating accusations of un-American fascism and affirming white citizen farmers' relationship to land. Mitchell represents California as a pastoral utopia where hierarchies of class, citizenship, and race are respected. Her novel renders unfeeling communist agitators as threatening the nation by seducing the young, manipulating the weak, and spreading lies about hard-working American farmers. Comparing her novel to *Factories in the Field* highlights the texts' shared vision of white settlers as land owners even though the threats they identified differed greatly.

The struggle for control of California agriculture's image hinged, in part, on determining who the real Americans were. In his series for the *San Francisco Chronicle*, John Steinbeck proclaimed his aim to show "how [the Dust Bowl migrants] live and what kind of people they are."[73] Mitchell's fictional response could be described as an illustration of how the Associated Farmers live and what kind of people they are. Mitchell asserts the Associated Farmers' pioneer roots. She describes the protagonist's family as "the Banner Family, San Joaquin Valley pioneers, third generation in California; plain people, poor people, proud people; salt of the earth" (5). She emphasizes their frontier heritage and lack of inherited wealth. Mitchell's novel explicitly counters the depiction of California's land owners that one would draw from McWilliams's work.

Of Human Kindness gives significant attention to the family's regional roots. This family heritage, dwelled upon in the novel, emphasizes that the tale is of national importance, representing the future of not only the region but the nation. Mary is the child of Southern gentility, an orphan with Tennessee roots raised in the San Francisco home of her frail aunt with Chinese servants. Her husband's father is a French immigrant with a fancy for the fiddle who married a "New England woman, strict churchwoman, no foolishness about her; hard worker" (217). By the novel's end, the daughter's husband, Lute Willow, has joined the Banner bunch, adding some Oklahoma blood to the national mix. In case the reader missed the association of the family name, the daughter Sally is nicknamed "Star-Spangled." The Banners embody the flag as a symbol of national unity and pride.

The novel further emphasizes the family's Americanness through their relationship to the land. As descendants of pioneers, the Banners know how to till the soil: "Salt of the earth the seat of their toil had dripped down into, the earth they loved and labored over and worked their will upon" (5). They are Jeffersonian farmers and the inheritors of the western frontier. Both Banner children spend time working in the fields alongside field hands, and their parents toil endlessly, "sixteen hours out of the twenty-four" (6).

Mitchell repeatedly emphasizes the pastoral beauty of the landscape. As Mary asks the reporter Dexter, "Can you see the beauty of it here?" (257). Even on the novel's final page, Mary finds comfort in the earth, which is "relaxed, exuding the warmth it held in the day" (359). The seasons dictate their lives, and relief is found in the cool breeze outside. Jeffersonian democracy lives on in the men's informal councils, in which the men consult family matriarch Ma Banner as well as their wives. Mitchell describes a land in which farmers are still farmers, not businessmen. They are not as "some chap called them—'Bankers with pitch forks'" (258). The novel denies the industrialization of agriculture.

Of Human Kindness emphasizes that the Banner wealth is hard-earned and well-deserved. The text introduces Ed as a poor man. One of his professors states, "I wish he had capital behind him; he'd go far. Well, I believe he will anyway, with only his head and his hands" (13). The novel also downplays Mary's wealth. Rather than the fortune she believed she would receive, Mary discovers her inheritance is only one hundred dollars a month. Ironically, the insignificance of such an amount to the narrator (who bursts into tears discovering she is not rich), might have confirmed the Banner family's unearned wealth for a Depression-era audience. Rather than capital for the farm, Mary's money goes into personal luxuries as she adjusts to life on the Banner's ranch.

At the end of the novel, the Banners suddenly discover oil on their land, promising substantial future wealth. The oil appears in the final pages as if a blessing on the Banner name; indeed the house they move to is called "Banner's blessing" by neighbors. Mitchell implies that the future senator's fortune comes as a benediction after a time of hard work and struggle. In this way, the novel counters accusations of corrupt land deals and inherited wealth found in works such as *Factories in the Field*. Moreover, it offers a vision of the American Dream as reality: success will come to those who work hard; those who fail are weak and lazy.

Of Human Kindness also acts as a reinvestment in Manifest Destiny, a divine blessing bestowed on the Banners' "land hunger." The novel depicts what Mitchell terms the Banner family's "land hunger" as natural, legitimate, and endorsed by God. There is never an implication of land bought unfairly or of land purchased that keeps another from owning. Rather, their land hunger is a driving force behind Ed and his mother, who is described as "dragging a living and more out of her flat acres, reducing her mortgage, buying more land, a bit here and a little there to straighten her lines. Land hungry always" (24). The Banners even have a "land look" on their faces when discussing the purchase of new tracts (123). In the novel, acquiring more land is a labor of love, like the upkeep of the "flat acres" themselves. Mitchell says, "Land was a hunger and a thirst to them, a lure and a challenge" (123). It is the American march across the continent; we are told that Mary Banner's name had a "marching" sound (58). Land purchases are justified by the Banners' hard work; there are no fallow acres in *Of Human Kindness*. In the novel, Dust Bowl refugees squat on farmers' lands for living quarters; they do not till the soil. The novel depicts the Associated Farmers as working the land while the migrants, unduly influenced by agitators, expect free rewards while refusing to work.

McWilliams, like Steinbeck (see chapter 2), asserts that California's elite treated white Dust Bowl refugees as poorly as if they were not white. The threat to white citizenship was at the crux of the injustice to which they responded. Mitchell's novel counters by tentatively embracing the possibility of white citizenry for Dust Bowl refugees if they adopt the right American values.[74] Her Dust Bowl refugees are "ignorant and shiftless" but capable of assimilation in a way nonwhite workers are not.[75] The Banners' inclusion of Lute, "the okie-dokie boy," through his wedding to Sally demonstrates that the right kind of Oklahomans will get ahead.[76] When Ed spouts his prejudiced views of "Okies," Mary reasons, "Oh, come, now, surely they're not all like that!"[77] Indeed, we are assured that Lute, despite his apparent laziness, is different from the other "Okies." He was not tractored out, and his family still owns land in Oklahoma. Land ownership is central to Lute's respectability. Although his daughter's choice initially horrifies Ed, by the novel's end he accepts and defends Lute.

The novel characterizes "Okies" as salvageable citizens. As Helga, a family friend and Ed's former love interest, expresses it, "They're good people Ed; come of decent American stock."[78] As such, they have the seed of potential within. The novel repeatedly emphasizes Helga's work with the relief agencies, where, as Mary says, "Helga's going to help make citizens for us."[79] Strikingly, this configuration denies Dust Bowl migrants their citizenship.

Legally they are citizens, but in the eyes of the Associated Farmers, they lack the characteristics that grant them citizenship privileges. Okies have the whiteness that will allow their citizenry; they must simply be instructed in it. The novel's rhetoric is reminiscent of Progressive Era assimilation programs aimed at Eastern European immigrants.[80] Such a narrative strategy allows the Associated Farmers to claim ownership over New Deal relief programs. Mary says to one Dust Bowl family, "See—I've written it down on this paper for you—where the nearest Government Camp is, and the FSA—that means Farm Security Administration—where you can get food until you find work."[81] For McWilliams the government camps are only a demonstration of what might be possible on a much larger scale; for the migrant workers Mary directs, the camps in themselves are the solution. The knowledge that local officials impart there may provide the Dust Bowl migrants' salvation, turning them into upstanding citizens. What the white Dust Bowl migrants need is not land but instruction in proper citizenship.

The novel represents "Okies" as future citizens through their implicit contrast to an "unassailable alien" Asian work force. As literary critic Colleen Lye argues in *America's Asia*, Depression-era representations of Dust Bowl migrants reconstituted the image of rural whiteness through contrast with the Asiatic racial form.[82] The relationship to the land was central to this definition of citizenship. The specter of Asian immigration had become linked to land ownership earlier in California history and particularly fueled concerns about growing Japanese tenancy. The Alien Land Act of 1913, which barred "aliens ineligible for citizenship" from land ownership, was a reaction to these fears. In Walter Irwin's racist *Seed of the Sun* (1921), the Japanese are characterized as having a primeval "land hunger." This allows us to see the Banners' "land hunger" in a new light. Mitchell suggests that the Banners have a patriotic duty to own and work land to prevent Japanese land ownership. The Banners' "land hunger" must compete against the "land hunger" of the unseen Oriental. This is a logic repeated in other right-wing texts of the time. *The Grapes of Gladness: California's Refreshing and Inspiring Answer to The Grapes of Wrath*, a novella by real estate developer M. V. Hartranft, urges white Dust Bowl migrants to find and settle land in California because, "if we don't fill every rich tillable acre in California with our own American folks, then the Orient will fill it for us."[83] Hartranft, like Mitchell, suggests that only laziness and ignorance prevent white Dust Bowl migrants from climbing the agricultural ladder and owning land in California. Both contrast the laziness of the Dust Bowl migrants with the perceived physiological efficiency of the Asian work force. In *Of Human Kindness*, it is the Dust Bowl refugees' lack of land ownership that reveals their need for citizenship education. Once educated, these Dust Bowl migrants are expected to take their place in the harmonious race and class structure the novel envisions as characteristic of California's agricultural relations. In doing so, they will help the United States defeat Asiatic land hunger.

Mary frequently models the racialized society in which properly educated Dust Bowl migrants may participate. One example is her relationship to the white painter Abernathy. Abernathy offers to paint Mary's new house for free in payment for the care she previously took of him when he fell ill. Mary says, "You were working for us when it happened and we were so glad to take care of you" (141). The novel presents Mary as a good employer who takes personal responsibility for her employees' health and well-being. The payment she receives for her kindness illustrates the loyalty and hard work appropriate to the employee. After accepting Abernathy's offer, Mary observes that "he looked and moved like one of Snow White's most amiable dwarfs but his little figure blurred in her gaze" (143). She figures herself as a princess and her employee as her personal servant. The dwarf simile belittles Abernathy, whose size is mirrored by his place in the pastoral hierarchy. The Snow White reference exposes the inequality and patronizing attitude of the novel's idyllic image of class relations in California. *Of Human Kindness* depicts white workers such as Abernathy, and nonwhite workers such as Mary's cousin's Chinese servants, her friend Duane's black servants, and her friend Glenda's Mexican servants, as being content with their positions and generally treated well by the white people for whom they work.

Disturbingly, the novel makes clear that Mitchell sees a parallel between her model of good employee-employer relationships and the Southern plantation system. Joe Cosgrove, the novel's "bad" farmer, is called a "Simon Legree" (123). The emphasis on Cosgrove as an exception to the majority reads almost like a defense of slavery (221). Moreover, after Mary treats an old black migrant farmer with respect, he exclaims, "You' quality, ma'am, I can tell that; southern quality" (175). When her son asks how the old man guessed his mother's origins, she explains, "I suppose he always associates decent treatment with the old ideal. But I'm a Californian, Ashley. Southern quality is a picturesque thing, but California common sense and common humanity is necessary for us!" (178). This exchange implies that Mary's vision of California kindness resembles the imagined benevolence of the former plantation system with added western practicality.

The disruption to the pastoral idyll in *Of Human Kindness* is not generated by organic worker discontent but by communist agitators who manipulate ignorant Dust Bowl migrants. Whereas fascism threatens McWilliams's utopia, communism threatens Mitchell's. By figuring the disruptive forces in the text as white communist agitators rather than nonwhite or poor white laborers, Mitchell further naturalizes a false vision of California's fields as harmonious and California's laborers as content.

Of Human Kindness portrays the novel's two communist characters as immoral and sexually deviant women. They are unnatural in their inclinations, and they seek to poison and pervert California's class and race relations. A seemingly empathetic but grotesque portrait is rendered of the communist sympathizer, schoolteacher Pinky Emory. As Ashley's sweetheart Nadine expresses it, "Why, we call her Pinky because she's pink, and I guess maybe she'll be a red some day" (89). Mary perceives Pinky as being ugly, ungainly, and neurotic; she sees her as unnatural, possibly homosexual. As Pinky discussed the plight of the migrant workers, "her face was crimson and tears filled her eyes and ran down over her sallow face. Her hands were clenched and her whole thin body shook and jerked. Mary felt an admixture of apprehension and compassion. Here was utter sincerity, hysterical but genuine" (91). Pinky is a character to pity. She evokes Mary's sentimental feminine sympathy: "All the way back to the Banner Ranch Mary wondered about [Pinky]. What had happened to her—or what hadn't happened to her—to make her like this? A bleak and bitter childhood? A wrong, long festering? Or just a starved emotionalism feeding hungrily now on the raw meat and rank wine of revolutionary thinking?" (92–93). Such concern provides a thin veil for Mary's harsh critique. According to Mary's logic, something must have gone terribly wrong to make Pinky "like this" (a communist). The novel depicts Pinky as always hungry but denying herself food, in contrast to the land-hungry and land-consuming Banners. She is a character who fails to reproduce, in contrast to Mary's fertile Sally, whose frequent pregnancies announce the passage of the time in the book. Pinky appears dead set against the laws of nature, and she dies pathetically for her crimes. After being scorned by the beautiful Black Widow, she throws herself under the wheels of an ambulance. It is not clear if she dies for "the Cause" or because of the denial of the Black Widow's affections. Either way, her actions are to be perceived as perverse and her radical inclinations as indicative of neurosis.

The novel's other communist, nicknamed the Black Widow Spider by Mary Banner, is unfeeling, cruel, and beautifully seductive: "She was a tall girl, willow slim in her white slacks and the thin white sweater which was drawn down revealingly over her round little breasts. Her ebony hair grew in a perfect widow's peak and her eyes were black and lustrous under sharply arched black brows. Her face was all mother-of-pearl save for the crimson mouth which was full and rather loose, and there was the same crimson covering her nails" (205). It is not simply the woman's beauty that is re-marked upon, but her revealing style of dress and indulgent use of make-up. Her "rather loose" mouth implies her rather loose sexual mores. The Black Widow's voice is "sultry, persuasive," linking her communist rhetoric to her sex appeal (207). We are told, "The girl insinuated herself between two men who looked like cotton-pickers, putting red-taloned fingers on the shoulder of each, and leaning so low over one of them that the white wool over her breasts grazed his face" (206). The implication is that her physical beauty allows her evil sway, as she slinks past men's rationality to manipulate them through her sexuality.

Her sexually tinged communism is as poisonous as the venom of black widow spiders, as her relationship with Ashley demonstrates. To get re-venge on Mary, she seduces and then scorns Ashley. The scene in which she casts him out is fantastically cruel. The Black Widow's love for Ashley is as hollow as her love for the working class. She uses this group for her own means and does not care if their children starve. In the novel's title scene, Mary discovers migrants squatting on her land. Trying to avert a confrontation involving her husband and the other farmers, she brings milk for their baby, directions to the Government Camp, and gas money to get them there. She succeeds in winning them over just as the Black Widow arrives. The Black Widow declares the milk poisonous and knocks it out of the desperate mother's hand, where dogs and a hungry toddler lick it off the ground. One of the migrants cries out, "That thar's not poison! That's th' milk a' human kin'ness!" (348). The Black Widow represents the absence of kindness. With her black widow's peak, blood-red lips, and dark eyes under sharply arched brows, she even bears a noticeable resemblance to the Queen in Disney's *Snow White and the Seven Dwarfs* (1937). While the similarities between film and novel are perhaps coincidental, Mary's kindheartedness ultimately protects her from the Black Widow's "venomous poison." This poison offers simultaneous associations to the red apples of *Snow White*, the snake in the Garden of Eden, and, of course, the bite of black widow spiders. Mitchell associates communism with all three.

Through her portrait of the Banner family, Mitchell insists upon the dangers of communism to the family and the nation. In the novel's narrative, Ashley is seduced by the Black Widow. The loss of their son to communism threatens Ed and Mary's marriage. Enraged by his son's betrayal, Ed proclaims his marriage to Mary to be the biggest mistake he ever made. Broken-hearted, Mary considers divorcing Ed. Ultimately, Mary and Ed realize that the abandonment of their marriage will hurt their entire community. Ed's friends inform him that he will win his Senate seat because of Mary as the community sees great value in "what we'd [Mary and Ed] stood for—our family life—our—our marriage—" (356). The pastoral order at the heart of Mary and Ed's marriage provides the strength to overcome the communist plot in America's garden. Mary and Ed reunite their family to save not only themselves but their entire community. Similarly, Ashley survives his encounter with communism and finds that his pastoral roots are deeper than before. Restoring Ashley to his proper position as future Banner patriarch establishes the family's triumph over the communist threat to America's agrarian order. As *Of Human Kindness* draws to a close, Mitchell reasserts the picture of California as a pastoral elite utopia. Despite communist agitators' best efforts, the categories of class, race, and citizenship are never fully disrupted in the novel. As the family romance registers as a regional and national crisis, the Banner family triumphs against the communist threat. White land owners retain control over their Edenic garden.

CONCLUSION

The Great Depression generated a crisis in the ideological relationship between white citizenship and land ownership in California. Three hundred thousand white migrants from the Dust Bowl moved into California during the 1930s, marking the sole period in which white workers were the state's dominant agricultural labor force. Both *Factories* and *Of Human Kindness* responded to the visibility of exploited white workers in California's fields. White farmworkers' presence allowed McWilliams, an antiracist radical, to paint the Associated Farmers as fascist and un-American because they prevented white Dust Bowl migrants from owning land. Mitchell, a stalwart conservative, defended the Americanness of white farm owners by suggesting that Dust Bowl migrants were being treated as potentially white and as potential land owners. Neither *Factories* nor *Of Human Kindness* argued for Japanese American, Chinese American, Filipino, or Mexican American ownership of California farms as a productive possibility for democracy. This is despite the fact that McWilliams actively worked in other venues to enhance the civil rights of communities of color in the United States. There can be no doubt that he endorsed the idea of noncitizen and nonwhite land ownership. The absence of this vision in *Factories* results from the way the book's binaries (fascism/democracy and monopolization/colonization) leverage the plight of white Dust Bowl migrants to indict the Associated Farmers. In an agricultural context, white citizens could be more easily imagined as legitimate US settlers than Mexican, Filipino, or Japanese workers. The discursive power of California agrarianism resulted in a narrative logic in *Factories* that obfuscated McWilliams's active political alliance with California's communities of color, in some places aligning his vision of white citizenship uncomfortably and surprisingly with Mitchell's racist views.

CHAPTER 2

From Farmer to Farmworker

Representing the Dust Bowl Migration

D URING THE GREAT DEPRESSION, AMERICAN FAMILIES took to the highways with unprecedented visibility.[1] Of these families, none was more publicly represented than the white migrants from the economic, political, and ecological disaster known as the Dust Bowl. During the 1930s, 315,000 to 400,000 migrants from the states of Arkansas, Missouri, Oklahoma, and Texas headed to California.[2] As historian James N. Gregory has argued, it was not the sheer number of migrants that gained attention so much as their perceived social class. Popular representations of Dust Bowl migrants emphasized the privation that pushed them into California.[3] Migrants' visibility served as a public reminder of the dislocations and the uncertainty the Great Depression had caused. As one of Dorothea Lange's photographic subjects asked, "Do you reckon I'd be out on the highway if I had it good at home?"[4] The mobility depicted in Dust Bowl migration narratives challenged popular representations of the nation's onward march toward a better and brighter future. The Dust Bowl as ecological and economic collapse challenged narratives of progress that relied on capitalism and modern technological achievement.[5] Representations of highway travel became a constant reminder of the failure of America's rural fantasy.[6]

Dust Bowl migration narratives conveyed anxieties not only about the nation's prosperity but also about the crisis that the Dust Bowl migration and the exploitation of white migrants in California's fields posed for national agrarian fantasies. Dust Bowl migrants suggested a failure of Jeffersonian agrarianism that challenged the relationship between white citizenship and land ownership that structured understandings of national belonging. Both John Steinbeck's *The Grapes of Wrath* (1939) and Sanora Babb's *Whose Names Are Unknown* (written in 1939, published in 2004) respond to this crisis in white land ownership. These novels reveal that when white farmers lose their land and are forced to become farmworkers, their whiteness is questioned. The ideological connection between land ownership and whiteness is so strong that landless farmworkers become not quite white. *Grapes of Wrath* responds to this crisis by affirming the Dust Bowl migrants' whiteness. The novel relies on migrants' whiteness to indict those who deny them land. A renewal of American democracy, according to Steinbeck's novel, requires restoring white Dust Bowl migrants' status as landowning citizens, even as it embraces collective ownership over Jeffersonian individualism. In contrast, Babb's *Whose Names Are Unknown* (hereafter referred to as *Whose Names*) refuses to affirm Dust Bowl migrants' white privilege. Babb's novel focuses on white landless workers' similarity to other oppressed groups, including Mexicans, Filipinos, and blacks. *Whose Names* suggests that all workers deserve dignity, freedom, and security, regardless of race. Instead of a return to Jeffersonian agrarianism, Babb's novel calls for a multiracial industrial union movement among both farmers and farmworkers. In suggesting a parallel between Jeffersonian agrarianism and industrial unionism, the novel naturalizes Babb's radical rhetoric, suggesting the possibility of a communism that is truly American. Babb's novel, moreover, endorses a proto-ecofeminist view by paralleling equitable partnerships between humans and land with equitable marriage partnerships. She celebrates the agency of land and women as important to American democracy and class unity. Despite these differences, both novels depict farm labor and farmland ownership as sites that determine national belonging and citizenship. They reveal the importance of American agrarianism for producing, contesting, and affirming the categories of abject alien worker and white citizen farmer.

"WE AIN'T FOREIGN"

Until the Great Depression, California's boosters claimed it as America's Eden.[7] According to American mythology, national prosperity resulted from the availability of land. White settlers could find a place to farm, and with work, they could build a successful life for themselves. Such farmers were the foundation of the nation, exemplifying the best of the American character. California, with its bountiful fields, showcased this greatness. Its abundance revealed God's blessing on US expansion across the continent. Agrarian advocates such as John Steinbeck, Dorothea Lange, Paul Taylor, and Carey McWilliams told the nation a different story about California. In books, articles, and photographs, they showed hard-working displaced farmers pouring into California only to find themselves as expendable farm-workers with no chance of owning land or even of feeding their children. Scholars have long located *Grapes of Wrath's* popularity in the ways it ad-dressed Great Depression anxieties about the future of the nation, revealing the hardships that people faced and showcasing their ability to survive.[8] Both geographer Don Mitchell and historian Douglas Cazaux Sackman con-tend that the novel's power relies partly on the harsh realities it revealed about California agriculture, undercutting the state's Edenic image.[9] How-ever, the novel's power also comes from its affirmation of the Dust Bowl migrants' whiteness and its contention that white Americans should be farmers, not farmworkers. Underlying the novel's racial logic is the senti-ment that white citizens deserve land.

Extensive attention has been paid to Steinbeck's environmental imagi-nation, especially his relationship with biologist Edward Ricketts. Scholars have found tendencies toward naturalism, environmental determinism, and deep ecology in Steinbeck's oeuvre.[10] In contrast, surprisingly little work has been done to analyze the formation of race within *The Grapes of Wrath*. Occasionally scholars draw attention to the Joads' whiteness, as when Alexander Saxton points out the slippage between radical egalitarian-ism and racial egalitarianism in the work, or when Michael Denning asserts that "racial populism deeply inflects" Steinbeck's works, whereby the "noble whiteness" of the Joads contrasts with "the minstrelsy of *Tortilla Flat's* Mex-ican Americans."[11] With the notable exception of Louis Owens's chapter on representations of Indians in *Grapes of Wrath* and Ashley Craig Lancaster's recent article on Steinbeck's response to eugenics, race has largely been positioned as marginal to the novel's major themes.[12] Yet the careful con-struction of the Joads' whiteness is at the novel's core. The injustice facing the Joads and the novel's proposed resolution, giving Dust Bowl migrants farmland, relies on readers' desire to see white citizens own land.

The novel's conception of whiteness corresponds with legal standards of citizenship that emerged in the decades prior to its production. New immigration and citizenship laws implemented during the 1920s and 1930s reified the relationship between whiteness and citizenship. The 1924 National Origins Act, part of the Johnson-Reed Act, consolidated the category of whiteness by defining all Europeans as white. The "national origins" categories in the law contrasted with racial categories that lacked national specificity. According to Mae Ngai, "The new taxonomy was starkly represented in a table of the population of the United States published in 1924, in which the column 'country of birth' listed fifty-three countries (Australia to Yugoslavia) and five 'colored races' (black, mulatto, Chinese, Japanese, Indians)."[13] The population table defined national belonging as white and denied nationality to those categorized as one of the five "colored races." Whiteness, as much as legal citizenship, legitimized one's belonging to the nation.

In the context of whiteness's reification as a marker of citizenship, *Grapes of Wrath* established the Joads' Americanness as a way of establishing their whiteness. The collective narrator in the novel states, "We ain't foreign. Seven generations back Americans, and beyond that Irish, Scotch, English, German. One of our folks in the Revolution, an' they was lots of our folks in the Civil War—both sides. Americans."[14] With roots in the American Revolution and in northern Europe before that, the reader is assured of the Joads' whiteness. As a family, the Joads embody the nation's official history from the revolution to the novel's present, including both sides of the Civil War.

More specifically, the Joads epitomize the mythic American westerner, a figure often envisioned as embodying the best of the American character.[15] The Joads are descendants of pioneers, and their relationship to the land evokes this pioneer mentality. The collective narration says, "Grampa took up the land, and he had to kill the Indians and drive them away. And Pa was born here, and he killed weeds and snakes."[16] The suggestive equivalence of conquest ("kill the Indians") and cultivation ("killed weeds and snakes") fits with the frontier model of settlement. In both colonial and frontier traditions, white settlers claimed ownership over the land because they saw themselves as "improving" the landscape in contrast to the perceived negligence of Native Americans.[17] The white family's labor made the land productive. When the Joads claim ownership of their homestead through improvements wrought by their hard work, they participate in the literary conventions of frontier narratives.[18]

This frontier heritage is deeply gendered. In *The Lay of the Land*, Annette Kolodny exposes the colonial legacy of depicting the American landscape as a woman, simultaneously a virginal landscape to be sexually subdued and a nourishing maternal force.[19] Steinbeck situates the Joads among these gendered frontier conventions when Tom asserts a racialized masculinity through the conquest of a feminized landscape.[20] He uses the body of a woman to inscribe his relationship to the Oklahoma homestead: "Joad carefully drew the torso of a woman in the dirt, breasts, hips, pelvis."[21] In his act of drawing the female figure on the Oklahoma earth, Tom proclaims ownership over it.

Within the frontier myth, the white American pioneer emerges as the "true" American through conquest of Native Americans and the feminized landscape. Through the death of the Indian, the pioneer becomes native; the continent becomes his.[22] This tendency is at work in Steinbeck's novel. Native Americans, as a living presence in the United States, are of little interest to the text, as shown by a trite statement that full-blooded Indians have it rather good on reservations.[23] Dead Indians, in contrast, carry significant symbolic weight in the novel. As Louis Owens has argued, when one of Steinbeck's migrants tells of his adventures as a recruit fighting against Geronimo, he not only destroys the Indian, he takes on the qualities associated with Native Americans.[24] This is also how we can read the half-Cherokee character Jule, who retained just enough "Injun blood" to have more carefully honed intuitions than the other characters.[25] The presence of one half-Indian character among the mass of white Dust Bowl migrants captures the novel's appropriation of indigenous qualities into white national identity.

As Owens contends, the Indian, as imagined in the American Wilderness, stands in for lost American potential. Within the novel, Indians carry the lost quintessential spiritual relationship with nature necessary for human happiness and survival. Owens argues, "In attempting to destroy the Indian, Steinbeck suggests, Americans damaged, if not destroyed that element within themselves that connected them with the earth, the intuitive self."[26] In *Grapes of Wrath*, the Indian becomes symbolic of the landscape itself. The shooting of the "brave on the ridge" described by a white migrant stands in for the destruction of American nature by the American army.[27] Through this depiction, *Grapes of Wrath* considers Native Americans and nature as part of the same category. This process both racializes nature and naturalizes race, much the way Steinbeck's feminization of the landscape simultaneously genders nature and naturalizes gender.

In addition to establishing the Joads' whiteness through their heritage and participation in the settling of the frontier and the genocide of Native peoples, *Grapes of Wrath* carefully constructs the Joads' whiteness against blackness.[28] References to blackness, and particularly to black slavery, haunt the novel. In *Playing in the Dark: Whiteness and the Literary Imagination*, Toni Morrison asserts that blackness operates as an oppositional force to construct whiteness in the works of many white American authors. Moreover, Morrison asserts, blackness and the black body in American literature has been central to shaping national identity. There are no black characters in *Grapes of Wrath*. Steinbeck, however, repeatedly references the specter of slavery through the owners' comparison of the white Dust Bowl migrants to blacks in the South and through the Dust Bowl migrants' affirmation of their whiteness through joking and derogatory reference to blackness. White Dust Bowl migrants distance themselves from African Americans to separate themselves from the caste markings of racialization, to establish themselves as superior, and to mark themselves as freemen. United States political history makes the connection between freedom and citizenship clear. One could not be a citizen if one did not have the ownership over oneself to consent to be governed. The slave citizen was an impossibility.[29] *Grapes of Wrath* affirms the Dust Bowl migrants' whiteness as way of proclaiming the migrants' freedom and resisting the slavelike exploitation they face in California.

White Dust Bowl migrants in the novel repeatedly distinguish themselves from blacks as a way of establishing their whiteness.[30] In the book's opening, Tom bonds with a white truck driver to catch a lift. The truck driver is not supposed to give rides, but Tom places him in the position of either giving Tom a ride or being someone "any rich bastard could kick around."[31] This class-based relationship is cemented through whiteness when the driver tells a joke about a "nigger" that Tom appreciates enough to try to remember later.[32] In another scene, as Dust Bowl refugees gather around the campfire, they relate an incident about a white woman, "a lady back home, won't mention no names—had a nigger kid all of a sudden. . . . Never did hunt out the nigger."[33] These shared racial anecdotes not only link the migrants to one another but also communicate the Joads' whiteness to the reader.

The Joads' whiteness affirms their status as freemen rather than slaves. Popular mythologies depicted the West as the region where the white male citizen could be free, exemplified by Huck Finn's desire to "light out for the territories." In Steinbeck's novel, the wavering line separating slave from freeman in California threatens the West as a site of American freedom. The anti-Chinese movement in late nineteenth-century California mobilized similar fears that Chinese "coolies" threatened white men's freedom in the West. As Colleen Lye has shown, these anxieties persisted into the 1930s.[34] Depictions of the Joads' descent into slavery alongside affirmations of their whiteness mobilized racial scripts around both slavery and Asian immigration.[35]

Grapes of Wrath portrays California's land owners as similar to plantation owners, treating white Dust Bowl migrants as if they were Southern blacks. One owner states, "Why, Jesus, they're as dangerous as niggers in the South! If they ever get together there ain't nothin' that'll stop 'em."[36] This comparison between western white migrants and Southern blacks establishes the way owners see the white migrants underpinning California's agricultural economy. Such comparisons make the threat to the Joads' freedom clear.

As free white labor comes to be treated as coerced slave labor, the white migrants become racialized as "Okies." The Joads first hear the term "Okies" when they travel west. As they enter California, a gas station attendant comments to a fellow worker, "Well, you and me got sense. Them goddamn Okies got no sense and no feeling. They ain't human. A human being wouldn't live like they do. A human being couldn't stand it to be so dirty and miserable. They ain't a hell of a lot better than gorillas."[37] This dehumanizing and animalistic language echoes racist and derogatory stereotypes traditionally used against people of color. Exposing this racialization of migrancy is a double-edged sword. By highlighting the falseness of the accusations against the Joads, the novel seems to critique the power of racism by exposing its underlying operations. At the same time, part of the novel's outraged tone depends upon white migrant workers being forced to experience the racism more frequently endured by African Americans. The indignation the novel creates depends upon the readers' realization that white American citizens are being treated as if they were black or foreign, not like white Americans, who presumably deserve better. In other words, the novel critiques racist prejudice when it is visited upon white migrants, but falls short of criticizing racism against people of color.

The assumption that white workers deserve better treatment than nonwhite workers recurs in the novel's implicit comparison of Dust Bowl refugees to Asian and Mexican laborers. White migrant workers are repeatedly called "outlanders" or "foreigners" by better-off Californians,[38] making the rebuttal "We ain't foreign" all the more poignant.[39] Because the text provides descriptions detailing the depth of the migrants' Americanness, the accusation rings shockingly false. Yet the same treatment is not given to nonwhite workers in the text. The narrator says, "They imported slaves, although they did not call them slaves: Chinese, Japanese, Mexicans, Filipinos. They live on rice and beans, the business men said. They don't need much. They wouldn't know what to do with good wages. Why, look how they live. Why, look what they eat. And if they get funny—deport them."[40] The description of Asian and Mexican workers as "imported slaves" affirms the Joads' status as white freemen. Nonwhite workers' deportability emphasizes their presumed foreignness and lack of citizenship. While the tone of the passage signals to the reader that the owners' words are not to be believed—"They wouldn't know what to do with good wages"—the narrative does not explicitly contradict the lies told about nonwhite laborers, as it does for white laborers. Rather, the text implies that while these lies may work against foreigners, they will not work against white Americans.

Given the context in which Steinbeck wrote and the knowledge available to him, his refusal to counter such images of Asian and Mexican workers was likely a conscious narrative decision. Steinbeck was not ignorant of Mexican and Mexican American labor militancy. As Steinbeck knew, Mexican American and Mexican migrants were often far more organized than white migrants were.[41] During the Great Depression, at least four hundred thousand persons of Mexican descent were "repatriated" to Mexico, including the illegal deportation of two hundred thousand Mexican American citizens.[42] Race, more than citizenship, protected workers from deportation. Steinbeck chose to make his migrants white in *The Grapes of Wrath*, just as he transformed the Mexican and Mexican American strikers he used for models in *In Dubious Battle* (1936) into white workers.[43] Some have asserted that Steinbeck strategically highlighted workers' whiteness, believing a national audience would be more sympathetic to them.[44] It seems equally likely that Steinbeck truly believed that only white workers could successfully unionize. He makes such a case in *The Harvest Gypsies*, contending that white workers are more disposed to fight for their rights, are beholden to higher living standards, and are more likely to garner public sympathy than nonwhite workers. This was a common refrain among white progressive farmworker advocates of the time, despite Mexican worker militancy in the strikes of 1933–34.[45]

Regardless of Steinbeck's motivations, his novel depicts "foreign workers" as a nonthreat to the agricultural industry. The narrator says, "The imported serfs were beaten and frightened and starved until some went home again, and some grew fierce and were killed or driven from the country. And the farms grew larger and the owners fewer."[46] According to Steinbeck, the resistance these workers offered failed to stop or even slow industrial agriculture's growth. In contrast, white workers emerge as an unstoppable threat to California's agricultural industry. *Grapes of Wrath* portrays their exploitation as the grounds for a new American revolution: "In the souls of the people the grapes of wrath are filling and growing heavy, heavy for the vintage."[47] Steinbeck constructs white workers' potential militancy against a false depiction of nonwhite worker passivity and complicity in labor exploitation.

Steinbeck's indictment of California's land owners' exploitation of white workers relies on Jeffersonian agrarianism. While the novel establishes the Joads' white citizenship through their Americanness, it questions the Americanness of California's farm owners. The novel depicts owners as un-American in part due to their distance from actual agriculture. We are told,

"Now farming became industry, and the owners followed Rome, although they did not know it."[48] The statement is an accusation. Americans desire an emulation of Greek democracy, not the fall of decadent and imperial Rome. By comparing California to Rome, Steinbeck represents it as a place outside of the United States. The Joads have to go through "border patrol" to gain entrance. Of the government camp, where the Joads are treated like "people," we are told, "This here's United States, not California."[49] The lack of democracy and respect for white American citizens such as the Joads mark the owners' oligarchy as unpatriotic. Additionally, the owners' relationship to nature further sets them apart as being less American than the Joads, who exhibit the desire for a truly American (Jeffersonian) relationship to nature. The owners, who "imported serfs," moved toward a feudal relationship to land. They "farmed on paper; and they forgot the land, the smell, the feel of it, and remembered only that they owned it, remembered only what they gained and lost by it."[50] In contrast, the Joads formerly worked their own land and aspire to work their own land again.[51]

In contrast to un-American land owners and foreign nonwhite workers, Steinbeck paints the Joads and other white Dust Bowl migrants as Jeffersonian democracy's true heirs. The Joads and other migrants are deeply connected to the land. Their community and culture are built into the soil they till. Tenant farmers think, "This land, this red land is us; and the flood years and the dust years and the drought years are us."[52] When the Joads abandon their homestead, they abandon a certain sense of themselves: "How can we live without our lives? How will we know it's us without our past?"[53] Their relationship to the earth connects them to their history, their memory, and their identity. Through the Joads, the novel questions how much the changed relationship to land will change the American people. Without a frontier to conquer, and without land to till, will men still be men? Will old traditions be lost? Grandpa and Grandma cannot survive the journey. They are too old to change. When the Joads were kicked off their farm, "it took somepin outa Tom. Kinda got into 'im. He ain't been the same ever since."[54] Yet the novel repeatedly reminds the reader that the Joads' changed relationship to the land and to each other, fostered by their dispossession, does not alter their status as white American citizens. Their inherent Jeffersonian qualities remain.

The novel reinforces the Joads' Jeffersonianism through their democratic tendencies. Wherever the Dust Bowl refugees go, democracy springs
up with them. This democracy emerges in the squatting circles of the men,
as literary critic John Timmerman has noted.[55] Squatting circles represent
the American citizen as a property-owning white male. At the novel's start,
we are told, "The bigger boys squatted beside their fathers, because that
made them men."[56] One's relationship to the squatting circle signals one's
role in the family decision-making process.[57] On the road, this democracy
is altered but still exists.[58] Steinbeck writes, "At first the families were timid
in the building and tumbling world, but gradually the technique of building worlds became their technique. Then leaders emerged, then laws were
made, then codes came into being."[59] Democracy springs organically from
the roadside campsites. *Grapes of Wrath* depicts this urge toward self-government as intrinsic but as threatened by the loss of land.

The loss of stability and rootedness is one of the greatest challenges
Grapes of Wrath confronts. The Joads lack both the economic independence
and geographic stability of the Jeffersonian farmer, which renders them
and other migrants a particularly unstable political force. The novel depicts
migrancy as a type of political repression. A fellow migrant worker explains
the burning of Hoovervilles to Tom: "Some says they don' want us to vote;
keep us movin' so we can't vote. An' some says so we can't get on relief. An'
some says if we set in one place we'd get organized."[60] Instead of democracy,
the Joads encounter a protofascist state that will respond only to violent
revolt.

The repression of democracy in the Hoovervilles contrasts with the self-
organization the Joads find at the government camp, where they are able, at
least temporarily, to settle on a piece of land. Of the road, we are told, "The
movement changed them; the highways, the camps along the road, the fear
of hunger and the hunger itself, changed them. They were migrants."[61] But
in the government camp, stability, self-government, and respect quickly
turn migrants back into "people"—that is, American people. When the
Joads arrive at the government camp, Tom asks the watchman, "You mean
to say the fellas that runs the camp is jus' fellas—campin' here?" "Sure," is
the reply. "And it works."[62] Once the Joads have settled into the government
camp, Ma exclaims, "Why, I feel like people again!"[63]

Through the government camps, Steinbeck posits land ownership as central to the re-emergence of American democracy in California. Michael Denning argues that a liberal reading of the novel would view the government camp as a celebration of the New Deal, while a radical reading would see it as merely a small prototype of what might one day be possible.[64] In my reading, the government camp is neither a celebration of the New Deal nor an example of the good things to come under Communism. Rather, the government camp reveals the New Deal's shortcomings. The Joads have to leave the camp, as there is no work; they would starve if they stayed. Respect and democracy are nothing without farmland. The possibility for improvement throughout the novel is always referred to as "if a fella had an acre. . ." (Steinbeck, *Grapes of Wrath*, 338). Ma, the family's voice of reason and virtue, refuses to dwell on the past, because, she says, "This here's purtier—better lan'" (422). Her words signal land's importance to the Joads' investment in California's promise, even after their travails in the state. Rather than wish for a return to Oklahoma, the Joads and other white migrants are preparing to demand ownership of California's fields. As the novel proceeds, it becomes clear that if the denial of land ownership to white Dust Bowl migrants is not rectified by California's oligarchy, the migrants will remedy the situation on their own.

The novel depicts the development of a collective (white) class consciousness as central to the migrants' ability to change conditions in California and acquire land. At the novel's beginning each character more or less looks after his or her own individual best interests. Ma looks after the family's interests, but slowly the importance of family breaks down. By the novel's end, Ma states, "Use' ta be the fambly was fust. It ain't so now. It's anybody. Worse off we get, the more we got to do" (444). Critics often describe this as a move from "I" to "we" in the text. This is the moment of revolution the text warns us about. The narrator says, "You who hate change and fear revolution. . . . Here is the anlage of the thing you fear. . . . It was my mother's blanket—take it for the baby. This is the thing to bomb. This is the beginning from 'I' to 'we'" (152). This new collectivity, "we," threatens to create a new society.

This prompts the question, who is the "we" in the novel? What is the new collective identity being formed? The migrants are displaced white US citizens who are treated like foreign, nonwhite slaves rather than as consenting free white labor. As such, they are prevented from realizing the privileges of their citizenship. At the same time, the owners who deny them those rights are marked as un-American; the owners "stole" California and transformed it into an un-American landscape. White migrants emerge as the true Americans. As Ma prophetically proclaims, "We're the people" (280). The migrants reinvent their identity based not on the family but on a larger sense of the community. Both individuals and families move toward a broader definition of themselves.

It is within this framework that we need to consider the novel's culminating scene, in which Rose of Sharon, following the stillbirth of her child, offers her breast to a starving man, feeding a stranger rather than her own progeny. As she did so, "her lips came together and smiled mysteriously" (453), echoing the moment of Casy's sacrificial arrest: "on his lips there was a faint smile and on his face a curious look of conquest" (267). As numerous scholars have argued, these are the moments of Christlike spiritual transcendence in the text.[65] With Rose of Sharon's selfless act, the family breaks down entirely and what Steinbeck calls "manself" arises. The family reconfigures around a collective American identity.[66] The Joads' triumph over bitter cruelty, seen through Rose of Sharon's final act, offers a particular type of American redemption.

One might read the Joads' deliverance to "manself" in light of the spiritual redemption captured in the frontier myth narratives that Richard Slotkin details: The Joads descend into the violent conflicts of California agriculture and re-emerge in a purified state (collectivity). Rather than purification from the ills of European civilization, the Joads are cleansed of the ills of industrial capitalism and the environmental sins that lead to the Dust Bowl, re-emerging as the quintessential (but still white) Americans.[67] Just as Frederick Jackson Turner's "new man" required a different government than colonialism and a separate culture from Europe, Steinbeck's new "manself" requires a transformation of government and American culture away from oligarchic land ownership toward more democratic models of white land access.

In *New Deal Modernism*, literary critic Michael Szalay argues that New Deal fiction, including *Grapes of Wrath*, depicts a transformation of the citizen's relationship to government whereby men become the principal of public policy through bodily absence from the family, while women's bodies move from the private sphere to serve a public role of nourishment. Tom exemplifies this absence. He departs even before the novel's final action. He appears almost to dissipate into air or spirit. He tells his mother, "I'll be in the way guys yell when they're mad an'—I'll be in the way kids laugh when they're hungry an' they know supper's ready."[68] The political transformation of the nation requires Tom's absence, just as it requires Rose of Sharon's body for the public good. Thus, the Joads, as the new American family, and Tom and Rose of Sharon, as the new American citizens, have completed their transformation.[69] Yet this transformation is ultimately about the right of white Americans to claim ownership over land. Farming becomes a site through which to reify whiteness as synonymous with land ownership and citizenship while dismissing black, Latina/o, and Asian workers' belonging to the nation and claims to land.

Grapes of Wrath insists upon Tom's and Rose of Sharon's whiteness and American heritage. Steinbeck's vision of "the people" or "manself" does not include black, Asian, or Latina/o workers. The text repeatedly refers to white owners and other white Californians as potentially part of the citizenry the migrants create. We are told, "The quality of owning freezes you forever into 'I,' and cuts you off forever from the 'we.'"[70] White owners had the opportunity to be part of this new American unity but were cut off from it through their selfish individualism and fascist behavior. In contrast, Asian, Latina/o, and black migrant workers were never included in the growing "we."[71] In the novel, race matters in determining membership to "the people." The novel depicts land ownership as central to the establishment of national identity. It responds to the threat to Dust Bowl migrants' white citizenship by envisioning a collective white underclass that may reclaim land from un-American owners and rebuild democracy in California through white land ownership. In doing so, the novel capitalizes on the presumed slippage between the category of white and the category of American. In reaffirming the Joads as the essence of "the people," *Grapes of Wrath* relies on a racial logic of land ownership.

BABB'S MULTIRACIAL WORKING-CLASS CONSCIOUSNESS

Steinbeck's racialized vision of citizenship and land ownership contrasts with the multiracial class consciousness articulated through Sanora Babb's novel *Whose Names Are Unknown*. Written in 1939 but not published until 2004, *Whose Names* rivals *Grapes of Wrath* in its artistry. Like Steinbeck's novel, *Whose Names* focuses on the displacement of an Oklahoma farm family, the Dunnes, and the exploitation that they and fellow migrants encounter in California. The title references Depression-era eviction notices, "To John Doe and Mary Doe whose true names are unknown."[72] While a case cannot be made that Babb's unpublished novel influenced the national consciousness in the same way as Steinbeck's best seller, her text is as deserving of attention as more popular works. Babb's novel testifies that an alternative response to the Dust Bowl migration was possible. Rather than reify the migrants' whiteness in the face of their dispossession, Babb disrupts the boundary between white farm owner and nonwhite farmworker. *Whose Names* suggests that the dignity and purpose that Jeffersonian democracy once offered white Oklahomans can be rebuilt through multiracial industrial unionism.

To understand Babb's ideological differences with Steinbeck, it is necessary to know something about her life experiences and political beliefs. Babb was born in Oklahoma Territory in 1907, the year Oklahoma became a state. Her fictionalized autobiography, *An Owl on Every Post* (1970), recounts this period of her life, which influenced her depiction of the region in *Whose Names*. She also spent significant periods of her childhood in Kansas and Colorado. After attending college, Babb worked at local newspapers and magazines, deciding to depart for California in 1929. She intended to become a newspaper reporter in the Golden State, but the Depression interfered, and she ended up unemployed and even homeless for a time, an experience that radicalized her. She joined the local communist-led John Reed Club in the early 1930s, traveled to the American Writers Congress in New York in 1935, and to the USSR in 1936. As she was writing *Whose Names*, she became a Communist Party member. She published short stories and poetry in papers such as the *California Quarterly* and the communist-sponsored *New Masses* and the *Daily Worker*. Her personal circle included Tillie Olson, William Saroyan, Richard Wright, Carlos Bulosan, and Ralph Ellison, with whom Babb had an affair. Ellison commented on drafts of *Whose Names*, encouraging Babb to further develop her African American characters.[73] Babb's political work included efforts on behalf of migrant farmworkers, the Spanish Republic, and the Anti-Nazi League. She spent the height of McCarthyism in self-imposed exile in Mexico City, in part to protect her husband, world-renowned filmmaker James Wong Howe, from further blacklisting.[74]

While Babb and Steinbeck met only once, the similarity between their two books is not coincidental.[75] In 1938, Babb volunteered for the Farm Security Administration in the San Joaquin and Imperial Valleys. Through this job she became close to Weedpatch Camp manager Tom Collins. Collins was Steinbeck's major informant; *Grapes of Wrath* is dedicated in part to him. Collins asked Babb to keep notes and, impressed with her observations, asked to show them to Steinbeck. Babb shared her notes and shortly thereafter completed *Whose Names*, which was under advance contract with Random House. Steinbeck's novel came out just prior to the scheduled publication of Babb's work. Her editor, Bennett Cerf, pulled her publication, writing, "What rotten luck. . . . Obviously, another book at this time about exactly the same subject would be a sad anticlimax."[76] *Whose Names* remained unpublished until 1990, when an excerpt appeared in the *Michigan Quarterly Review*.[77] The University of Oklahoma Press finally published the book in 2004, one year before Babb's death.

The political distance between *Grapes of Wrath* and *Whose Names* is striking, given their superficial similarities in form and content. Both *Grapes of Wrath* and *Whose Names* reveal the ideological crisis that ensues when white US citizens lose their farmland. When white farmers become exploited farmworkers, it threatens the nation's foundational myths. Whereas Steinbeck affirms Dust Bowl migrants' whiteness in the face of this crisis, Babb depicts a multiracial "we." The dispossession of white Americans from their land provides an opportunity for white migrants to develop solidarity with black, Asian, and Latina/o workers, remaking a more inclusive political community. At the heart of Babb's work is not only a new multiracial model for land ownership but also a model for more equitable gender relations aligned with a vision of successful agriculture as a partnership between humans and the earth. This model of shared agency contrasts with Tom Joad's demarcation of both land and women as property. Instead, Babb emphasizes the active, equal, and willing participation of women and land in any relation of possession.[78]

At the novel's start, the protagonists' partnership with nature provides their sense of purpose and human dignity. Their work on the land inspires them. Every morning Milt Dunne and his father, Old Man Dunne, "felt renewed in themselves" as "they looked at the land they had planted the day before, and the land they would plant this day, and they felt a sense of possession growing in them for the piece of earth that was theirs" (Babb, *Whose Names*, 6). Like the Joads, their toil in the earth, rather than legal title, gives them this sense of possession. In Marxist terms, the Dunnes are not yet alienated from their labor. Of Milt we are told, "Nothing was quite like the satisfaction he felt after he planted or harvested a crop. *This kind of feeling is one of the things a man lives for*, he told himself on one of the long walks to a neighbor's farm, *the feeling that I made something*" (58). Milt feels pride, accomplishment, and a sense of ownership about his work. Yet, unlike the Joads, he shares this sense of accomplishment with the land: "*I made something with the soil, together we made a crop grow in order and loveliness*" (58). What nature and humans jointly produce has value that is more than monetary.

Babb's novel depicts agriculture as a partnership between humans and the earth. The earth is generous; it has agency. The land on which the Dunnes labor not only helps grow crops but also expands their horizons. It stretches their hearts and minds. According to Old Man Dunne, "The earth was generous and could give him his needs, and stir his heart and soul. Did he not many times stand and look at the far horizon, feeling the tug deep in his thoughts as if his being were stretching and drawing out beyond him?" (39). The earth provides the foundation for the Dunnes' political and philosophical analysis of the human condition. Staring at the earth with which he works, Old Man Dunne realizes "that man was capable of making a good life for himself, of guiding his existence, of finding a better answer to the longings of his spirit, once he learned a way to throw off the halter of power on earth that controlled the things men created in their work" (39). The characters recognize that the abstract property relations that dominate agriculture separate humans from happiness. A partnership with the land brings dignity and purpose that capitalist land relations deny them.

In Babb's novel, the capitalist system of absentee land owners and large banks disrupts the characters' idyllic relationship to the land. The Oklahoman Brennermann family embodies this system. They own more land than

anyone around, while the father works for the local bank. The Brennermanns do not work their own land; unlike the other characters, they are
divorced from the soil. The father's profession connects land monopolies
directly to the banking industry. The Brennermanns' youngest daughter,
schoolteacher Anna, describes the banking system as "a monster gorging
itself on the farmlands and crops of the people she knew, who had lost their
independence either through accidents of nature or through the fluctuat-
ing prices for crops and animals—and—in general—the depression" (33).
Capitalism takes advantage of peoples' misfortunes. Whereas the novels'
farmers rally around those who are sick or suffer from accidents, the bankers turn a blind eye, seeing only profit-making opportunity. Banks lack a
regard for human dignity and disrupt the community's safety net.

The novel most explicitly demonstrates the consequences of capitalist
greed when Mrs. Brennermann, the banker's wife, sends the pregnant Julia
Dunne home in a fierce storm to avoid feeding her dinner. Julia miscar-
ries from exposure, and her husband, blaming Mrs. Brennermann, shouts,
"Goddamn that old woman!" (41). Julie's miscarriage suggests that future
generations cannot be maintained on the farm because of the greed of the
rich. The young are born dead. The loss of the baby, the family's only son,
represents the final break in the Dunne family's patriarchal lineage. Milt
is brought to his knees by the loss, sobbing for the first time since he was
a boy, until finally "in anger he shook his fist, shook it hard and fierce at
something in the world" (45).

It is not merely the cold hearts of a few local bankers and the faraway
orders of eastern banking establishments that result in the Oklahoma farmers' suffering. Governmental policies encouraged farmers to overcultivate
the plains, resulting in the ecological devastation of the dust storms. In the
"Author's Note," Babb writes, "It was a mistake to plow the plains in a land
of little rain and wind, wind, wind, and the mistake resulted in dust, which
covered fields and buildings, killed people and animals, and drove farmers out with nothing."[79] Overplowing disrupted the sustaining partnership
between people and land. Humans disregarded the earth's generosity, and
the Dust Bowl resulted.

If the characters in the novel want a return to the security and dignity
of their Jeffersonian days, *Whose Names* suggests, they must embrace industrial unionism. This industrial unionism is the solution for both the

farmworkers in California and the farmers who remain in Oklahoma. Oklahoma's biggest advocate for industrial unionism is Max, a farmer's educated son. As he explains to a group of farmers, "One thing sure, farmers have got to realize that they belong with others who work. We've got to wake up and find out about things and stick together more, the way the workers do in the cities."[80] Echoing Carey McWilliams's take on the Kaweah Cooperative, the characters dream of using the power they could obtain through collective action to demand inclusive technologies rather than the exclusive technologies placed on their land by private capital. Max states, "We need dams . . . but we need big ones, not just private ones with high-price water the way it is here now."[81] Because of technological innovation and large-scale irrigation projects, individualized Jeffersonian farming is not the best solution. Like McWilliams, Babb believes ownership of infrastructure and collective agrarianism would give farmers the power to take on the greed of banks.

Whose Names captures the potential power of collectivity through family narratives and romances. Julia and Milt's reproductive failure in Oklahoma contrasts with Max's procreative potential. Max is the only character to establish a romantic relationship in Oklahoma. When the other characters depart for California, he stays with Anna. Max's industrial unionism offers Oklahoma's only reproductive hope. A new life there will be built when he and Anna's shared philosophies are put into practice. Similarly, Anna's sister Frieda, a spinster in Oklahoma, finally finds her own potentially generative relationship after her conversion to revolutionary unionism in California. She longs for a husband throughout the novel and finds a man to marry only after she is jailed for fighting for the union. Political conversion precedes lovemaking in the novel. Successful reproduction becomes a symbol for the possibilities of equitable production. Moreover, the partnership between humans and the earth prior to industrial capitalism's interference mirrors the fulfilling and willing partnership Babb depicts in many of the novel's marriages.[82] As scholar Erin Battat points out, the novel's final climax involves "not a conversion to class consciousness but a commitment to an egalitarian marriage."[83]

Equitable production in *Whose Names* requires a rejection not only of patriarchy and human domination of nature but also of racial privilege. As

Anna says to Max, "Interesting too . . . how we're not really divided according to our nationalities, but by how much or how little money we have."[84]
Class trumps race in the novel. Poor whites realize that their class status
determines the way they are treated more than their racial privilege. Like
Steinbeck, Babb depicts the process through which Dust Bowl migrants
lose their white privilege upon entering California. The children are teased
and called "Okies" at school. This change affects the children's psychology
as they think, *"'Okie' is a funny word, and an okie is me. Someone different.
Someone not as good."*[85] This racialization serves as a form of labor control.
Julia says that some of the clubwomen "want to have us all sterilized," to
which her husband responds, "Yow, they want to fix us like horses. Just
good for work. . . . I felt desperate when he said they don't like their kids
mixing."[86] Racist accusations in the novel serve as political repression. At
one point, the bosses charge into a group of Dust Bowl migrants, screaming "White niggers!," and attempt to remove one man in particular.[87] The
scene is reminiscent of lynch mobs that murdered African Americans; the
targeted man, Martin, is falsely accused of sexually assaulting the boss's
wife. Milt explains that Martin was actually attacked because "he's trying
to organize us."[88] In Babb's novel, bosses employ oppressive tactics against
white migrants that are commonly directed at black communities. This suggests the economic motivations for oppression and repression, echoing the
economic understanding of race advanced by McWilliams's *Factories in the
Field*.

   Whereas *Grapes of Wrath* responds to the denigration of white migrants
by affirming their whiteness, Babb's characters empathize with workers of
color. The characters' growing understanding of their class position leads
them to a sense of cross-racial solidarity: "You were just growling about the
Mexicans the other day working for nothing," Julia says testily. Her husband responds, "Oh well, I reckon they work for nothing for the same reason
we do."[89] Similarly, when Milt first meets Garrison, who is black, he thinks,
*"We're both picking cotton for the same hand-to-mouth wages. I'm no better'n he
is; he's no worse.* The memory of being called a white nigger in Imperial Valley
lay in his mind unforgotten, sore, like an exposed nerve."[90] Milt's experience of being called a "white nigger" allows him to see his similarity to black
workers. Rather than reassert a racial hierarchy, Milt dissolves that hierar-

chy. All farmworkers, no matter their race, are equal.[91] Babb's characters, moreover, look to black and Filipino characters for leadership. Her white characters are tutored by Garrison and the Filipino union organizer Pedro, who was likely based on Carlos Bulosan.[92] Babb's white migrants learn from those whose resistance to oppression preceded them. Milt senses the skills that Garrison has acquired in a lifetime of dealing with oppression. He thinks, "Somehow he wanted this man's respect, and suddenly he was not ashamed to acknowledge it himself."[93] Milt's instincts are not misplaced. When Garrison learns that a strike by inexperienced workers is under way, he calls in the union for backup. It is Garrison's house at which the organizers gather. Babb suggests that without the union and Garrison's leadership, the uprising would have been crushed far more easily.

Babb's inclusion of Garrison, along with his wife Phoebe, cements rather than fragments the Dust Bowl migrants' class bonds. It affirms Babb's vision of a racially inclusive "we" constituting "the people." Black workers were present in California's fields and active in some agricultural strikes.[94] Jesse McHenry, a black Communist Party member, organized agricultural labor throughout the 1930s, and Babb modeled Phoebe on a black chairwoman she witnessed in the camps.[95] Yet Popular Front representations of California agriculture rarely featured African Americans. Both McWilliams and Steinbeck ignore black workers. While Dorothea Lange photographed black agricultural workers, they were not included in her major publications.[96] Aside from Babb's novel and recently published photos by her sister Dorothy, one of the only other progressive works to foreground black farmworkers in California during this period was Langston Hughes's little known play, *Harvest*.[97] Why this absence of attention to California's black farmworkers? The popular discourse around Dust Bowl migrants focused on white farmers losing their land. Advocates (such as Steinbeck in his pamphlet "Their Blood Is Strong") countered depictions of "Okies" as being less than white, calling for the restoration of their white privilege. Babb's novel is unique because her characters refuse to claim white privilege and instead forge a multiracial class consciousness under the leadership of black and Filipino labor organizers.

The solidarity the Dunnes enact with Garrison and Pedro further illustrates the novel's reconceptualization of political belonging. Black people were excluded from substantive citizenship privileges during this period, while Filipinos were deemed "noncitizen nationals." Yet in Babb's novel, Pedro and Garrison become "the people's" leaders. Through Pedro's and Garrison's leadership, the novel offers a new vision of the nation's citizenry and a new possibility for its government.

Throughout the novel, we are told that the old system is dying and a new system is being born. Julia thinks, "Seems the world's like an old horse that's had spells of colic ever so long and finally has such a bad one he can't get up and knows he's about quit kicking. If it was a horse, his master would shoot him and break in a new horse."[98] According to the characters, more is needed than a simple reform of capitalism and the United States. The world needs to be built anew. Babb naturalizes this process when Max states, "It's like nature, maybe it's human nature, that when something dies and rots something new and healthy grows up to take its place."[99] Capitalism is rotting; industrial unionization is growing up "new and healthy" from the novel's multiracial working-class alliance. Revolutionary rhetoric rises from the salt of the earth, those who work the soil. It grows as an American crop. Babb follows in the footsteps of Thomas Jefferson, J. Hector St. John Crévecoeur, and Frederick Jackson Turner in looking to the landscape to define the American character. But the crop that she grows is a revolutionary one. It embraces racial inclusivity, earth's agency, and more equitable gender relationships.

Through their collective relationship in unionization, the characters find the satisfaction they once had in relation to the earth. Through union activity, the workers begin to feel the freedom that Old Man Dunne felt from his land. Milt realizes, "It was better to starve than to become the shadow of a man on this earth that could give him a full, whole life. . . . He wants more than bread and sleep; he wants himself—a man to wear the dignity of his reason."[100] In the text's final moments, humanity is reborn: "The word *love* lay in the warm air of the little tent for each of them to feel in the unashamed and simple truth of his knowing."[101] The bonds of nation reliant on human division and labor segmentation are broken as the multiracial community of workers become "as one man."[102] Thus, Babb's novel finds the possibility for human potential, the ability to simultaneously achieve freedom and security, in multiracial revolutionary unionism. Multiracial revolutionary unionism offers the spirituality and sense of purpose that Dust Bowl migrants once found in their relationship to the soil.

CONCLUSION

Both *Grapes of Wrath* and *Whose Names* affirm the racial politics of land ownership explored in the first chapter. The novels present Dust Bowl migrants' dispossession as a crisis of white citizenship. Like Carey McWilliams and Ruth Comfort Mitchell, Steinbeck and Babb both see white migrants' loss of land ownership as threatening to their racial privilege. While Steinbeck's novel affirms the citizenship of white migrants through their race and inherent Jeffersonian qualities, Babb's characters replace their allegiance to racialized citizenship with a multiracial class consciousness. In this way, Babb's novel escapes the racial pull of California agrarianism in a way that even McWilliams's *Factories in the Field* was unable to do. In imagining black and Filipino leadership, Babb's work stands apart from that of many other Popular Front representations of white Dust Bowl migrants' plight in California's fields.

CHAPTER 3

The "Clouded Citizenship" of Rooted Families

Japanese American Agrarianism in *Rafu Shimpo*, *Kashu Mainichi*, and *Treadmill*

W HILE WHITE DUST BOWL MIGRANTS FOUND THEIR whiteness under question when they lost ownership of their farms, Japanese Americans found themselves unable to gain access to white citizenship even through land ownership. Until World War II, Japanese immigrants and Japanese Americans sought to deploy Jeffersonian racial scripts to their own advantage. Yet these attempts, in newspapers, short stories, and novels, proved largely unsuccessful. While land ownership could Americanize poor whites, some political and business organizations saw Japanese American land ownership as a treasonous transfer of US land to Japan. As Austin Anson, the managing secretary of the Grower-Shipper Vegetable Association of Central California put it, "It's a question of whether the white man lives on the Pacific Coast or the brown man."[1] Under this racial logic, American agrarianism could not assimilate the unassimilable Asian other. Japanese immigrants and Japanese Americans remained cast as perpetual foreigners who could transform American nature but could not be transformed by it.

This chapter explores the racial politics of land ownership at work in Japanese American claims to national belonging during the 1930s. It analyzes two Los Angeles Japanese newspapers, *Kashu Mainichi* (Japanese California Daily News) and *Rafu Shimpo* (Los Angeles Japanese Daily News) alongside Hiroshi Nakamura's novel *Treadmill*. In attending to these cultural documents, this chapter considers the ways some Japanese Americans used agriculture to situate themselves in relation to other nonwhite groups in California, such as Filipinos, blacks, and Mexicans. Japanese American attempts to claim agricultural citizenship not only relied on the whiteness of land ownership but also required a distance from other groups racialized as abject aliens. It is only when such texts question the racist foundations of Jeffersonian agrarianism that interracial solidarity becomes possible.

Throughout the 1930s, *Kashu Mainichi* and *Rafu Shimpo* portrayed agriculture as proof of Japanese immigrants' economic and cultural contribution to the United States. They emphasized the shared class position of white and Japanese American growers in the face of strikes by Mexican and Filipino workers, obscuring the presence of Japanese strikers. Through criminalized depictions of Mexicans, Filipinos, and blacks, the newspapers affirmed racialized images of the strikers as violent and threatening. They reinforced the racial logic of the construction of the "abject alien" laborer by racially aligning Japanese Americans with white farmers.

In contrast, Nakamura's *Treadmill* examines agrarianism's failure to protect the characters from internment during World War II. *Treadmill* follows the protagonist Teru as she is uprooted from her family's farm, suffers physically and emotionally during internment, and eventually is sent to Tule Lake to await deportation, or "repatriation," to Japan, a nation she has never visited. The novel charts the characters' realization that their performance as loyal American farmers offers them no protection from the most virulent forms of US racism, setting the stage for an interracial solidarity not seen in the 1930s newspapers. Teru finds that she can best embody the democratic ideals of the nation once she has left its territory, turning her back on her parents' pre-internment agrarianism. A deterritorialized identity allows her access to Americanness in ways that a rooted relationship to the nation never did. Only in escaping the nation and its racial script of land ownership can her citizenship be recognized.

"THE SPECTER OF THE JAPANESE FARMER"

Farm labor shaped pre-internment Japanese American lived experiences on the West Coast.[2] From 1900 until 1913, the majority of California's agricultural laborers were Japanese.[3] When Pearl Harbor was bombed, between one-third and one-half of all Japanese immigrants and Japanese Americans were farmers or farmworkers.[4] Japanese Americans responded to the material and ideological positioning of their agricultural contributions.

From the early days of Japanese immigration, anti-Japanese agitators built on anti-Chinese sentiment to depict Japanese immigrants as a threat to California's economic and moral order.[5] Following Japan's victory in the Russo-Japanese War (1904–5), exclusionists such as California senator James D. Phelan positioned Japanese immigrants as a military threat as well.[6] Invoking Japan's rising status as a modern power, they purported that Japanese American agricultural success put US land in the hands of a foreign government, creating the possibility of fifth column activity.[7]

While Chinese exclusion activities highlighted the threat that Chinese workers supposedly posed to white workers, anti-Japanese agitation focused on Japanese Americans' growing land ownership as jeopardizing white farmworkers' ability to climb the agricultural ladder.[8] According to Senator Phelan, the Japanese "are not content to work for wages, as do the Chinese, who are excluded, but are always seeking control of the farm."[9] Anti-Asian agitators specifically decried Japanese American women's participation in family farm labor as an unfair economic advantage and a perversion of US family values.[10] Senator Phelan viewed the very traits that seemed most American in white workers, such as the desire to own land rather than work for wages, as particularly suspicious in Japanese immigrants. Anti-Japanese agitation culminated in California's Alien Land Laws, first passed in 1913 and strengthened in 1920.[11] These laws aimed to prevent Japanese immigrants from owning or leasing farmland, though many were able to get around the provisions.[12]

Despite this rhetoric, Japanese agricultural workers and farm owners rarely, if ever, posed an economic threat to California's white population, either to its agricultural elite or to its working class.[13] Japanese Americans expanded the productivity of land through intensive labor practices rather than extensive land holdings.[14] Japanese Americans operated only 2 percent of all farms and 0–0.3 percent of the total farm acreage in California.[15] The average farm owned or leased by first-generation Japanese immigrants, or Issei, in 1940 was forty acres, compared to the state average of two hundred acres.[16] Even when Japanese Americans owned farms, they competed mainly with other small-time growers, not the powerful Associated Farmers.

Japanese Americans were, however, essential to California's booming agricultural industry. While white farmers focused on crops suited to large tracts of land and mechanized methods of harvest, such as wheat and potatoes, Japanese American farmers produced labor-intensive crops such as strawberries and tomatoes.[17] Japanese Americans produced 30 to 42 percent of all truck crops.[18] In certain areas they held a virtual monopoly, producing 90 percent of strawberries, 73 percent of snap peas, 75 percent of celery, and at least 50 percent of tomatoes.[19] Through these niche crops, Japanese Americans contributed to the West Coast's agricultural identity without directly threatening white growers' markets.[20] In 1940, there were 6,170 Japanese-operated farms, of which 70 percent were tenant-operated. Many of the rest were owned, at least in name, by Nisei.[21] The extent of Japanese immigrants' agricultural contributions, despite the relatively limited amount of land they controlled, resulted from their intensive methods of cultivation and crop specialization.

Although Japanese Americans' farm ownership was not extensive, it still threatened the racial meanings endowed in white farmers' relationship to the soil. Japanese Americans were more easily imagined as farmworkers than as farmers. This is apparent in suggestions following Pearl Harbor that Japanese Americans be used as a labor force under military guard on agricultural land owned by white Californians. For example, the Pacific League, a Southern California civic organization, issued a resolution on February 2, 1942, advocating "that all Japanese people of both foreign and American birth, be drafted into an agricultural division under supervision of the Department of Agriculture of the Federal Government in the same manner as draftees of the United States military forces are inducted into service . . . creating a great agricultural army providing both a humanitarian and practical solution of this immediate problem and eliminating a menace to our general welfare."[22] Exhortations to employ Japanese Americans as coerced field laborers highlighted the threat that Japanese American economic mobility and land ownership posed to racialized conceptions of the US citizen as farm owner. Recasting Japanese Americans as deterritorialized workers reinforced their status as aliens and reified the relationship among whiteness, citizenship, and land ownership.

While the Pacific League's proposal did not come to fruition, interned Japanese Americans were used as agricultural labor during the war. The

camps were to produce their own food, with surplus going to the war ef-
fort.²³ Additionally, the first Japanese Americans to receive clearance from
the internment camps were sent out on work crews to save Idaho's sugar
beet crops from a labor shortage.²⁴ In Colorado, Arizona, Utah, Montana,
and Wyoming, interned Japanese Americans labored in the fields, sometimes alongside German POWs, while Mexican "guest workers" worked
California's fields under the Bracero Program.²⁵ This reality reveals the desired place of the alien citizen (both Asian American and Latina/o) in US
agriculture. Farmworkers were perceived as temporary migrants and not as
full participants in the nation. As laborers, Japanese Americans, US-born
or immigrant, economically and ideologically fit the bill. They could be used
to support the nation's goals as long as they remained workers rather than
landowning citizens.

Not all white citizens, of course, perceived Japanese Americans as always and inevitably workers rather than farmer-citizens. While the Grower-
Shipper Association and the Pacific League positioned Japanese Americans
as abject aliens unsuited for farm ownership, some New Deal liberals cast
Japanese Americans as potential citizens. As a New Deal project, internment camps appeared capable of assimilating Japanese immigrants and
Japanese Americans.²⁶ Ansel Adams's famous Manzanar photographs exemplify this ideology. As Elena Tajima Creef writes, "In the logic of Adams's
narrative, the Japanese Americans are fortunate to have been transported
to the desert where they can be transmuted by the landscape and disciplined
through the camp's self-sustaining work into productive citizens ready to
pursue the 'opportunity of America' upon their eventual release."²⁷ Adams's
description of internee agricultural production captures this philosophy:
"There is nothing in the world, perhaps as poignant as the emergence of
crops from harsh and barren land. . . . With irrigation—sparse as it is in
this land from which most of the water has been appropriated—and with
hard work, the men and women of Manzanar have brought forth food from
the earth and brought pride of achievement to their hearts."²⁸ According
to Creef, Dorothea Lange's internment photographs used images of Japanese American land loss to a more radical purpose. She visually paralleled
the tragedies of Japanese American internment and Dust Bowl migration,
suggesting the similar ways both groups covered over their vulnerability
with dignity. In Lange's vision, white Dust Bowl migrants and Japanese

Americans had equal claim to substantive citizenship. Their loss of land was similarly disastrous.[29]

Thus, some white representations of Japanese agrarianism positioned Japanese Americans as abject aliens better suited to wage or slave labor than land ownership. Others, such as Adams and many internment officials, saw Japanese Americans as being in need of assimilation, and envisioned agricultural labor in the internment context as being redemptive, creating loyal citizens ready for release. A few, such as Lange, positioned Japanese Americans as proper citizens prior to internment, recognizing internment as the racist tragedy it was. This is the complicated discursive landscape navigated by Japanese American agrarianism.

THE BACKBONE OF JAPANESE LIFE

In 1935, *Kashu Mainichi* columnist Larry Tajiri wrote, "The backbone, the spinal column, of Japanese life in the United States then, is the farmer."[30] Throughout the 1930s, such sentiments filled the pages of the English-language sections of the two major Los Angeles Japanese American daily newspapers, *Rafu Shimpo* and *Kashu Mainichi*.[31] In the 1930s, these newspapers represented agriculture as being central to the Japanese American experience and as the primary medium for Japanese Americans to establish their national belonging.[32] Both *Rafu Shimpo* and *Kashu Mainichi* were published predominantly in Japanese yet contained at least one page a day (more on Sunday) in English that catered to a Nisei, or second-generation, audience.[33] The articles were not translations of the Japanese features; they were written by a separate staff, including their own English-language editors. The English-language sections provided a forum for the rising stars of the Nisei generation. Despite the papers' slight political differences, their depictions of agriculture were quite similar.[34]

During the Great Depression, *Kashu Mainichi* and *Rafu Shimpo* used agriculture to establish the Issei as being historically important to California. As Larry Tajiri wrote in *Rafu Shimpo*, "Though slighted by historians who dipped their pens in blood and thunder, the growth of a great state, California, has been coupled with the growing importance of the Japanese in agriculture in the state."[35] The Japanese, Tajiri insists, deserve credit for California's glory. The newspapers' depictions of Issei agricultural contributions correlate with the Issei pioneer narrative identified by historian Eiichiro Azuma. The pioneer narrative "challenged the Anglo-American monopoly of frontier expansionism, arguing for [Japanese American] relevance to the settling of the west."[36] According to Azuma, this pioneer thesis, promoted by amateur Japanese American historians, catered to colonialist desires of both US Manifest Destiny and burgeoning Japanese imperialism. In the newspapers' descriptions, Japanese pioneers, like white pioneers, struggled against economic uncertainty, but prevailed due to their hard work and perhaps the favor of God. Japanese pioneers served alongside white pioneers as Manifest Destiny's laborers, providing the work that transformed America's resources into the nation's wealth.

Farming played a pivotal ideological role in the Issei pioneer narrative. Consider this *Kashu Mainichi* editorial: "The soil has been kind to the Japanese pioneers in California. Back-breaking toil, the many years of sweaty, hard labor which the first generation Japanese have given the land have been returned in full measure in abundant crops, and in later years in the transition of virtual control of many of the Japanese agriculturists."[37] In contrast to the white labor movement's narrative of Asian immigrants as slaves lowering working standards for white agricultural workers, *Rafu Shimpo* and *Kashu Mainichi* portray the Japanese immigrant as Jeffersonian farmer. Figuring Japanese immigrants as pioneers places them in a mythic time prior to agricultural industrialization. The Japanese immigrant's rightful place as US land owner becomes naturalized through descriptions of the willing American soil producing plentiful crops. Such descriptions obfuscate Japanese immigrants' location in a racialized labor hierarchy. It also obscures that many Issei never transitioned from farm laborer to farm owner. Instead, the newspapers' narrative offers a progressive timeline in which the Issei's hard work provides the stepping-stone for the building of cultured community, advancing from its frontier roots.

Such a formulation dominated the Central Farmers Association's "Back to the Farm" campaign, launched in 1933 and heavily supported by both papers.[38] The campaign urged Nisei to pursue farming as a career.[39] It argued that Japanese success in America would be measured by participation in the farming industry. Writers proclaimed, "Without the farming industry the Japanese could not have reached the present status that they now enjoy," and "Agriculture is seen as best vocation to attain recognition by American [sic]."[40] The newspapers emphasized that Nisei could increase the recognition of their parents' contributions by furthering the Japanese American presence in California's agricultural industry.[41] Farming provided an assured way for Nisei to establish a positive Japanese American legacy in California.

According to the papers, returning to the farm not only respected Issei sacrifices but also recognized the Nisei duty to their American homeland. George H. Nakamoto, *Rafu Shimpo*'s English-section editor, proclaimed, "As citizens of America, the nisei can best serve the country to which they owe their education and citizenship by developing the industry that is purely American in product."[42] According to M. M. Horii, "As American citizens, we must and should attach ourselves permanently to society and the State by acquiring land and other property."[43] Such articles positioned farm ownership as evidence of Nisei's loyalty.

The newspapers depicted farming as being modern, scientific, and the ideal occupation for Nisei to advance themselves. Nisei faced severe employment limitations, regardless of educational level, due to racial discrimination. The papers depicted agriculture as a welcoming field in which Nisei success was possible.[44] As Azuma notes, "It is ironic that the overall exclusion of the Japanese from most other economic sectors, which caused their lopsided involvement in agriculture in the first place, gave them this hope, when in reality Issei farming underscored the severe limitations to Japanese livelihoods in the United States."[45] The newspapers suggested that farming could be the avenue through which Nisei could engage with other vocations, as they worked within an increasingly modernized, scientific agriculture. As "a Nisei Farmer" wrote, "The time when a farmer could make profit in farming by just swinging a hoe, or driving an ill smelling horse from sunrise to sunset is gone. At present, and even more so in the future, a farmer must be a combination chemist, biologist, entomologist, meteorologist, and economist in order to derive proper returns."[46] Agriculture could encompass other professions from which Nisei were unfairly locked out. Kamata Ota, president of the Cooperative Farm Industry of Southern California, explained that Nisei should not "[limit] themselves in production alone, but by advancing into the distribution, transportation, and marketing. . . . There should be a gradual diminishing of the so-called problem of the lack of vocations for the second generation."[47] One author suggested that the Nisei farmer need not even live in the country. He could run the farm from a city office.[48] Thus agriculture was transformed from an industry of sacrifice to a business requiring advanced education and allowing endless opportunities.

The newspapers positioned the Japanese American community as unified in their class position as small farmers, obscuring the community's true class diversity. This is apparent in the papers' nearly daily coverage of the agricultural strikes that raged in the southland during the early 1930s.[49] Although Japanese Americans were involved in strikes as growers and as laborers, the Japanese American press related a "critical wage war between Japanese farmer and Mexican ranch laborer."[50] This narrative obscured Japanese laborers' presence among the strikers. The construction of the strikes as racially rather than economically based obscured the material interests at the heart of the struggle by promoting ethnic identity over class-consciousness.[51] This aligned Japanese growers with white growers against Mexican and Filipino workers.[52]

The papers articulated their investment in ethnic solidarity by emphasizing Japanese workers' support for Japanese growers. *Kashu Mainichi* vehemently contested the existence of Japanese strikers: "Contrary to the news item in 'Western Worker,' communist weekly, the Japanese grape pickers have not sent in delegates from the fields declaring that they are ready to strike with others."[53] *Kashu Mainichi*'s attack on the *Western Worker* was part of a broader red-baiting strategy.[54] As one article suggested, "Although many Japanese have left the fields here at the insistence of agitators, many returned immediately after the agitators have left."[55] Such rhetoric both rejected the possibility of class-conscious Japanese American workers and depicted legitimate union activity as anti-American communism. The papers conveyed that Japanese Americans would only participate in such actions under duress.[56]

In addition to obscuring and dismissing the actions of striking Japanese laborers, the papers highlighted Nisei strike-breaking actions and the Japanese American Citizens League's (JACL) support for such endeavors.[57] Coverage of Nisei strike breakers emphasized their heroism, as *Kashu Mainichi* proclaimed: "Venice Japanese Rescued by Nisei Volunteers: To Continue Celery Packing; Farmers Grateful."[58] Another article celebrated, "Sixty nisei volunteer workers cleaned one field in spite of threatening strikers."[59] In this formulation, brave Nisei risked violent retaliation by strikers to assist victim-like growers. The papers celebrated Issei laborers' refusal to strike and the Nisei generation's scab labor as a signs of loyalty to the United States.

The papers' red-baiting strategies furthered this loyalty narrative. A *Rafu Shimpo* editorial asserted, "California agriculture is harassed by labor disturbances, practically all of which are instigated or participated in by Communists and other un-American elements."[60] Similarly, *Kashu Mainichi* stated that "the movement was instigated by paid agitators and for the most part was not the expression of the workers as a whole."[61] Strike participants' un-Americanness affirmed the loyalty of Japanese growers, workers, and Nisei (who such articles depicted as neither growers nor laborers). An editorial in *Rafu Shimpo* stated, "Though denied the rights and privileges accorded the full fledged American citizens, though classed as 'aliens' ineligible to ever attain that status, the Issei Japanese have long proved themselves worthy of American principles and have maintained their stand against radicals and Communists consistent with the attitude of the nation as a whole."[62]

The desire for the Japanese American subject to be consistent with "the attitude of the nation as a whole" is apparent in the papers' depiction of Mexicans, Filipinos, and blacks. The language of racial strife was seldom far from articles, such as in the headline "Fear Racial War as Farm Labor Strike Spreads in Santa Maria Valley Area."[63] The depiction of racial strife obscured the material interests at the heart of workers' struggles. Moreover, the Japanese press employed derogatory racial stereotypes of Filipinos and Mexicans to depict strikers as violent, irrational, and controlled by communists. *Kashu Mainichi* stated, "Striking in an effort to force Japanese ranchers of Southern California to meet their demand for exorbitant salaries and the hiring of 90 per cent unionization, a belligerent group of Mexican and Filipino farm-hands led by representatives of the United-Agricultural Workers' Union of America yesterday fought a stern battle with several policemen seeking to quiet the 300 rioters."[64] *Rafu Shimpo* stated, "Aroused over the unreasonable demands by the Mexican labor union, officials of the San Diego and Chula Vista Chambers of Commerce stepped into the controversy between the Japanese growers and the Mexicans and issued a warning that unless the Mexicans conform to the terms set down by the Japanese, drastic action will be enforced."[65]

This portrayal of Mexican and Filipino workers as "unreasonable," "belligerent," and requiring state discipline was not a racial formation emerging solely out of class interests in the contexts of the strikes. Similar depictions in *Rafu Shimpo* and *Kashu Mainichi* appeared throughout the 1930s in reports on crime, automobile accidents, and love affairs. The criminalization of Filipinos, Mexicans, and blacks can be seen in just a small sampling of the headlines: "Filipino Bandits Rob Nisei Couple, Threaten to Kill Baby Daughter"; "Mexican Gunman Wounds Nipponese Woman in Robbery"; "Three Nisei Robbed in Super Market Hold-Up by Negroes"; "Lil' Tokio Raids Confessed; Two Mexicans Jailed"; and "Filipino Trio Arrested in Police Drive to Protect Lil' Tokio."[66] Such headlines generated the distinct sense of a crime wave and articulated the Japanese population's fear of Filipinos, blacks, and Mexicans. The papers depicted all three groups as disorderly and deadly.[67]

The consequences of this criminalization campaign can be seen in the case of twenty-year-old Harou Tanaka, who, in 1937, apparently murdered his ten-year-old niece and blamed it on two Mexicans, spurring a manhunt before confessing. Despite the cloud of suspicion the police cast over Tanaka, the Japanese papers initially offered support. *Rafu Shimpo* dedicated a full column to the story of the "indignant" Tanaka:

> My niece and I had spent the day visiting in San Diego and were returning home by automobile when we stopped at Manchester and Inglewood to watch the setting sun and to get a view of the city below. Shizuko had to get off the car a minute, and while I was waiting, two Mexicans approached and began acting queerly. I immediately took out the Colt gun which was in the pocket of the car, but before I knew what was happening, they were upon me. They succeeded in wresting the gun away and were beating me, when Shizuko, who was returning at the time, began to scream and then run way. One of the Mexicans shot her, and as I rushed on him, he shot me point blank. When I awoke, I was laying beside her. I got up to summon aid, and remember crawling through the weeds. Then I woke up here.[68]

The ease with which Tanaka lied and the willingness of the Japanese community to believe him are chillingly similar to the story of Susan Smith, who murdered her children and then cast the blame on an anonymous black man. Tanaka, like Smith, responded to and affirmed society's criminalization of Mexican and black masculinity.[69] Through stories like Tanaka's, the newspapers contributed to a larger racial project of the criminalization of black, Mexican, and Filipino youth.[70]

The newspapers' criminalization of Mexicans and Filipinos contributed to the claim that Mexican and Filipino strikers threatened the Japanese American community. The newspapers depicted strikes as a form of economic harm (loss of agricultural profits) similar to the harm caused by kidnappings and robberies. The newspapers articulated the strikes' potential to imperil Japanese American agricultural prosperity as a direct threat to Japanese Americans' ability to claim the rights and privileges bestowed on white citizens. Throughout most of the 1930s, and in contrast to the class-conscious *Doho*, both *Rafu Shimpo* and *Kashu Mainichi* argued that Japanese Americans' socioeconomic status protected them from the most virulent forms of racism. *Rafu Shimpo* and *Kashu Mainichi* recognized that Japanese Americans were susceptible to the same low status as other racial minorities should their economic importance falter. One article warned, "[Agriculture] is the only means for the prevention of the Japanese people from falling into the bewildered obscurity of the Negro and the Mexican."[71] Articles claimed that agricultural success protected Japanese Americans from even worse incarnations of US racism. Rather than recognizing a shared struggle for multiracial equality, the papers contrasted Japanese American prosperity with the criminal behavior of blacks, Filipinos, and Mexicans. In doing so, they articulated a version of Japanese American identity that may be interpreted as a precursor to the modern model minority myth.

Agriculture was central to the articulation of this protomodel minority subject. *Rafu Shimpo* and *Kashu Mainichi* emphasized agriculture's ability to protect Japanese Americans from the exclusion and racism facing other racial minorities. By highlighting the racial tension between Japanese growers and Mexican and Filipino workers, the papers obscured the class diversity of the Japanese American community, envisioning Japanese Americans as the quintessential family farmers. Ultimately, these strategies failed to protect the Japanese American community from the dominant racial formations of Yellow Peril, and internment resulted in the significant loss of Japanese American agricultural holdings.

JAPANESE AMERICAN AMBASSADOR

Like *Kashu Mainichi* and *Rafu Shimpo*, the novel *Treadmill* opens by imagining Japanese American agricultural labor through the trope of the independent American farmer. The Noguchis' agricultural labor communicates their citizenship through their economic contributions and active cultural assimilation. This is similar to the case the newspapers made through their "Back to the Farm" campaign and pioneer narratives. Yet, while the newspapers envision a unified Japanese American community protected from the most virulent forms of US racism by their agricultural success, *Treadmill* suggests a common ground among disenfranchised groups, who are trapped on the same treadmill, chasing an American dream they can never achieve. The book grapples with the failure of farm ownership to protect Japanese Americans from the virulence of US racism and articulates instead an emergent internationalist human rights framework in its final pages.

Treadmill is the only known novel about internment written by a Japanese American during internment. Historian Peter Suzuki discovered it in the National Archives in 1952, publishing it in 1996. Little is known of Hiroshi Nakamura (1915–1973), who passed away before Suzuki contacted him. According to his family, he was born in Gilroy, California, and attended San Jose State College before transferring to the University of California, Berkeley. He graduated in 1937 with a degree in zoology. Prior to World War II, he penned several short stories under the pseudonym Allen Middletown, believing that an Anglo pseudonym would improve his chances of publication. Unfortunately, he received only rejections. Nakamura was interned in the Salinas Assembly Center, followed by the Poston camp in Arizona. He was eventually transferred to Tule Lake, California, and completed *Treadmill* while working for Tule Lake's Community Analysis Section. At Tule Lake he married Mary Sato Nakamura, who remembers "using our battered but serviceable old portable nightly to type the manuscript in our camp room." After the war Nakamura returned to Los Angeles and sent

Treadmill to a number of publishers, who liked the novel but, according to Nakamura's wife, "feared publishing it could damage their reputation."[72]

Despite its historical significance, *Treadmill* remains a largely unknown novel. It follows the experience of college-age Teru Noguchi, whose family—sister Sally, brother Tad, and parents—are small-time truck farmers in California. In the opening pages, Teru's father is unexpectedly arrested by the FBI. The remaining Noguchis are interned, and Mrs. Noguchi suffers heatstroke. The stroke, combined with negligent medical responses, leaves Mrs. Noguchi impaired. In camp, Teru begins dating a disillusioned young man named Jiro while Sally falls for Teru's former boyfriend, George.

While the government eventually returns Mr. Noguchi to his family, the loyalty oath further disrupts their lives. The government administered the loyalty oath to Issei and Nisei over eighteen years of age, failing to anticipate the confusion and resistance that the questionnaire generated. Question 27 inquired, "Are you willing to serve in the armed forces of the United States on combat duty, wherever ordered?" Question 28 asked, "Will you swear unqualified allegiance to the United States of America and faithfully defend the United States from any or all attack by foreign or domestic forces, and forswear any form of allegiance to the Japanese Emperor or any other foreign government, power, or organization?" Although George, Teru, and Mr. Noguchi answer "Yes-Yes," Jiro, Sally, and Mrs. Noguchi answer "No-No." Sally changes her answer to yes to marry George after he is drafted. Sally and Teru are separated when the Noguchis are moved to Tule Lake, where the government segregated "disloyals." When Teru is given the opportunity to relocate for a well-paid secretarial position, her father announces that he has decided to apply for repatriation because the Noguchis will never be accepted in the United States. Teru decides she cannot let her elderly father, young brother, and ill mother face hardships in Japan alone.[73] The novel's final pages consist of a series of pained letters from Teru to her sister Sally on the eve of her deportation to Japan.

The novel's depiction of internment's injustice pivots on its initial portrayal of Japanese Americans as loyal members of the nation and all-American farmers. The novel first asserts Japanese American belonging to the United States through the Noguchi family's relationship to US soil and dismisses legal citizenship as a marker of loyalty. When internment is announced, Issei community members contend, "We told you [Nisei] your citizenship was only good for fair weather" (Nakamura, *Treadmill*, 8). By referencing weather, *Treadmill* depicts legal citizenship as a changing status upon which Japanese Americans cannot rely. For farmers, the weather signifies economic instability. Floods or drought could cause ruin. In referring to "clouded citizenship," Nakamura implies that changing legal meanings of Japanese American citizenship threaten the Noguchi family's socioeconomic status (8). The narrative suggests that, like the weather, citizenship is outside of the characters' control. However, since its meaning is always changing, citizenship, like weather, serves less as a determinant of identity than as a practical concern shaping material conditions. By deploying weather metaphors in agricultural contexts, the text highlights the drastic influence such practical concerns have on characters' everyday lives while refuting any correlation between legal status and national loyalty.

While the novel describes legal citizenship through the agricultural metaphor of weather, it defines national belonging through figurative rootedness. Teru, in proclaiming her parents' Americanness, offers a string of questions as evidence: "Why their purchase of the land they farmed and the house they lived in? Why should they be sending their roots down so deep?" (24). This sentiment of "sending their roots down" establishes Japanese American national belonging as a choice made by active cultivation. Teru emphasizes her parents' decision to purchase, rather than lease, land. She emphasizes their status as land owners. The focus on her parents' agency disrupts a conception of national belonging as being inevitable or biological and outside of one's control. Through metaphors such as digging and rooting, the narrative grants Japanese immigrants agency in their Americanization process. Mr. and Mrs. Noguchi nurture and tend to their relationships to local communities, American values, and US soil. In this way, the novel allows first-generation Japanese Americans to "naturalize" even though, as Asian immigrants, they are denied the legal process of naturalization.

The narrative characterizes agriculture as central to the Noguchi family's political, social, and economic contributions. *Treadmill* credits the parents with their children's assimilation. Tad's success at the track meet, Teru's academic achievement, and Sally's popularity demonstrate the family's community involvement. These accomplishments result from more than the happenstance of location; they are one consequence of Mr. and Mrs. Noguchi's active loyalty. We are told, "Why had they made Sally quit her Japanese language school when she'd gotten poor grades her first year in high school? They'd been so proud, too, when Teru had given the valedictory address. And why their purchase of education endowments to ensure sending Tad through college?" (24). This social investment directly links to the Noguchis' agricultural activities. The above passage connects their investment in their children's Americanization to their purchase of farmland, demonstrating that the Noguchis had sent "their roots down so deep" (24). The novel implicitly compares the Noguchi parents to immigrant plants, recalling Crévecoeur's *Letters from an American Farmer*. Thus the novel affirms their Americanization, justifies their agricultural activities, and attributes their children's community involvement to their relationship to the land, specifically their successful cultural cultivation of their offspring.

In addition to agricultural metaphors, the novel insists on Japanese American loyalty through kinship metaphors. Nakamura writes, "Teru remembered a story in which a mother told her adopted child, 'You weren't forced upon us by circumstance like most babies. We chose you because you were the nicest child we could find.' Her father and mother too had come of their own free choice to make America their home" (24). Teru equates the nation with a child and the immigrants with adoptive parents. Her parents' love for the nation might be as fierce as that of a parent for a child and certainly no less strong because they selected the nation. In asserting the stronger loyalty of the immigrant over the native to the national family, the text refuses to conform to assimilationist narratives that perceive the second generation as more loyal or more assimilated into the United States than the first.[74] By explicitly embracing adoption as a form of family, *Treadmill* includes immigration as a natural form of national belonging. By expanding the nuclear family, a symbol through which the nation is naturalized, *Treadmill* imagines a more inclusive national family.

If the Noguchis' actions can be described as an active rooting of the family in the United States, both physically and metaphorically, the government's intrusions can be described as an uprooting. The novel blames the government's actions for the characters' disillusionment with the United

States and its progressive narrative of improving race relations. Whereas the characters previously worked hard to legitimize their relationship to the nation, internment leads them to see themselves as unwanted by the nation and as perpetual foreigners.

The novel represents internment as a threat to the nation's security and wartime productivity because the removal of Japanese Americans from their land prevents Japanese Americans from performing their agricultural duties. The Noguchis are small-time truck farmers working for the local market. *Treadmill* demonstrates the family's national allegiance as they insist on meeting their market commitments up until the last possible minute, despite personal hardships, out of "duty" (1). They are prevented from doing their duty by the FBI's removal of Teru's father and later by the violent racism Teru encounters on her vegetable route. The novel's first page makes apparent that the government men force Teru's parents to abandon their work in the yard hoeing parsnips and bunching carrots: "Must be important, [Teru] thought, for both of them to leave the last-minute work which had to be done" (1). Teru completes her father's work only to encounter youth who attack her truck, screaming racist epithets, and break gasoline-filled glass jars over her vegetables, rendering them unsalable. Within the novel, white racism enacts economic sabotage on the American nation by disrupting the war contributions of loyal Japanese Americans.

Internment not only disrupts the parents' agricultural endeavors but also removes the children from the activities that signal their American-ness. We are told that "Teru, Sally, and Tad had made arrangements to quit junior college and high school that very day" (5). Tad is in first place in the track meet when Teru rushes him home—mid-meet—to say good-bye to his father as the government men take him away. His father's arrest prevents Tad from achieving his athletic potential. Likewise, Sally must be pulled away from joyriding with friends as a result of the FBI's presence in their home. By removing the Noguchi children from their social, athletic, and academic contexts, the US government disrupts the processes that produce "good Americans." One character says, "Look, we talk American. We act American. We are Americans. It'd be strange if we weren't, after being exposed to it all these years in school and at work" (51). Internment pulls the characters further and further away from the rest of the nation. Teru's friendship with best friend, Janet, who is French American, is symptomatic. After Janet's first visit to the internment camp, Teru "felt unwillingly that their friendship would never be the same again. They were being exposed to such totally different environments and interpretations and as time passed they would inevitably grow away from each other" (55). Internment not only removes Teru from a typical American youth but also creates a set of new experiences to which only Japanese Americans are exposed. This fosters a growing gulf between Japanese Americans and white Americans.

In depicting the material and ideological changes undergone by Mr. and Mrs. Noguchi, Jiro, and Teru, *Treadmill* blames internment for the characters' increasing distrust of the US government and disillusionment with American ideals. Internment creates rather than responds to Japanese American disloyalty. Mrs. Noguchi suffers heatstroke as the internees languish in overheated buses in weather upward of 122 degrees Fahrenheit. Teru says, "No one can say that the heat is killing these people, but our hygiene teacher at J.C. told us that the death rate definitely rises during a heat wave, and so, I myself believe that those people would be living today if they hadn't been forced to come to this awful place" (79). As Mrs. Noguchi develops a mental illness following her heatstroke, Sally explicitly condemns the government, stating, "Look what they did to Mother" (153). Mrs. Noguchi's illness leads her to turn against the United States, captured in her No-No response on the loyalty questionnaire. Her disloyalty can be traced back to the negligence that led to her altered state of mind. Mrs. Noguchi's No-No answers result in the Noguchi family's segregation at Tule Lake and lead Mr. Noguchi to apply for repatriation. Through Mrs. Noguchi's deterioration, Nakamura blames the government for the family's "repatriation."

Whereas the early pages of the novel establish the characters' Americanness through family farming, after internment, the novel grapples with the characters' increasing frustration and disillusionment with the US government and the nation's rampant racism. One character says, "There's no use trying to delude ourselves that we're American. If our skins were white, it would be another matter. Look at the Indians around here. They say they're discriminated against even yet. Then look at the white-skinned immigrants.

They don't even have to be born here to be considered full-fledged Americans" (135). This passage establishes that loyalty and recognized national belonging have little to do with the place of one's birth. Discrimination is race-based, and the characters labor under a national system of white supremacy. The characters perceive US racism to be an unconquerable foe, an inextricably American enemy.

The characters' growing awareness of the racism affecting other non-white Americans shapes their despondency about the potential for antiracist progress. Whereas newspapers such as *Kashu Mainichi* and *Rafu Shimpo* distinguished the Japanese American community from Mexican American and black populations, *Treadmill* depicts the experience of Native Americans and blacks as being similar to that of Japanese Americans. After the announcement of Executive Order 9066, Teru notices "an increasing friendliness on the part of Germans, Negroes, Italians, and Mexicans" (24). German disloyalty and Italian materialism (25), as represented by the novel, contrast with the analysis of racism offered by blacks and Mexicans, who "don't like Americans. They treat us like dirt" (25). Responding to the small pittance the internees received for harvesting the cotton crop, Teru realizes, "No wonder the negroes can't get ahead" (94). Similarly, the "dilapidated shacks" of the Indian reservations shock her, as "she'd always pictured Indian Reservations as well kept because they were under government protection" (193). The novel's characters perceive the government's treatment of other racial minorities, and the resultant economic immobility, as indicative of their own future. Teru uses information shared by local Indians—"over half the total number of Indians who were earmarked for this reservation died either on the march here or within the first months after arriving"—to understand the wave of sickness and death passing over the internment camp (79). Internment leads Teru to a new understanding of racism's consequences and slowly forces her to perceive the United States as being dominated by Anglos who prevent nonwhites from truly participating in democracy. Interracial solidarity emerges after Jeffersonian agrarianism fails to protect the Noguchis from US racism.

The novel depicts the characters' desire to leave the United States as a direct consequence of internment. When Mr. Noguchi, Teru's father, states his decision to return to Japan, it is prefaced by several pages listing the discrimination that he, his family, and his friends faced. He explains that prior to internment, he ignored it all, convinced that America "was really a land of opportunity with a limitless future for anyone with ability" (168). This list suggests that characters such as Mr. Noguchi previously persevered through many forms of racism. Their loyalty is not only "fair weather," like Nisei citizenship (8). Yet internment differs drastically from earlier incidents. As Teru's boyfriend Jiro states, "Any debt of gratitude [to the United States] I may have acknowledged was wiped out at evacuation" (139). With internment, Mr. Noguchi and Jiro come to believe that the white supremacy of American society will not be transformed in their lifetime or the lifetimes of their children. As Jiro puts it, "I'm afraid I'm not idealistic enough to want to die for my great, great grandchildren" (131). Instead, Jiro celebrates Japan, believing that its pan-Asian imperatives offer the only true hope for challenging the United States' white supremacy. He expresses the belief not only that Japan's triumph will demonstrate the possibility of Asian equality but also that Japan's actions support an anticolonial mission. He claims, "Japan has already done a great deal. Look at the record. America has given up all claims to extraterritoriality in China. England promises independence to India after the war. Holland promises a greater measure of self government for the East Indies" (130). In rearticulating the stakes in World War II, Jiro attributes to Japan the struggle for the Four Freedoms that Roosevelt ascribed to America.[75] *Treadmill* represents Jiro as a man of virtue; his citizenship renunciation is only "a natural outcome which was inevitable, at least for him, after evacuation and segregation . . . he had no choice."[76] The government remains culpable for Jiro's renunciation of his US citizenship. As evidence of the United States' hypocrisy in a war fought for "oppressed minorities . . . [and] democracy," internment represents a loss for the United States in the war's ideological battlefront. The direct casualities of this loss are loyal Americans, the Japanese American internees.

Yet Teru's impending deportation, her removal from the nation-state, turns out to be key to her ascendancy as American subject par excellence. At the heart of the novel is Teru's struggle to fulfill the role of universal US citizen, or what cultural theorist Lauren Berlant terms "abstract personhood."[77] The universal citizen or abstract person is an ideal. It is the disembodied

abstraction of citizenship that renders the presumed whiteness and maleness of the citizen invisible. The universal citizen or abstract person receives
the promises of equality before the law. Yet because society's construction
of race renders whiteness and masculinity as invisible and universal, the
nonwhite nonmale subject becomes embodied and marked as different. This
embodied subject is denied the equality promised to the universal citizen.[78]
Teru finds that, as a Japanese American woman, she can inhabit the space
of the universal citizen or abstract person only once she has left the nation.
To become the universal citizen or abstract person, she must first escape the
relationship between racialized landscape and racialized citizenship that
structures her family's previous agrarian life.

This transformation is figured through the possibility of Teru serving,
metaphorically, as an ambassador. Her white boss in the internment camp,
Mr. McBain, provides her an opportunity to leave the camp for a well-paid
secretarial job. He says, "You'll make the best ambassador I know."[79] His
description of the job of ambassadorship renders the Japanese American
community as outside of the United States, as an ambassador builds relationships between two sovereign nations. As Mr. McBain explains, Teru's
job would be to demonstrate the loyal citizenship of the Nisei population to
white America, to prove "that they [Japanese Americans] are no different
from your sons or my daughters."[80]

The novel depicts ambassadorship as a form of marriage. As a young,
strikingly pretty, and single daughter, Teru provides the prospect of intermarriage. Mr. Noguchi makes this connection when he states, "Teru is also
a girl and I regard relocation and marriage in the same light."[81] She will leave
her family to belong to the American state as a woman traded (in a deal
brokered between white men) to affirm friendship between the Japanese
American community and the white American community. This is not just
a metaphorical marriage. Teru believes that to relocate to Cleveland for
the job would require her to marry a white man, "with delivery waiting
to complete the cycle of assimilation."[82] When Teru rejects the concept of
marrying white, she repudiates that model of assimilation as well as the
Oriental exotification it would require of her. While Teru remains unable to
"put her finger on the cause," she remembers her distaste of a white school-
mate's attraction to her, expressed through comments about "the half-caste

heroine" and "hybrid virility."[83] Teru does not want a man who will love her because of his conception of her Oriental identity, built from Hollywood movies, nor does she wish to be an ambassador to the United States by modeling a Japanese American identity in which she would be required to "lose her identity as Japanese" through intermarriage and assimilation.[84] As an ambassador to white America and as an Orientalized woman expected to marry a white man, Teru would remain embodied as a Japanese subject whose foreignness would remain racially marked. She would not be able to take on the mantle of universal citizenship, even if she could remain in the United States and escape the camps.

Teru rejects this offer of relocation, opting instead for relocation to Japan with her family. Her language here is telling. She says, "Friendships were so fine and heartwarming but they didn't always last. You had to be there to tend them like a fire. They were broken, they languished, they cooled, they met with intolerance, they met with forced evacuations."[85] In this passage, Teru considers her relationship to the United States a friendship. This is strikingly different from the adopted family metaphor Teru offers at the novel's start. Teru's rejection of kinship marks her deepest statement of disillusionment. The United States had never truly integrated her family into the nation, and even if she were to "intermarry" now, choosing the United States as her spouse, she recognizes that she would remain outside of the national family. Such a marriage would only mask her subordination to the nation under the guise of romantic love.[86] Teru rejects the ambassadorship offered her both because it requires her to model a form of American identity in which she would lose her Japanese American specificity and because she recognizes that under the racial logic of the United States, white America would always see her as an outsider.

Teru instead chooses to be a different kind of ambassador, electing to relocate to Japan. In making this choice, Teru asserts an identity that allows her to become an abstract American citizen without sacrificing her Japanese American subjectivity. The final chapter takes place after Teru has been sent to Tule Lake with her parents and brother. Her sister Sally remains behind with her drafted Nisei husband, George. The novel ends as a series of pained letters from Teru to Sally. These letters imply her distance from the rest of America, as if she has already departed. Yet her letters to her sister remind the reader of her bond to the United States. They are letters written by one who is away from home and as such remind the reader of Teru's true home. In centering on the sibling relationship between Teru and Sally, *Treadmill* re-establishes a familial bond between Teru and the United States.

These letters to Sally capture Teru's voice, her individuality, and her subjectivity. They represent her communication and her consciousness as increasingly set aside and separate from the rest of the work. Here the novel transforms from its earlier alternating modes of modernist fiction, documentary realism, and sentimental melodrama. It takes on the form of an epistolary novel. Scholars from Lynn Hunt to Nancy Armstrong perceive an eighteenth-century cultural transition visible in the popularity of epistolary novels and domestic fiction (such as Samuel Richardson's *Pamela*) that allowed the production of modern individual subjectivity.[87] The interiority central to these novels articulated the consciousness that allows universal subjectivity. The citizen-subject of the modern nation-state relies on this conscious universal subject. Teru strives to be the abstract and ideal American citizen who has access to the nation's promise of equality, and who has achieved subjecthood, the modern marker of personhood. *Treadmill* documents Teru's moves toward universal western subjecthood (or abstract personhood) by blurring the boundaries between protagonist and narrator, and eventually uses epistolary conventions to erase this distinction altogether. In doing so the novel documents Teru's ascent to universal US citizen at the very moment of her exclusion from the nation. Indeed, such a transformation can be complete only once Teru has left the United States. It is only when Teru escapes from the nation that marks her visibly as Oriental (an unassimilable alien) that her position as abstract person or universal citizen can be truly textually recognized.

If, prior to internment, Teru's father struggled to naturalize his family through their agricultural roots, after internment the Noguchi family no longer has faith that the American soil will accept them. Teru does not see herself as capable of transforming US agricultural discourse. Her only hope of ensuring her American identity is to escape the tropes of nation and nature that shaped her pre-internment experiences. The pre-internment hopes of naturalizing through American agriculture no longer exist. Thus *Treadmill* refutes the ability of agricultural land ownership to provide access to citizenship for Japanese Americans even as the text initially establishes the political and cultural belonging of its family through agricultural motifs and metaphors.

Significantly, the relationship between individuals in the Noguchi family and the United States depicted through Teru's experience of exile conforms to the New Deal tropes that Michael Szalay argues typified much modernist literature of the period. As discussed in the previous chapter, Szalay asserts that in New Deal literary works, the male citizen often vanishes while the female citizen moves from the private sphere to the public sphere. In such texts, women transition from selfish maternal acts of nurturing to public forms of aid provided by their bodies, such as when Steinbeck's Rose of Sharon breast-feeds a stranger in *The Grapes of Wrath*. Men too must vacate their familial roles. They become abstract citizens of the new American collective through bodily absence, such as when Tom Joad metamorphoses into a "spirit."[88] Likewise Teru's father and Jiro are textually absent from *Treadmill*'s final pages. Both are banished from the United States, as Teru's father applies for repatriation and Jiro renounces his citizenship. Denied entrance to the collective abstract male citizenship of the New Deal, they are relegated to the outside of the nation-state. In the context of the relationship between the US state and the US citizen, both male subjects are removed.

Simultaneously, as an ambassador, Teru becomes the public citizen Szalay describes. She achieves citizenship through public sacrifice rather than private intimacy. Teru becomes both abstract person and public citizen in her removal from the nation-state. Like Jiro and her father, who are exiled from the nation rather than admitted to the collective national body, Teru can assume the mantle of universal citizenship only by departing from the nation. In *Assimilating Asians*, literary critic Patricia P. Chu argues that Asian American literature transforms the bildungsroman. Typically bildungsroman narratives create national subjects through an erasure of differences. Asian American texts instead tend to demonstrate a form of "authorship [that] signifies not only the capacity to speak but the belief that speech—or literary representation—is also a claiming of political and social agency."[89] *Treadmill*'s bildungsroman narrative combines with its incorporation of epistolary conventions to characterize Teru's exile from the United States as a move that allows her differences to speak for the nation. Her emigration marks her maturity into political speech. With her transformation in political consciousness, the novel's cartography shifts. Teru transitions from an unrecognized US citizen rooted in a California agricultural landscape to a recognizably US subject, an ambassador, traveling and transforming international space. This geographical transition recasts the international implications of her public American persona.

The internationalism of the novel's antiracist activism appears in Teru's final personal plea. Because *Treadmill* is such a little-known novel, the passage is worth quoting at length:

> Beyond this treadmill that saps our will to do good, there must be some common meeting ground where all peoples can mingle with liking and with trust. There must be within our lifetimes, a day when all people will be humble enough to know that whether we are born in a palace or a hovel, from a black, white or yellow womb, we share the common bond of being human, with sensibilities that can be hurt, pride that can be injured, honor that can be admired.
>
> We've got to come to realize that the atom bomb in Hiroshima didn't just wipe out a city, remote and far removed from our own existence. We've got to feel the horror of knowing as we would know if it happened to loved ones of our own, the grief of a mother looking at her new born babe smashed to a bloody pulp in her arms, the dying gasp of a child with his eyes searching in vain for someone to comfort him. . . . We who have passed through evacuation have learned a lot. We mustn't forget.[90]

The treadmill referenced here is not the exercise machine. Rather, it is a banned form of forced labor and punishment common in nineteenth-century British prisons. The treadmill the characters run on is a form of punishment by which their labor is extracted for the gain of others. In figuring the United States as a treadmill, good citizens strive for democracy but the energy they exert fails to move the nation forward.

In fleeing the United States, Teru rediscovers her faith in the tenets of American democracy and civil rights that she lost through internment. Reinvesting in a commitment to antiracist democracy, she writes to Sally, "I wish sometimes that I were staying to help fight that battle with you but it's a comforting thought to know we'll both be working for the same thing though we'll be separated by the ocean."[91] Teru may relocate to Japan, but her commitment to democracy and freedom continues to inform her life goals. These values become transposed as an international antiracism in an incipient human rights framework in Teru's final speech.

Indeed, Teru's relocation implies that it is only in this postwar international context that such values may thrive both in the domestic nation and on the global scale. In her letter, she moves from the experience of evacuation to the injustices of war. The passage moves from the local contained spaces of treadmills and wombs positioned in the United States to Japan and specifically Hiroshima. This transition marks not the move from one nation to another nation but from national to global concerns. Teru transforms from an unrecognized US citizen rooted in a California agricultural landscape to a recognizably US subject, an ambassador, traveling and transforming international space. This geographical transition recasts the international implications of her public American persona, a transition possible only when she escapes the prescribed script linking race and nation through nature. Teru ultimately abandons her attempt to claim national belonging through agricultural metaphors and instead achieves abstract citizenship through the deterritorialized language of international ambassadorship.

CONCLUSION

In the 1930s and 1940s, Japanese American representations of agricultural labor in California negotiated the same cultural binary of citizen land owner and abject alien farmworker that the Dust Bowl migrants encountered. As articles in *Kashu Mainichi* and *Rafu Shimpo* reveal, some Japanese Americans distinguished themselves from Filipino and Mexican farmworkers by insisting that Japanese immigrants and Japanese Americans inhabited the subject position of the farmer alongside whites. *Treadmill*, too, begins with the assumed relationship between citizenship and farm ownership in an attempt to bridge the perceived opposition between Asian heritage and American citizenship. Yet it quickly exposes the inability of the family's status as rooted American farmers to protect them from internment and from virulent government racism. The novel reveals internment as a disjuncture that dislodges Japanese American narratives about agriculture, opening the possibility for an interracial solidarity not possible within agrarian narratives that emphasize Issei and Nisei as all-American farmers. It suggests that recognition of Teru's abstract personhood will come not from a return to the land but as she distances herself from national territory. The novel recognizes the failure of farming narratives to successfully incorporate Japanese Americans into the nation and instead turns toward an emergent international and interracial human rights discourse as offering a new possibility for asserting Japanese American rights.

CHAPTER 4

"The Earth Trembled for Days"

Denaturalizing Racial Citizenship in Hisaye Yamamoto's Fiction

I N THE LATE 1940S AND EARLY 1950S, HISAYE YAMAMOTO wrote a series of well-received short stories about Japanese American agriculture during the Great Depression, including "Seventeen Syllables" (1949) and "Yoneko's Earthquake" (1951). While literary critics have widely celebrated these works, little attention has been paid to Yamamoto's choice of setting. The racial and gendered politics of California farm labor are central to the political interventions made by "Yoneko's Earthquake" and "Seventeen Syllables." Yamamoto's short stories, written just a few years after internment, critique the naturalization strategies at work in the pre-internment representations of agriculture discussed in the previous chapter. Her short stories reveal the shortcomings of *Rafu Shimpo*'s and *Kashu Mainichi*'s depictions of Japanese immigrants as being aligned with white farmers against Filipino and Mexican workers.[1]

"Yoneko's Earthquake" and "Seventeen Syllables" expose the violence required to enforce racial hierarchies and the inability of racial hierarchies to provide substantive citizenship rights to the Japanese community. The stories, moreover, use interracial romance to suggest the ways differently oppressed groups might unite in their efforts to resist domination and exploitation. While some Japanese American texts of the Great Depression, as well as those of the early Cold War, naturalize Japanese Americans' national belonging, Yamamoto's fiction denaturalizes that relationship by depicting Japanese American agrarianism as being reliant on racial, gendered, and economic exploitation enforced by violence.

These radical politics embedded in "Yoneko's Earthquake" and "Seventeen Syllables" reflect Yamamoto's increasing interest in the Catholic

Hisaye Yamamoto. © 1992 by Marilyn Sanders—all rights reserved.

Worker movement during the years she penned the stories. In 1952, just months after publishing "Yoneko's Earthquake," Yamamoto declined a prestigious writing fellowship at Stanford University, effectively abandoning her writing career, to relocate to a Catholic Worker farm in New York, where she lived alongside Dorothy Day. Yamamoto's fiction considers the contradictions of Japanese American agriculture as part of her engagement with Catholic Worker back-to-the-land projects. "Seventeen Syllables" and "Yoneko's Earthquake" address the division of manual labor from intellectual creativity, a separation that Catholic Worker cofounder Peter Maurin purported to address through farm cooperatives. Through her depictions of the domestic tensions of Japanese family farms that result from the racial project of abject alienage, Yamamoto brings Japanese American specificity to the Catholic Worker critique of capitalism.

PATHWAY TO RADICAL AGRARIANISM

Yamamoto had both a personal and a philosophical relationship to agricultural labor. Her family's experiences with farming contributed to her understanding of the racialized nature of property relations and likely spurred her interest in anarchist agrarianism. Born in 1921, in Redondo Beach, California, Yamamoto grew up among Japanese farming communities in Southern California. Her father worked as a farmer throughout her childhood.[2] While many of her friends helped out with their families' harvests, Yamamoto, who wrote a regular column for *Kashu Mainichi*, did not.[3] Executive Order 9066, authorizing internment, interrupted both Yamamoto's farm-labor–free lifestyle and her *Kashu Mainichi* column. In 1942, Yamamoto's family was growing strawberries on land her father owned through a Japanese farming cooperative, a system devised to evade California's Alien Land Law. With internment pending, the cooperative sold the land to a man named Pearson. Yamamoto's father received his portion of the cooperative's payment, and instead of profiting from the crop he planted with his own hands, his family was hired to pick strawberries for wages.[4] Yamamoto joined her family in the fields. She recalls, "Pearson divided the Mexicans in one group, with a Mexican foreman, and the Japanese in another group, with a Japanese foreman, and that's the way we worked, until we got evacuated."[5] Yamamoto thus experienced life both as the daughter of a small farmer and, briefly, as a laborer on a larger tract of land under a racialized system of management.

While Yamamoto lost her column at *Kashu Mainichi*, which suspended publication until 1947, she found other venues to continue publishing. At the age of twenty, she was interned at the Colorado River Relocation Center in Poston, Arizona, where she stayed for three years.[6] There she wrote for the camp newspaper, the *Poston Chronicle*. After the war, she was hired by the *Los Angeles Tribune*, an African American newspaper looking to engage Japanese Americans returning after the war. She published increasingly frank articles about racial inequality in "Small Talk," her *Los Angeles Tri-*

bune column. As historian Matthew Briones argues, the *Los Angeles Tribune* shaped Yamamoto's approach to race. As she deepened her analysis of the relationship between anti-Asian and antiblack sentiment in the United States, Yamamoto began participating in the sit-in movement in Los Angeles.[7]

The *Los Angeles Tribune* also led Yamamoto to the *Catholic Worker*. It was one of several newspapers to which she was assigned to search for articles of note. Drawn to *Catholic Worker* philosophies, she began bringing the paper home with her.[8] Yamamoto left the *Los Angeles Tribune* in 1948 to concentrate on her writing and raise her adopted son Paul. She was supported at first by insurance money from her brother Johnny, who was killed in World War II as part of the celebrated Japanese American 442nd Regimental Combat Team, and later by receiving the John Hay Whitney Foundation Opportunity Fellowship.[9] Her fiction was met with acclaim; three of her short stories appeared in Martha Foley's lists of "Distinctive Short Stories." "Yoneko's Earthquake" was included in *Best American Short Stories: 1952*.[10]

Throughout this period, Yamamoto continued to read the *Catholic Worker*, subscribing for twenty-five cents a year, or a penny per issue. As Yamamoto said, "The more I read it, the more I wanted to be part of the movement."[11] Yamamoto also kept up a correspondence with Catholic Worker activist Yone U. Stafford that originated in a letter Stafford sent the *Los Angeles Tribune* in response to one of Yamamoto's articles.[12] After reading about the Catholic Worker movement for seven years, Yamamoto "finally got up the nerve, in 1952, to write to the Workers to express my desire to join up."[13] Yamamoto continued, "Dorothy Day didn't jump up and down for joy, but cautiously suggested I meet her later in the year when she was due in Los Angeles on a speaking engagement. I met her at a midnight mass at the Maryknoll Sisters in Boyle Heights, then later for lunch with a couple of others, one of whom was a priest she called a 'fellow renegade.'"[14] Following her meeting with Day, Yamamoto turned down a prestigious (and funded) opportunity to advance her career as a fiction writer by studying with the prominent poet, literary critic, and Stanford University professor Yvor Winters. Instead, she headed to New York, because, as she put it, "my heart chose *The Catholic Worker*."[15]

To understand why Yamamoto chose the *Catholic Worker*, it is necessary to know something of the movement and its interest in farming communes.

The *Catholic Worker* began as a newspaper, cofounded by Day and Maurin. The paper combined anticapitalist radicalism with Catholic pacifism. As Day wrote in the first issue, published on May Day 1933, "In an attempt to popularize and make known the encyclicals of the Popes in regards to social justice and the program put forth by the Church for the 'reconstruction of the social order,' this news sheet, *The Catholic Worker*, is started."[16] Catholic Workers considered themselves conscientious objectors to all wars, and many did not pay federal income taxes as a protest against both war and government. Volunteers at Catholic Worker centers around the nation provided food, shelter, and clothing to needy patrons.

Many Catholic Workers considered themselves Christian anarchists. Most notable among them were Robert Ludlow and Ammon Hennacy, who went on to publish *The Autobiography of a Catholic Anarchist* (1954). As Ludlow expressed it, "The Christian is opposed to all evil and in the field of government he must be opposed to all evil government and it is his contention that the state as we know it, the state as a historical entity, is an evil form of government." Hennacy rooted his anarchism in pacifism, believing that nation-states promoted the resolution of conflict through war.[17] Yamamoto subscribed not only to pacifism but also to the anarchist belief in participatory democracy. In an interview with literary critic King-Kok Cheung, she explained, "I'm a Christian because I believe that Jesus Christ is the Son of God. And an anarchist because I agree that 'the government is best which governs least.'"[18] This vision of anarchism contributed to the collective model of governance that many Catholic Worker projects used.

During the period in which Yamamoto began reading the *Catholic Worker*, the paper had more than sixty-six thousand subscribers and had recovered from its wartime loss of supporters due to Day's adamant pacifism during World War II. The paper argued for integration and reported on the arrests of Catholic Workers picketing alongside the National Association for the Advancement of Colored People (NAACP). The paper put reports of lynching and labor struggles side by side. It followed the rise of McCarthyism, described the US occupation of Japan, and bemoaned the hunger and poverty of children across Europe and Asia in the war's aftermath. It promoted organic farming and critiqued the Soviet Union's reliance on technology to increase agricultural production. According to the *Catholic*

Worker, resource scarcity could be solved not by technology and industry but by a return to the natural agrarian way of life, voluntary poverty, and the teachings of Christ.

Many of the Catholic Worker movement's core tenets can be traced back to Maurin. He was never as well known as Day, but she often credited him as being her inspiration. Maurin provided Day with the possibility of reconciling her Catholic faith with her social conscience and history of political involvement, and the *Catholic Worker* newspaper was initially his idea.[19] Maurin expressed the ideas that most appealed to him in blank verse. His "Easy Essays," which the *Catholic Worker* frequently published, conveyed a complexity of thought through repetitive word play. Yamamoto was particularly influenced by these essays. When corresponding with Cheung about her interest in anarchism and the Catholic Worker movement, she referenced Maurin directly.[20]

Maurin was the first and most influential proponent of back-to-the-land projects within the *Catholic Worker*. He originated from a village in the South of France where residents worked communal pastures. This experience shaped his political commitment to cultivation. Maurin understood farming as a solution for many of the social ills that he believed were caused by capitalism and industrialization, including an individual's alienation from the land, labor's loss of craft and artistry, and rural communities' destruction as cities grew.[21] Maurin viewed farming as a way of returning the means of production (the land) to a collective social body and as a way of returning dignity to work. He termed his vision of farming, which went hand in hand with the Catholic Worker movement's promotion of manual labor and voluntary poverty, "the green revolution."[22]

While Maurin's green revolution had its roots in his memory of French peasant life, which he described nostalgically as "precapitalistic," it was more than just a return to the past.[23] Rather, Maurin viewed farming as a way of reimagining and reinventing society.[24] Farming communes offered an opportunity to put into action many of the ideas that fueled his interest in Catholic social radicalism. He believed the farms were not just solutions to underemployment and poor labor conditions. He referred to them as agronomic universities where "the scholars must become workers/so the workers may be scholars."[25] According to Maurin, intellectuals and laborers needed to learn from each other. He envisioned the life of the mind integrated into a life of manual labor, evenly dividing each day between study and labor. There would be little to no separation between the laborer and the scholar. They would not serve as separate classes.

Maurin's vision of the philosopher-farmer coincided with the Catholic Worker movement's belief that labor confers a spiritual benefit. Historian Mel Piehl describes "a commitment to satisfying and socially useful labor" as a core Catholic Worker tenet, alongside voluntary poverty and pacifism.[26] In an unpublished biography of Maurin, Day wrote, "On the farming commune, there was plenty of work for all, another reason why Peter was always extolling the land. People could not live without working. Work was as necessary as bread. But what was needed was a philosophy of labor. Work was a gift, a vocation."[27] One could not lead a fulfilling life without labor, and farm labor offered a particularly uplifting form of labor, ensuring that farm residents contributed to their own well-being rather than living off the exploitation of others.

In the 1930s and 1940s, dozens of Catholic Worker farming projects sprang up.[28] In the years preceding Yamamoto's New York move, the *Catholic Worker* included articles in almost every issue discussing the benefits of back-to-the land experiments. These articles emphasized the difficulties of farming endeavors, including practitioners' lack of agricultural knowledge and their frustration at resulting farming failures. Yet almost all of these articles also proclaimed the experience worthwhile and encouraged others to join in.[29] An article by agrarian novices Thomas Campbell and his wife is representative. Of their farming experience, they say, "We are both brand new, having lived in big cities all our lives and, hence, would like to address ourselves to those who are attempting to make a decision: 'Shall I—or we—try life on the land?' . . . The initial step taken of actually leaving the city and going to the country is an act which will be deep satisfaction in most cases. . . . You cannot read yourself into any worthwhile experience, least of all those connected with the land. So, if you are stopped in the first step, muster your courage and go."[30] The articles that Yamamoto read in the months and years preceding her decision to go "back to the land" included such pleas to follow one's heart and try out an agrarian lifestyle, regardless of the hardships that would follow.

The twenty-two-acre farm that Yamamoto and her son moved to was purchased in the late summer or early fall of 1950 and was named after Maurin, who passed away in 1949. The farm was only in its third season of Catholic Worker cultivation when Yamamoto arrived, around Labor Day 1953.[31] By this time Day often resided at Peter Maurin Farm, and her grandchildren became playmates of Yamamoto's son Paul.[32] The farm was not in prime condition. Shortly after Yamamoto's arrival, Catholic Worker Rollande Potvin described it as consisting of "very poor and run down soil. Compared to the farm at Newburgh it is not very productive."[33] The project's difficulty conferred status. Agriculture appealed to Catholic Workers in part because of their belief that humans require meaningful labor to thrive. The work's physical intensity was more important to the project than agrarian self-sufficiency.

Yamamoto's work at the farm combined the intellectual with the domestic. Writing for the *Catholic Worker* became one of Yamamoto's primary duties. Her first article highlighted the parallels between New Jersey's "worst agricultural strike" in 1934 at Seabrook Farms and more recent walkouts there by Nisei workers.[34] Yamamoto also took over a monthly column containing day-to-day updates on Peter Maurin Farm. She described her farm life as a mishmash of animal tending, housekeeping, and intellectual labor, saying, "I fed the chickens and rabbits usually, sometimes cooked if there was no one else around to do it, cleaned cupboards, sorted clothing that came in, and wrote for the paper."[35] Her account highlights the gendered nature of her labor assignments. Indeed, Day publicly celebrated Yamamoto's work ethic, going so far as to label her as the farm's "best example of manual labor."[36] Day's description of Yamamoto underscores Maurin's agronomic university ideal. Day wrote, "She works without effort, quietly, efficiently, taking care of rabbits, chickens, washing up the kitchen, dining room, hall, and corridors with a concoction of boiled onion skins and water which Mary Lisi, one of our Italian friends, introduced us to. Our house is spotless, thanks to her, and yet she always has time to type articles, to read, both to herself and to little Paul. What an example of tranquility."[37] Yamamoto embodied the scholar-worker ideal, at least in Day's eyes.

Yet Yamamoto's columns consistently register the difficulty of trying to live out Catholic Worker ideals in everyday life. They testify to the adversities of communal living. As Yamamoto expressed it, "It is still a daily miracle how we, coming from such diverse backgrounds and thrown together by our common needs, live as one family, struggling to respect one another's personalities."[38] According to her columns, life at Peter Maurin Farm could be quite unpleasant. She wrote, "For some reason, Advent—liturgically a season of joyous waiting—turned out to be rather grim at Peter Maurin Farm, with the communal nerves on edge and dissension prevailing."[39] Another time she complained, "Even here at Peter Maurin Farm, where we are actually living on the land, the harassments that come with living in the community often loom larger than the agricultural problems, so that we must occasionally remind ourselves that it is, after all, a farm."[40] Yamamoto later stated that the intensity of the conflicts between community farm members was unexpected, remarking that, "Dorothy Day never wrote about the darker aspects of living in community in her column, which had so enchanted me."[41]

Other Catholic Worker projects shared the communal discord Yamamoto found at Peter Maurin Farm. Historical theologian Jeffery Marlett, in describing Maryfarm, said, "Although many, including seminarians, children on vacation, and college students, crowded in during summers, the permanent residents were a motley crew of families, unemployed laborers, and the urban homeless. A more volatile group unprepared for the tensions of communal living could scarcely be found."[42] Catholic Worker William Guachat, who spent over twenty years as part of a Catholic Worker farming collective, complained that participants were often reluctant to become scholar-laborers: "The scholars insist upon being scholarly, and the workers insist upon working physically for weal or woe, and the twain never met."[43] Maurin's ideals rarely materialized in practice.

There is no evidence that Yamamoto's departure from Peter Maurin Farm resulted from frustrations with communal living. Her move, rather, appears motivated by love. She returned to California in 1955, following her marriage to Anthony DeSoto, whom she met at Peter Maurin Farm. Yamamoto continued throughout her life to affiliate with Catholic Workers and to believe that small communities could empower the individual, explaining that "the government by mutual consent in small groups—communities— is the ideal form of democracy."[44] She published occasionally in the *Catholic*

Worker as well as in other venues until her death in 2011. Over thirty years after leaving Peter Maurin Farm, Yamamoto professed, "I believe Dorothy Day is the most important person this country has produced."[45]

"SEVENTEEN SYLLABLES" AND "YONEKO'S EARTHQUAKE"
AS CATHOLIC WORKER TEXTS

In the same years in which Yamamoto read the *Catholic Worker*'s call for cultivation, she revisited pre-internment Japanese American farm life through her fiction. Her counter-narrative of Japanese agrarianism reveals the appeal that *Catholic Worker* visions of farming held for her. Yamamoto explained her attraction to the *Catholic Worker* in terms of Maurin's ideal of the scholar-worker: "Peter Maurin believed in a synthesis of what he called 'cult, culture, and cultivation,' which meant going back to the land. His ideal was that a person could work out in the fields maybe four days—four hours a day—and then go back to the farmhouse and paint or write or do printing or whatever, all centered around the Catholic Church."[46] "Seventeen Syllables" and "Yoneko's Earthquake" illustrate the impossibility of the worker-scholar under the United States' racialized conditions of agricultural production. The *Catholic Worker*'s idealistic visions of nonhierarchical communal farming appear as an implicit resolution to many of the problems explored by Yamamoto's fiction. This is not to suggest that Yamamoto consciously shaped her short stories to express a Catholic Worker agrarian ethos. Rather, as Yamamoto acknowledges, an author's politics may shape a text in ways in which the author may be unaware. As she explained to one interviewer, "I call myself a Christian anarchist, but I'm not sure my beliefs come through in the stories. If they're part of me, however, some sense of it must be evident. . . . A fiction writer who has a political agenda will probably consciously or unconsciously incorporate it into his work, don't you think?"[47] Yamamoto's short fiction is in implicit, rather than explicit, conversation with Catholic Worker philosophies.

Maurin's desire for property relations enabling scholar-laborers echoes what many have read as the central tension in "Seventeen Syllables," between the mother's desire for art and the father's desire for labor, or what Sau-ling Cynthia Wong has called the conflict between necessity and extravagance.[48] In "Seventeen Syllables," Tome Hayashi transforms into the poet

Ume in the evenings. As Tome, she contributes to the family's domestic economy; she "kept house, cooked, washed, and . . . did her ample share of picking tomatoes out in the sweltering fields and boxing them in tidy strata in the cool packing shed."[49] In contrast, Ume not only ignores her social obligations to her husband but also threatens the family's economic well-being. When Ume wins first prize in a haiku contest sponsored by *Mainichi Shimbun*, a San Francisco paper, the editor drives down in person to deliver the prize. Tome abandons the tomato harvest to have tea with the editor on a day when time is of the essence and all help is necessary to salvage the family's investment. Yamamoto writes, "The lugs were piling up . . . and the ripe tomatoes in them would probably have to be taken to the cannery tomorrow if they were not ready for the produce haulers tonight."[50] Mr. Hayashi has already informed his daughter, "We've got no time for a break today," when his wife offers tea to the editor bearing her award.[51] Significantly, when Mr. Hayashi sends a message to Ume/Tome, it is a reminder about the tomatoes.[52] When she still does not return to the fields, Mr. Hayashi storms up to the house and destroys the prize, ending Ume's poetry career. Mr. Hayashi's outrage is not simply about Ume's creative success or independence, as scholars often contend.[53] He is upset that this success directly interferes with the family's urgent need to harvest tomatoes. That Ume's "life span, even for a poet's, was very brief—perhaps three months at most," suggests the impossibility of Maurin's ideal, the scholar as worker and the worker as scholar, under the economic constraints facing Japanese immigrant farm families.[54] Achieving such an ideal is particularly unlikely for Japanese immigrant women given the family's gender dynamics.

Similarly, in "Yoneko's Earthquake," the Filipino farmhand Marpo transgresses not only in his affair with Yoneko's mother, Mrs. Hosoume, but also in striving to be more than a laborer. Early in the story we are told that Marpo displayed dynamic and varied interests and identities: "Marpo the Christian and Marpo the best hired man, . . . Marpo the athlete, Marpo the musician (both instrumental and vocal), Marpo the artist, and Marpo the radio technician."[55] This description seems to capture Maurin's ideal of a life engaging both body and brain. In contrast, the "old Japanese man" who replaces Marpo after the discovery of the affair has "no particular interests, outside working, eating, sleeping, and playing an occasional game of goh with Mr. Hosoume."[56] Marpo's multiple identities seem directly linked to his inability to perform the duty of farm labor (and only farm labor) in the way in which Mr. Hosoume considers appropriate, while the old Japanese man, with "no particular interests," can be more easily reduced to his labor. The racial and economic order in which Marpo toils does not allow artistry or other forms of creative expression to thrive.

In both short stories, Yamamoto describes farm laborers as machine-like and depicts the emergence of human qualities, especially creative and sexual passion, as economically disruptive. Yoneko and her brother Sergio "followed the potato-digging machine and the Mexican workers—both hired for the day—around the field."[57] The statement equates Mexican laborers with machines because of their capacity to be hired. There is no difference between the renting of a machine and the renting of human labor. Rosie, the daughter in "Seventeen Syllables," was capable of working in the fields "as efficiently as a flawless machine."[58] Like Yoneko, she becomes more like a machine than a daughter when she engages in farm labor. Yet, like Marpo, Ume, and Mrs. Hosome, Rosie's ability to function as a machine is reduced when her passions intrude; as her love interest, Jesus, approaches, "her hands went berserk and the tomatoes starting falling in the wrong stalls."[59] Through these descriptions, Yamamoto's texts employ a Marxist critique of wage labor's effect on workers. Under capitalism, the human qualities of the laborers become distractions and inefficiencies. Art and sensuality cannot survive within the racialized economic system of the pre-internment Japanese American family farm. They are in direct competition with marginalized individuals' economic survival.

The forces that prevent Yamamoto's characters from simultaneously attaining economic security and expressing their sexuality and creativity are rooted in racialized labor and property relations. Prior to the McCarran-Walter Immigration and National Act of 1952, Asian immigrants, including Japanese immigrants, were unable to gain US citizenship. They were labeled "aliens ineligible for citizenship," a designation rendering them perpetually foreign and unable to participate in electoral democracy. The state reduced the roles of men like Mr. Hosoume and Mr. Hayashi to their economic functions, while the Alien Land Law curtailed their ability to achieve economic success. As literary critic Grace Kyungwon Hong contends, Yamamoto's stories reveal the effects of the Alien Land Law through details such the Hosoumes' harvest of crops known for their short-term turnover.[60] Anti-Asian regulations affected which crops Mr. Hosoume and Mr. Hayashi could grow, their ability to invest long-term in a piece of land, and the conditions under which they could hire workers. The economic insecurity of the small family farms in Yamamoto's fiction emerges not only as a general result of capitalism but specifically as a result of the workings of race in a capitalist system.

Yamamoto's short stories also speak to the effects of denying naturalization to Asian immigrants through the frustration and powerlessness of the stories' patriarchs. Scholar Charles Crow reads Yamamoto's harsh depiction of male desire for authority over wives and daughters as a feminist challenge to patriarchal Issei culture.[61] Yet in "Seventeen Syllables" and "Yoneko's Earthquake," the father's frustrations emerge partially from his powerlessness in the face of the family's economic and political oppression. This was a period in which politicians, newspapers, and members of the general public expressed open hostility toward Japanese immigrants. Legal regulations and cultural manifestations in this era would have excluded Mr. Hosoume and Mr. Hayashi from US civil society in significant ways. Consequently, these men perceive their wives' insubordination as a threat to their masculinity that jeopardizes their sense of self-ownership in a nation-state and economic niche in which they can legally possess little and in which their political and cultural contributions are ignored and denied. Their feelings of impotence lead both men to resort to violence against their wives— reactions that stem the state and broader society's denial of the men's subjectivity and agency.

The burdens each character carries in "Seventeen Syllables" and "Yoneko's Earthquake" are linked to the capitalist conditions of labor migration and the racist conditions of US property ownership. Scholar Cheryl Higashida argues that Yamamoto's short fiction reveals the historical context for agricultural production's racialized structures. She contends that it is "the historical conditions of production that are integral" to "the text's subtle protest against racialized patriarchy *and* its sympathetic portrait of a rural *issei* woman's struggles as a mother, wife, and fieldworker."[62] These historical conditions include Mexican migration to the United States, Filipino migration to both Hawaii and California, Japanese migration to Hawaii and California, the shift of Japanese immigrants from farmworker to farm owners, and Japanese migrants' tensions with the Filipino community.[63] They also include the conditions of racialized property ownership that exclude Japanese immigrants, rendering their place in the economic and racial hierarchy always tenuous, just as Japanese immigrants and Japanese Americans are rendered perpetually foreign.[64]

Given the privileged position a critique of racialized private property holds in Yamamoto's fiction, collective ownership of agrarian land would likely have held great appeal for her. In "Yoneko's Earthquake" and "Seventeen Syllables," Yamamoto's characters are prevented from living lives that combine manual labor with sexual and creative expression. They face emotional and physical violence when seeking spiritual, sexual, and emotional fulfillment. Yamamoto depicts these forms of fulfillment as a threat to the family's economic survival and to the father's already-threatened masculinity. Maurin's farmer-scholar offers the possibility of the fulfilling life that so eludes Yamamoto's characters. Her fiction examines many of the problems for which Maurin's agrarian vision appears as the solution.

Maurin's writings, however, fail to incorporate the nuanced analysis of race, gender, and sexuality that Yamamoto's fiction provides. While Maurin viewed agriculture as the solution to the separation of craft and work, Yamamoto's stories reveal the inability of family farming to reconcile labor with art under a system of racialized property relations and unequal gender relations. Whereas Maurin's investment in Catholic Worker cultivation emerged from his desire to return to the agricultural conditions of his childhood, Yamamoto's short fiction suggests the desire to distance herself from the racialized and gendered realities of industrial capital, labor relations, and property ownership that structured her earliest memories and her parents' lives. Her work brings Japanese American specificity and historical consciousness of race to the Catholic Worker ideal.

EXPOSING RACIAL FAULT LINES

"Seventeen Syllables" and "Yoneko's Earthquake" contribute an explicitly Japanese American context to Catholic Worker agrarianism through the ways in which the short stories counter the popular narratives of Japanese American farming that circulated in pre-internment Japanese American newspapers. As detailed in chapter 3, the agrarian narrative that US Japanese newspapers popularized during the Great Depression aligned the Issei farmer with the white farmer against threats by Filipino and Mexican farmworkers. In Yamamoto's fiction, the danger comes not only from Mexican and Filipino field hands but also from the sexuality and creative artistry of Issei wives and Nisei daughters. It is the patriarchs who resort to violence, not disobedient family members and employees. Whereas *Rafu Shimpo* and *Kashu Mainichi* naturalize Japanese belonging to the United States through a strategy of racial othering, Yamamoto's short stories naturalize interracial resistance to systems of subordination. Rather than portraying pre-internment Japanese American agriculture as a peaceful and productive community of obedient Americans disrupted by violent racial others, Yamamoto portrays pre-internment Japanese agriculture as a system of exploitation in which a patriarch denied power outside of his farm responds violently to threats to his limited authority. According to *Rafu Shimpo* and *Kashu Mainichi*, farming protected the Japanese immigrant from society's racism and provided an opportunity for success. In contrast, Yamamoto's short stories express the powerlessness of the Issei farmer. Rather than provide Japanese immigrants with access to white citizenship, farming in Yamamoto's fiction exemplifies the Issei farmer's marginalization.

The stories communicate Issei marginality in part by invoking Cold War gender anxieties.[65] Yamamoto wrote "Seventeen Syllables" in 1949 and "Yoneko's Earthquake" in 1951, the early years of the Cold War. Scholars such as Elaine Tyler May contend that during this period domesticity operated as a process of containment and was inseparable from foreign policy goals. Business and political leaders presented heterosexual family life as a "sphere of influence" that protected the nation from the interconnected threats of communism, nuclear annihilation, and nonnormative sexualities.[66] They encouraged men and women to root their identities in their home lives rather than in their sites of employment. They discouraged dissent in asserting that racial and economic home-front tensions threatened the cultural battle of the Cold War.[67] Yamamoto's short stories depict uncontainable wives, daughters, and employees. The stories suggest that only physical and emotional violence could maintain the racial and gendered subordination and exploitation required in Japanese American agriculture. In this way, they challenge the naturalization of domestic hierarchies and counter the narrative of Japanese American agrarianism that newspapers such as *Kashu Mainichi* and *Rafu Shimpo* relied on prior to internment.

Mrs. Hosoume's and Tome's behaviors, which literary scholars often read as acts of feminist agency, exemplify Cold War anxieties about uncontainable women.[68] Popular representations and political rhetoric during the Cold War characterized nonnormative power dynamics within families as a perversion. In "Seventeen Syllables," Ume's poetic creativity threatens the Hayashi nuclear family by challenging Mr. Hayashi's patriarchal authority. Her threat to his dominance through her success as a poet aligns with Cold War fears of disobedient wives. Her poetic ambition imperils her husband's masculinity and echoes fears prevalent in the period's mass media of overambitious mothers who refused to put parenthood before their careers.[69] Mrs. Hosoume, through her affair with Marpo, demonstrates a sexual freedom that emasculates her husband.

In "Seventeen Syllables" Ume's insurrection reminds the reader of Mr. Hayashi's tenuous role in the domestic life of the nation. Ume interrupts Mr. Hayashi's familial relations, the one area in which his identity is grounded and his belonging affirmed. She manages to disrupt both the economic and cultural life of the family. With her appearance, the regular patterns of the family's life are lost. The narrative renders the negative effects through Mr. Hayashi's social deprivation. He plays solitaire in the evenings, a time he formerly spent socializing with Tome.[70] Moreover, after Ume's arrival the family separates even when company comes over, as Ume takes center stage with her poetry. As an Asian immigrant, barred from naturalization, Mr. Hayashi lives an existence peripheral to the mainstream. With the incursion of Ume, he becomes marginalized even within the realm of his own family. He can no longer ignore the contrast between his political exclusion and his domestic inclusion, for he maintains no place of belonging.

Mr. Hayashi's increased marginalization also manifests outside of the home, as when the Hayashi family visits their friends, the Hayano family. Ume discusses haiku with Mr. Hayano while Mr. Hayashi sits next to the disabled Mrs. Hayano. The actively engaged role of the evening goes to Ume, Mr. Hayashi's wife, while he, Mr. Hayashi, is rendered parallel to a woman disfigured by childbirth. We are told, "Something had been wrong with Mrs.

Hayano ever since the birth of her first child."[71] Mr. Hayashi finds himself positioned not only as partner to the most powerless person in the room but alongside a person whose disfigurement resulted from her female anatomy. Ume's appearance emasculates Mr. Hayashi. In contrast, Ume becomes the equal of the powerful other male in the room, Mr. Hayano. Pairing Ume with Mr. Hayano highlights the extent of Mr. Hayashi's fall in social status. It links Mr. Hayashi's degradation to his national exclusion by recalling stereotypes of Asian men as effeminate.[72] Ume questions the legitimacy of Mr. Hayashi's familial authority just as images of Asian men as sexual others attacked the ability of Asian immigrants to become US citizens.

"Yoneko's Earthquake" and "Seventeen Syllables" address the Cold War crisis of masculinity in light of Asian American gender stereotypes and racial exclusion. With the loss of autonomy in the workplace, media representations instructed white middle-class men to find their source of authority in the home.[73] Yamamoto's Japanese immigrant men, denied authority and authenticity as abstract citizens of the nation-state, attempt to affirm their masculinity through their authoritative roles in the domestic economy. Because the family farm setting comingles the location of family with the location of labor, rendering the domestic and the economic inseparable, the rebellion of women in the family and of men employed on the farm is doubly threatening to Issei patriarchs. This is compounded by Mr. Housome's and Mr. Hayashi's exclusion from full participation in the public sphere.

Mr. Hayashi and Mr. Hosoume react to threats to their limited authority with violence. Yamamoto explicitly refers to Mr. Hayashi's destruction of Ume's haiku prize as the "violence of the hot afternoon."[74] Yamamoto describes the picture's destruction as an "explosion."[75] The story suggests that Mr. Hayashi effectively murders Ume, as we are told, "Ume Hanazono's life span, even for a poet's, was very brief."[76] Similarly, Mr. Hosoume, threatened by his wife's perceived insolence, "slapped her smartly on her face."[77] The abortion he forces his wife to have is described in the metaphor of the "beautiful collie" he runs down with his car.[78] While *Kashu Mainichi* and *Rafu Shimpo* emphasized the dangerous criminality of black, Mexican, and Filipino workers, Yamamoto depicts violence as part of the nation's domestic strategy of containment, a strategy enacted upon Issei wives by already marginalized Issei patriarchs attempting to retain in the domestic sphere the power and respect they were denied in the public sphere.

The short stories evade Cold War censorship by employing what liter-ary critic Traise Yamamoto terms "strategic resistance" in their depiction of domesticity. "Yoneko's Earthquake" and "Seventeen Syllables" conform to hegemonic narratives of race and gender by encompassing both Cold War criticism of oversexualized and overambitious mothers and Cold War narratives in which Asian daughters achieve liberty in their escape from traditional Asian fathers. Yet in their "articulate silences" Yamamoto's nar-ratives also critique the capitalist nation-state in which economic survival mandates dehumanization, requires authoritarian rule, and demarcates the boundaries of racially appropriate bonding.[79] When read through the lens of Cold War cultural politics, Yamamoto's depictions of family dynamics question the nation's ability to overcome these inequalities inherent to its system of rule.

In discussing the function of familial metaphors as national symbols through the structure of gendered inequality, postcolonial scholar and gen-der theorist Anne McClintock asks "whether the iconography of the family [can] be retained as a figure for national unity, or must an alternative, radi-cal iconography be developed?"[80] This question underscores Yamamoto's fictional examination of family dynamics. Yamamoto's short stories por-tray families as sites of inequality and hierarchy. The patriarch violently reprimands those who assert their individuality, their creativity, or their sexuality. His identity depends on their subordination. The nuclear family fails as a model of democracy, equality, and freedom. Yamamoto's depic-tion of Issei patriarchs suggests that the stories' malfunctioning families may result from the nation's failure to fully include racial minorities. The violence of political and economic oppression in the stories allows the do-mestic violence depicted in the text. The father's oppressive actions cannot be understood outside of his limited economic options. Thus, the short stories are not simply an indictment of patriarchy but also an explanation of domestic inequity embedded in the nation's larger racial project as part of a capitalist system.

DENATURALIZING THE NATION-STATE

Yamamoto's critique of the nation through her depiction of family dynam-ics relies on the short stories' agricultural setting. The conventions of Japa-nese American agrarianism are central to the ways in which Yamamoto denaturalizes national belonging and suggests the radical possibilities of alternative kinship formations. Pre- and post-internment Japanese American literature frequently portrays Japanese Americans as "naturally" being part of the nation-state. They grow like plants in the soil and in some representations are endemic to the Americas. The relationship between Japanese Americans and American nature is peaceful, harmonious, and productive. In contrast, Yamamoto uses representations of violence to suggest the cruelty of the relationship between Japanese Americans and the nation-state. Interracial and intergenerational resistance blooms, while the seasonal cycles of nuclear family reproduction lead only to decay and death.

The texts question the naturalness of traditional heterosexual reproduction within the nuclear family by showing the cyclical process of fertility, growth, and harvest to be quite cruel. In "Seventeen Syllables" Mrs. Hayano's seasonal reproductive capacity ("there were four Hayano girls, all lovely and each one named after a season of the year") results in her decay.[81] In birthing her children, she ceases to bloom, as "something had been wrong with Mrs. Hayano ever since the birth of her first child."[82] Natural reproduction, linked to the seasons, ravishes the mother. Is her decline natural? Rosie responds to Mrs. Hayano's condition "wonderingly. . . . But it was not a matter she could come to any decision about."[83] Rosie's ambiguity regarding Mrs. Hayano's illness hints at Yamamoto's refusal to portray physical and emotional suffering as part of a natural order that the characters must simply endure and accept. The case of Ume is similar. Yamamoto names Ume for a flower that lives only three months, the length of a season. In many farm narratives, seasons represent processes to which humans must align their lives. Life and death, like the harvest of crops, become part of life one must simply accept, although they are at times unpleasant. Yet Rosie's discomfort with both Ume's death and Mrs. Hayashi's disfigurement counters such agrarian literary traditions.

In contrast to the violence of conventional reproductive structures, Yamamoto's stories naturalize interracial romance through pastoral imagery. Many of the women choose paramours who are inappropriate according to Japanese American community norms.[84] Rosie's interest in Mexican American farmhand Jesus and Mrs. Hosoume's romance with Filipino farmhand Marpo cross class, race, and religious lines. While Mrs. Hosoume's romance is also inappropriate because it is adultery, Rosie's could be interpreted as an act of seduction synonymous with prevalent Japanese American stereotypes of threatening Mexican and Filipino male sexuality. Yet the short stories naturalize these two relationships through their association with farming.

Both romances bloom among the rows of plants in the field. Rosie and Jesus fall for each other while racing to see who can pick the most tomatoes. Later, Rosie "ran between two patches of tomatoes" to join Jesus in the barn for their first kiss.[85] Yamamoto renders the sexuality captured in the sweethearts' agricultural pursuits by the "truly monstrous, pale green worm" that Jesus surprises Rosie with; it looked "like an infant snake."[86] This imagery depicts Jesus's lust for Rosie as seductively sinful (a snake in the garden), as well as innocent in its immaturity (an infant). The text also associates Rosie with the ripe tomatoes of the harvest season. When she screeches at sight of the worm, Jesus points out the "immature tomatoes" she holds.[87] Her sexuality matures with the tomatoes, and she later consumes a ripe tomato in the instant before he kisses her. Yamamoto alludes to the Garden of Eden with the tempting snake, the tomato as apple, and the kiss as initiation into forbidden knowledge. The Edenic imagery contrasts with the hard labor in which Rosie and Jesus participate, just as the text further justifies Rosie's taboo encounter through her inability to fully separate Jesus the farmhand from Jesus the savior. At one point, she was "not certain whether she was invoking the help of the son of the Carrascos or of God."[88] Similarly, the romance between Marpo and Mrs. Hosoume grows after the days she spends with him in the fields. When Mrs. Hosoume returns "breathless" one day, with "a gold colored ring with a tiny glasslike stone in it," the text implies that their sexual engagement began among rows of plants.[89] Both romances ripen with the crops and are consummated during the harvest. The pastoral imagery of these images contrast with the harshness used to depict relations among the nuclear family at the story's center. It suggests that alternative kinship formations might be more natural, peaceful, and loving than the hierarchical structures employed for capitalist gain.

Yamamoto's agrarian narratives question not only the naturalness of the nuclear family but the legitimacy of the nation-state. The violence of seasonal change in "Seventeen Syllables" and "Yoneko's Earthquake" contrasts with romantic images in pastoral narratives where seasonal change represents harmony between the state of nature and the American farm family. The Japanese American relationship to agrarian nature in Yamamoto's texts signifies the destruction of economic exploitation rather than a peaceful precapitalist agrarian existence. Yamamoto narrates this seasonal violence onto Asian American bodies, such as Mrs. Hayano, whose duty to her family comes at the cost of her physical and emotional well-being. Her reproductive labor, resulting in her four beautiful daughters, mirrors the Japanese American productive labor of cultivation resulting in the abundant crops that provide California's wealth at the expense of Japanese American material, emotional, and physical health.

The earthquake in "Yoneko's Earthquake" suggests the instability of the kinship relations that bind Japanese Americans to the US nation-state. Yamamoto describes the earthquake as "though some giant had seized [the house] in his two hands and was giving it a good shaking."[90] Aside from evoking the fairy-tale worldview of the children, the image of the giant characterizes the family as being under attack. The text depicts the earthquake, and the hand of nature that it represents, as being active. The ground the Hosoume family stands upon lacks stability. Their roots are viciously yanked up amid the "tremendous roar," with all they had come to see as stable "shuddering violently."[91] The metaphorical giant forcibly pulls the Hosoume family off of their land. As the narrator puts it, "The earth trembled for days afterwards."[92] The earthquake destabilizes both the land on which they stand and the house in which they live.

The earthquake dislodges the relationship between the Hosoume family and their house, hinting at the tenuous nature of the relationship between the Japanese American family and the US nation. As historian Wendy Kozol argues, the postwar (suburban) house increased its ideological significance in the Cold War, the period in which the stories were written. The Cold War house offered protection and security against atomic weapons and communists.[93] Yet for Yoneko, the home not only fails to offer protection during the earthquake, afterward it becomes a dangerous place that must be avoided, first because of aftershocks, and later because of her housebound father's quixotic actions, which "cramped her style."[94] Every time Marpo ventures into the house after the earthquake in search of supplies, Yoneko screams,

"No, Marpo, no!" (Yamamoto, "Yoneko's Earthquake," 48). The earthquake establishes that the family, in contrast to the house, is composed only of human relationships rather than being rooted in the ground. When Mrs. Hosoume drags the children out of the crumbling house, Marpo "gathered them all in his arms, as much to protect them as to support himself" (47). Marpo's arms provide the alternative and more protective shelter. Marpo's response to the earthquake evokes his new role in the family. He becomes the provider of shelter and protection in the absence of the children's father and in the face of their house's structural vulnerability. This hints at the ability of interracial solidarity in the text to offer shelter and protection to those most vulnerable to exploitation. The earthquake exposes the family's fragile relationship to the home (family/nation) that shelters them.

As entering the house becomes dangerous, the text depicts young Yoneko awakening to the instability of her familial, national, and natural belonging. The earthquake, in its natural violence, exposes the underlying power inequities within the family and denaturalizes the nuclear family relationships that stand in for national belonging. The narrative refuses to disentangle the earthquake, the father's injury, and the mother's affair. They are swept up in the description of a "monstrous upheaval" that shakes Yoneko's faith in God, Marpo, and her place in the world.[95] As such, the earthquake suggests the instability of categories previously conceptualized as natural, and therefore timeless, stagnant, secure, and inevitable. The earthquake destroys the house as a symbol of the protection offered to Yoneko by her father, and, by association, the nation that shelters her. The earthquake also destroys Yoneko's newly acquired faith in God: "Yoneko began to suspect that God was either powerless, callous, downright cruel, or nonexistent. In the murky night, under a strange moon wearing a pale ring of light, she decided upon the last as the most plausible theory" (51). In losing her faith in God, Yoneko loses her faith in her family and nation to protect her.

Christianity represents a form of belonging for Yoneko that is similar to her longing for familial and national kinship. She "yearned at times after Christianity, but she realized the absurdity of her whim" (46). The "absurdity of her whim" represents recognition of her outsider status. She cannot attend the white Baptist church due to her Japanese ethnicity, yet there are not enough Japanese in her rural community for a Japanese church. The text captures her racial exclusion not only in the implicit implausibility of her attendance at the white church but also by equating her Japaneseness with the type of crops her family grows. The narrator explains, "They were the only ones, too, whose agriculture was so diverse as to include blackberries, cabbages, rhubarb, potatoes, cucumbers, onions, and cantaloupes. The rest of the countryside there was like one vast orange grove" (47). As Hong points out, the Hosoume family's diversity of crops results from the Alien Land Law.[96] Oranges require a long-term investment in one plot of land, which was unrealistic for Issei families in California under the Alien Lands Law. The instability of the family's relationship to the land that is represented textually by the earthquake evokes the racist exclusionary laws of the nation-state. Yoneko's desire to belong (have the same crops as others, attend the same church as others) links to her desire for a stable relationship to nature, and thus the nation.

Through Christianity, Marpo offers Yoneko the ability to belong, to fit in, and to be like others.[97] The Christianity that he dangles in front of her performs functions similar to the narrative of national community. It offers her a sense of belonging to an "imagined community" and a timeless creation story. She can begin to understand her place temporally and geographically through the mythic stories of Christ that Marpo offers her. When the earthquake causes Yoneko to lose her faith in God, the text insinuates that this is also a moment of losing her faith in the nation-state. Yoneko recognizes the falsity of the promise of belonging to the land and to a people who do not accept her, a promise embodied by her legal citizenship.

Yoneko's lost faith in God links to her later lost faith in Marpo. From Yoneko's perspective, Marpo abandons her just as God did during the earthquake. Indeed, Yoneko's adoption of Marpo's God initially results from her seeing Marpo as a God. With her acceptance of Christianity, Yoneko became "an ideal apostle, adoring Jesus," just as she adored Marpo, who the narrator, in her childhood crush, depicts as practically perfect.[98] Yoneko and her brother Sergio "visited with Marpo at least once a day and both of them regularly came away amazed with their findings."[99] Early on, before the affair, Mr. Hosoume detects a threat in his children's adoration of Marpo, as "Mr. Hosoume began remarking the fact that they dwelt more with Marpo than with their own parents."[100] For example, when Marpo builds a radio that the children cluster into his room to listen to, Mr. Hosoume buys the radio, and Marpo "put away his radio manuals and his soldering iron in the bottom of his steamer trunk."[101] Mr. Hosoume recognizes Yoneko's adoption of Marpo's God as a threat to her vision of her own father as godlike. With the earthquake, she loses faith in the ability of both Marpo's God and her father as God to protect her and her family.

The natural violence depicted in "Yoneko's Earthquake" becomes inextricably intertwined with the story's domestic violence, a pattern seen in "Seventeen Syllables" as well.[102] The earthquake leads to Marpo's affair with Mrs. Hosoume. The earthquake is also the most direct source of the father's injury. These events produce a "catastrophe" in the lives of the characters.[103] They lead to Mr. Hosoume's feelings of cuckoldry. He accuses his wife, Marpo, and his children of impudence: "Just because I'm ill just now is no reason for them to start being disrespectful." When he and his wife then argue, "Mr. Hosoume went up to where his wife was ironing and slapped her smartly on the face. It was the first time he had ever laid hands on her."[104] Yamamoto describes the children's reaction as "thunderstruck," another image of nature's violence.[105] This sudden stormlike interruption to the family cannot be separated from the "monstrous upheaval" caused by the earthquake.[106] The wrathful hand of the father mirrors the wrathful hand of the giant that shook the house during the earthquake. The protecting shelter of the house, the nurturing lap of nature, and the father as protector all turn violent, revealing the peaceful agrarianism popularly associated with family farms as an illusion.

Yamamoto's tendency to employ natural metaphors such as earthquakes as representative of violent threats to Japanese American families is at odds with many textual representations of the period that attempt to establish Japanese American national belonging through textual naturalization. Comparison to Monica Sone's *Nisei Daughter* highlights the distinct relationship among nature, nation, and violence in "Seventeen Syllables" and "Yoneko's Earthquake." Sone first published *Nisei Daughter* in 1953, not long after Yamamoto published her short stories. The book proved palatable to a broad American audience seeking to interpret the experience of Japanese American internment as ultimately being in line with American values. Sone reproduces the nation's narrative that young Nisei were better off (meaning more assimilated) as a result of internment. Critics retrospectively note the lack of anger and blame in the text.[107] Prior to internment, the young protagonist cannot reconcile her Japanese identity and her US American identity. She states, "I didn't see how I could be a Yankee and Japanese at the same time. It was like being born with two heads. It sounded freakish."[108] This image of double-headedness emerges in other Asian American texts of this period, such as *No No Boy* and *Fifth Chinese Daughter*.[109] The protagonist's racial identity (with its assumed foreign nationality) differs from the racial identity of the unmarked or abstract national subject. Since the racial identity of the unmarked national subject is presumed to be natural, the protagonist feels unnaturally burdened with two contradictory subject positions, echoing W. E. B. Du Bois's "double consciousness."[110]

The protagonist reconciles her double-headedness by verifying the naturalness of her Americanness, as exemplified in her family's visit to Japan. During this episode both her brothers become sick, and one of them, Kenji, dies of *ikiri*, a disease endemic to Japan.[111] Shortly before Kenji's death, the narrator's father says, "It's nearly July. . . . Children from America often get sick during these months."[112] With Kenji's death, Sone conveys the inability of American children to survive in the Japanese nation. This contrasts with the two daughters' triumph over tuberculosis in the United States. The parallel between the girls' struggle with tuberculosis and Kenji's failure to survive *ikiri* communicates the Americanness of the family, as much as the title of the chapter—"We Meet Real Japanese." As Monica comes of age, she realizes that she is not a freak of nature. Even if her cultural identity is plural, her national identity is singular. She says, "I used to feel like a two-headed monstrosity, but now I find that two heads are better than one."[113] This is because two heads ultimately give her "a clearer understanding of America and its way of life, and we have learned to value her [America] more."[114] Monica's cultural duality results in her national loyalty. The naturalness of Japanese American belonging to the American nation is re-established as *Nisei Daughter* demonstrates that "an elemental instinct bound" Japanese American families "to this soil."[115]

This comparison to *Nisei Daughter* helps us recognize the difference in Yamamoto's fictional families' relationship with the national soil. The violent characterization of nature in "Yoneko's Earthquake" is a rejection of the Hosoume family's peaceful agricultural existence. It suggests the violence that faced Japanese Americans as they sought national inclusion. Given Yamamoto's unwavering pacifism, the theme of violence described repeatedly in both "Yoneko's Earthquake" and "Seventeen Syllables" is particularly striking. The aggression and cruelty emerge predominantly from two sources in the short stories: nature (earthquakes, harvests, and seasons) and the patriarchs (Mr. Hosoume and Mr. Hayashi). Both nature and each family's father symbolically stand in for the nation-state in their brutality, in the Cold War embrace of the nation-state, and in structuring kinship metaphors of the nation-state philosophy.[116]

Throughout Yamamoto's fiction, cars serve as particular vehicles of the nation's violence against Japanese Americans. In her memoir "Life Among the Oil Fields," Yamamoto explicitly establishes a relationship between the automobiles and the United States. In this essay, a reckless automobile runs down the narrator's brother, Jemo. Initially he appears dead; "he does not move."[117] He returns from the hospital "clothed in bandages, including one like a turban around his head and face."[118] The white couple in the car who had hit him lack "even the decency to come and inquire after Jemo's condition."[119] This leads the narrator to say, "I sometimes see the arrogant couple from down the road as young and beautiful, their speeding open roadster as definitely and stunningly red. They roar by; their tinkling laughter, like a long silken scarf, is borne back by the wind. I gaze after them from the side of the road, where I have darted to dodge the swirling dust and spitting gravel. And I know that their names are Scott and Zelda."[120] As critics have demonstrated, this image ties the car to the uncompassionate nation-state Japanese Americans encountered in the 1920s, when the memoir takes place. The scene echoes the cruel carelessness of Myrtle's death in *The Great Gatsby* and recalls the moral emptiness symbolized by automobiles in Fitzgerald's novel, such as Daisy's refusal to take responsibility for her actions.[121] For Yamamoto, Scott and Zelda Fitzgerald represent privileged white Americans' selfish lack of consideration for those with whom they must share the national road. Yet Yamamoto's characters escape the deadly consequences of speeding automobiles that Fitzgerald's characters face. Instead, Yamamoto's narrator imagines herself dodging and darting out of the way so as not to be killed like "an animal."[122] She uses her wits and brawn to resist the dehumanization that their negligence enacts.

The necessity of survival against national violence that threatens the humanity of Japanese Americans emerges in the car accident of "Yoneko's Earthquake" as well. When a wire knocked down by the earthquake hits his car, Mr. Hosoume began to "writhe and kick and this had been his salvation."[123] As in "Life Among the Oil Fields," Mr. Hosoume lives only because of his darting and dodging. He survives by unconsciously writhing, causing his car to spin out of control and out from under the wire. While the earthquake is most directly responsible for Mr. Hosoume's injury, the car becomes the vehicle that allows it. His survival testifies to his instincts and his actions, not to any protection offered by the car. Nature and nation conspire in his emasculation. The car accident physically violates Yoneko's father. The electrocution injures him; he returns an invalid. The accident renders him impotent—perhaps even sexually, the text hints. He is confined to the house and to his wife's previous tasks of cooking and childcare. The gender ambiguity of his character mirrors the ambiguity pictured in the construction of the stereotypical Asian immigrant, specifically the Chinese coolie.[124] Yet Yamamoto does not portray such gender ambiguity as an Asian threat to the nation. Rather the nation threatens the Japanese immigrant with such violent and emasculating injuries.

In *Race and Resistance*, literary critic Viet Thanh Nguyen contends that in much Asian American literature, the Asian American body stands in for the Asian American body politic. This produces a tension in texts between hegemonic contentions that one body is representative of all Asian Americans and the Asian American response that there are multiple Asian and Asian American bodies.[125] In Yamamoto's writings, Mr. Hosoume's electrocution and Jemo's injuries offer material evidence of the nation's attack on Japanese Americans. Their wounded bodies stand in for the harm done by the privileged white American public and the callous US nation-state concerned more with its speed, modernity, and sleek image than with the actual inclusion of racially excluded subjects. Twentieth-century representations of automobiles often signify narratives of freedom and socioeconomic mobility. In contrast, as Sau-ling Cynthia Wong asserts, images of geographic mobility in Asian American texts are "usually associated with subjugation, coercion, impossibility of fulfillment for self or community."[126] While mobility and travel in hegemonic narratives usually lead the narrator to an "immobility of a desirable kind: that of having created a permanent home and cast down roots," Asian American texts frequently fail to achieve this immobility as a form of freedom.[127] As Yamamoto's image of Zelda and Scott Fitzgerald running down Jemo demonstrates, Japanese Americans were not included in the national socioeconomic mobility of the "roaring twenties." Throughout the pre-internment period, they instead faced the economic and ideological violence that "Yoneko's Earthquake" depicts. Japanese Americans were not just excluded from national socioeconomic mobility. They also were harmed by white Americans' access to it. The achievement of freedom, independence, and wealth by white national subjects came at the expense of this uprooting of Japanese American families.

"Yoneko's Earthquake" and "Seventeen Syllables" paint the relationship between Japanese Americans and the American nation as one of violence and harm, refuting the narratives of acceptance and progress offered by some pre-internment Japanese American newspapers and the narratives of belonging and healing offered by some post-internment Japanese American literature. These narratives frequently overlook the racialized abjection faced by Japanese immigrants and Japanese Americans and instead rely on the nationalized language of farm and earth to suggest a harmonious relationship between Japanese Americans and the nation. Yamamoto, in contrast, uses agricultural metaphors and depictions of nature to denaturalize the nuclear family and nation-state and to acknowledge the consequences of the racial and gendered hierarchies of capitalist agriculture.

CONCLUSION

Instead of upholding farming as a pathway to Japanese American racial acceptance or emphasizing nature as a site of healing for previously interned Japanese Americans, Yamamoto's fiction highlights the instability and unnaturalness of the categories of race, family, and nation that dictate the racial oppression and economic exploitation facing Japanese American families. Yamamoto's depictions of pre-internment Japanese American farms expose the complex interplay of race, class, and gender among nonwhite farmers and farmworkers. In doing so, she reveals the shortcomings of other Japanese American textual attempts, both pre- and post-internment, to naturalize Japanese American national belonging. She exposes the role of violence and exploitation at the heart of American agrarianism and implicitly endorses the *Catholic Worker* vision of the scholar-laborer as a solution to capitalism's hierarchies. While some naturalization narratives reinforce the racial gatekeeping of the nation, Yamamoto's fiction reveals the possibility of using agrarian discourse to question the processes by which the nation-state, the nuclear family, and the nation's racial hierarchies are naturalized. In concert with other Japanese American texts of the mid-twentieth century, Yamamoto's work affirms the centrality of US agrarianism to larger projects of racial exclusion and to Japanese American attempts to navigate, subvert, or simply shift position within the cultural apparatus that defined some subjects as citizen-farmers and others as abject alien farmworkers.

CHAPTER 5

"The American Earth"

Reclaiming Land and Nation in
America Is in the Heart and *Strangers in Our Fields*

I N THE FINAL PAGES OF CARLOS BULOSAN'S *AMERICA IS IN THE Heart* (1946), the narrator, Carlos, describes "the American earth" as being "like a huge heart unfolding warmly to receive me."[1] The loss, grief, fear, and flight that structure the work are resolved by intimacy with the earth itself. The earth embraces Carlos even as the nation pushes him aside. The narrator's desire for land runs through *America Is in the Heart*. Yet this yearning to merge with the earth is not primarily a desire for national inclusion. Rather, it addresses the larger imperial context in which Bulosan wrote and in which US agriculture is entangled. Carlos's passion for the American landscape becomes one location through which Bulosan articulates his aspiration for land reform in the Philippines.

Thus far, *The Nature of California* has considered migrant farmworkers' relation to the nation primarily as immigrants denied legal citizenship or as alien citizens deprived of recognition of their citizenship by the state and civil society. Yet, as Bulosan's writing reveals, American agrarianism is an imperial venture. US agriculture rests fundamentally on the backbone of stolen native land. The construction of the US farmer-citizen as land owner relies on the invisibility of indigenous land claims. Farming in the US is incapable of escaping its settler colonialist context. It also depends on a colonized labor force. In the southwestern United States, including California, Mexicans and Mexican Americans labor without fully recognized rights on land that belonged to Mexico before it was part of the United States. Other farmworkers upon whom US agribusiness relies migrate to the United States because of uneven and imperial relations among nations. As historian and Latina/o studies scholar Gilbert Gonzalez contends, Mexican migration to the United States results from a long history of US economic domination over Mexico.[2] The Mexican and Mexican American workforce, in Gonzalez's view, results from neocolonial political and economic relations that reached a particular zenith under the Bracero Program, a guest worker program that issued 4.5 million temporary contracts to workers from Mexico between 1942 and 1964.[3]

Filipino farmworkers, including Bulosan, labored in an even more explicitly colonial context than did Mexican workers. Spain ceded the Philippines to the United States in 1898, and the United States did not recognize the Philippines' independence until 1946, considering it an "unincorporated territory," ineligible for statehood. Like Mexico, the Philippines won its independence from Spain. In the Philippine-American War (1899–1902), as in the Mexican-American War (1846–48), the United States claimed the land but was hesitant to incorporate the people as full citizens. From 1901 to 1934, Filipino workers retained the status of "noncitizen nationals," and were encouraged to work in the United States but were denied citizenship rights. After 1934, Filipino migrants found their status even more tenuous as their legal status changed from noncitizen national to deportable alien.[4] With both Mexico and the Philippines, the United States desired the land and labor, but treated the subjects who performed the labor as abject.

Farmworkers and their advocates resisted this process of abjection. Bulosan's *America Is in the Heart* and Ernesto Galarza's *Strangers in Our Fields* (1956), a report critiquing the Bracero Program, refute the abjection of the Filipino migrant and the Mexican bracero, respectively. Bulosan and Galarza both fought to unionize California's agricultural workers and in doing so wrote texts that exposed agricultural workers as colonial subjects. *America Is in the Heart* and *Strangers in Our Fields* (hereafter referred to as *Strangers*) counter the United States' abjection of farmworkers by reimagining US agricultural landscapes. In both texts, reclaiming national landscapes forms an essential part of the process by which farm laborers assert their humanity, resisting the processes of their alienage and abjection. Galarza exposes the Bracero Program's landscape as one of denationalized capitalism. He calls for renationalization, for a return of Mexican workers to Mexican soil and US agricultural lands to the United States. Bulosan, in contrast, turns the imperializing processes of the United States around, claiming the American earth for the Philippines. He alters the national identity associated with US workers and US landscapes, creating an agricultural narrative grounded in the Philippines, even as it is set in the United States. For both Galarza and Bulosan, the relationship between nations concerns them more than the full incorporation of the racialized subject into the nation-state. Both Galarza and Bulosan depict US agriculture as a nexus through which uneven relationships between nations manifest, creating the conditions of alienage for workers and providing a key site through which workers could reclaim the status of citizen.

MARKED BY EMPIRE: A CONTEXT FOR CARLOS BULOSAN

Carlos Bulosan arrived in the United States on July 22, 1930, at the age of nineteen. He was born in the town of Binalonan, Pangasinan, in the Philippines in 1911.[5] His parents were peasants, though they were not as impoverished as Bulosan sometimes claimed. Once in the United States, Bulosan increasingly involved himself in political and intellectual circles, editing *The New Tide*, a radical literary magazine, in 1934. Through this magazine he came in contact with left-wing writers such as William Saroyan and Richard Wright. He wrote in English for a primarily US audience and contributed to union papers as often as he did to literary ones. From 1936 to 1938, Bulosan was hospitalized with tuberculosis yet continued to write furiously, often in the company of novelist Sanora Babb and her sister Dorothy (Alice and Eileen Odell in *America Is in the Heart*). Bulosan published poetry, short stories, essays, and novels, gaining national acclaim throughout the 1940s. On September 13, 1956, Bulosan died. He never returned to the Philippines, and he never became a US citizen.[6]

As renowned literary scholar of the Filipino diaspora E. San Juan Jr. notes, US imperialism in the Philippines provides an essential context for Bulosan's writing.[7] Following its victory in the Spanish-American War, the United States waged a brutal battle against Filipino independence fighters from 1899 to 1902. The United States deployed two-thirds of its army. Between 220,000 and 1,400,000 Filipinos were killed.[8] The United States agonized over its relationship with the Philippines as politicians and businessmen wanted to incorporate its territories but not its inhabitants. The

United States eventually claimed the Philippines, along with Puerto Rico and Guam, as "unincorporated territories," distinct from incorporated territories in which eventual statehood was assured. As noncitizen nationals, Filipinos could travel to the United States but were not eligible for citizenship. Between 1907 and 1936, 150,000 Filipinos, including Bulosan, migrated to the United States and worked in Hawaiian sugar plantations, Alaskan canneries, and West Coast agricultural fields. According to Mae Ngai, "nearly 85 percent of the Filipinos arriving in California during the 1920s were under thirty years of age, 93 percent were male, and 77 percent were single."[9] These young men faced intense vigilante violence such as in Watsonville, California, in 1930. Anti-Filipino mobs justified their brutality as a defense of white womanhood, while anti-Filipino organizations called for the exclusion of Filipino workers, using a logic similar to that applied earlier to Chinese and Japanese workers.[10] Such organizations partially achieved their goals with the Tydings-McDuffie Act of 1934 and the Welch Act of 1935. The Tydings-McDuffie Act granted the Philippines a modicum of self-government and reclassified Filipino noncitizen nationals as deportable aliens.[11] Filipinos resisted this discrimination and exploitation through labor organizations such as United Cannery Agricultural, Packing, and Allied Workers of America (UCAPAWA), and advocacy projects such as the Committee for the Protection of Filipino Rights.[12]

America Is in the Heart, a fictionalized autobiography, describes the narrator Carlos's childhood in the Philippines, his passage to the United States, where he rides the rails from one seasonal job to the next, his two years of convalescence with tuberculosis during which he grows as a writer, and his progressive political awakening as he struggles to unionize Filipino laborers. The book ends shortly after Pearl Harbor with Carlos's brothers and friends rushing to join the army to defend the Philippines and fight fascism worldwide. Bulosan intended the book to provide a composite view of the Filipino laborer's experience in this period. As Bulosan's friend, Carey McWilliams, writes in the introduction to *America Is in the Heart*, "One may doubt that Bulosan personally experienced each and every one of the manifold brutalities and indecencies so vividly described in this book, but it can fairly be said—making allowances for occasional minor histrionics—that some Filipino was indeed the victim of each of these or similar incidents."[13]

Carlos the narrator and Bulosan the author are not synonymous, and following scholarly convention in distinguishing between them, I reference the narrator by first name.

Family, land, and national identity are all closely linked in *America Is in the Heart*. Bulosan grounds his text in the Philippines, grappling from the first line with the material consequences of the archipelago's colonial status for his family's landholdings and thus for their emotional and material well-being. Although Carlos leaves the Philippines to spend the majority of the text in the United States, the book retains roots in the Philippines. Home is never far from Carlos's thoughts, and his survival strategy depends on noting the similarity between the US landscape and white US women to places and people in his country of origin. Through these proclamations of familiar women and landscapes, Carlos generates a new cartography for the Americas and a new kinship network in which the Philippines are at the core, not at the periphery. From Carlos's vantage point, the Filipino subject and the Philippines are at the center of the United States, including at the center of the US agricultural empire and resistance to it.

The first hundred pages of the book take place in the Philippines, and from the narrative's inception, *America Is in the Heart* insists on its readers' recognition of the US influence on the Philippines. The story opens with the return of Carlos's brother from fighting for the US Army in Europe. Leon's entrance embeds Carlos's rural farming life in an already established military relationship with the United States and Europe. The first line of the memoir reads, "I was the first to see him coming slowly through the tall grass in the dry bottom of the river."[14] Leon's "khaki army uniform" invokes the US military's incursion into the fields of the Philippines as well as into the private space of Filipino families.[15] When Carlos's father introduces Leon, he states, "It is your brother, son."[16] He names the relationship between Leon and Carlos as familial, yet Carlos responds, "Welcome home, soldier," refiguring his relationship to Leon.[17] The text exposes the naturalization of US involvement in the Philippines through the process whereby a child meets brother as soldier as well as greets soldier as brother. This appears as the rhetorical converse to US ideologies that patronizingly refer to Filipinos as "little brown brothers" of US citizens. In Bulosan's text, US army recruitment strategies and economic underdevelopment of the Philippines, alongside absentee landlordism, force Filipinos to play the roles of both US solider and "little brown brother." In this way, Bulosan's work exposes the "white man's burden" in the Philippines as being primarily ideological, while Filipinos themselves are forced to bear the material consequences of the United States' imagined burden.

The economic and political consequences of the Spanish-American War shape the book's narrative of agrarian loss. This first third of the memoir chronicles Carlos's family's loss of land, echoing John Steinbeck's *Grapes of Wrath*. Literary scholar Chris Vials believes that Bulosan's adaptation of the yeoman farmer's decline, a narrative popularized by writers such as Steinbeck, Pearl Buck, Erskine Caldwell, and Margaret Mitchell, enabled the book's widespread reach within the United States. As Vials argues, by turning to the yeoman farmer, Bulosan draws attention to the role of American imperialism in the oppression of Carlos's family.[18] In repeating the trope of farmland loss, Bulosan not only places his text in a recognizably American context but positions land dispossession as a primary consequence of US colonialism.

The ways in which Bulosan's memoir echoes the Joads' travails not only renders US imperialism legible for an American audience but also sets up the politics of land and earth that are central to Bulosan's broader project, including his incipient nationalism.[19] Carlos's claims to the earth emerge from his family's history. He says, "[Carlos's father's] parents and their parents before him had lacerated their lives digging away the stones and trees to make the forest land of our village a fragrant and livable place" (Bulosan, *America Is in the Heart*, 76). This pioneer narrative underscores the response of Carlos's father to his dispossession: "There is something wrong in our country when a man can take away something that belongs to you and your family" (55). Generations of sacrifice define the land as the family's property. Labor constitutes ownership, as his father inquires of Carlos, "Is it possible, son? . . . Can a stranger take away what we have molded with our hands?" (55). Bulosan figures the land as something produced by the Filipino peasantry and stolen by the colonial government of absentee landlords and bourgeois families. Just as the Joads' loss of land threatened their family unity, with the loss of Carlos's family's land, "My father knew then that it was the end of our family" (48). Just as Grandpa and Grandma

Joad are unable to survive the trip to California, Carlos's father cannot live without his land. Carlos describes "my father's struggle to hold onto the land he knew so well, fighting to the end and dying on it like a peasant" (27). When his father loses his land, Carlos's family become migrant farmworkers. Carlos works with his mother and sisters in the fields of the town of Tayug. One family owns all of the land in Tayug, as well as all of the land in two adjoining towns (38). Absentee landlordism is as rife in the Philippines as in California. Similar to white Dust Bowl refugees, Carlos's family endures deprivation that results from the theft of their farm. It is this loss of land that sets up Carlos's unending flight in the United States, and it is his love of land and family that sustains him in the United States.

When Carlos begins traveling around the United States, he retains his humanity in the harsh conditions he encounters because of his memory of the landscape of home and of female family members left at home, especially his mother. Carlos's ability to reconstitute his Filipino family in the United States assures his survival. He searches out his brothers Amado and Macario. Although they are seldom in the same place, the siblings retain a bond of loyalty throughout the text, especially as Macario and Carlos solidify their political camaraderie. Their shared love for their mother is central to their relationship. To demonstrate his identity to Macario, Carlos must provide his mother's name: "To him, and to me afterward, to know my mother's name was to know the password into the secrets of the past, into childhood and pleasant memories; but it was also a guiding star, a talisman, a charm that lights us to manhood and decency" (123). As literary scholar Patricia Chu asserts, Carlos's mother's "static remoteness serves as a foil, a ground by which to measure the change and progress of the uprooted Asian American male protagonist."[20] As a "guiding star," their mother provides the boundlessness and love that Carlos associates with the Philippines, helping him retain his humanity in the face of numerous travails.

The text's white women function similarly to Carlos's mother, helping him maintain a "decent" masculinity in the face of savage American exploitation. According to literary scholar Susan Koshy, Carlos yearns to possess white women romantically because he cannot possess land within the United States. He associates white women and pastoral visions of the US landscape with the transcendent democratic ideal of America, an ideal unrealized in his life. He seeks integration into the American nation through miscegenation.[21] However, Bulosan also associates these white women with the Philippines. Their beauty and desirability are recognizable to Carlos through their resemblance to his mother and his sisters. Similarly, Carlos identifies the beauty of the US landscape in the ways it reminds him of the Philippines. This use of analogy is an act of repossession rather than an attempt at assimilation or integration. Carlos claims both the white women and the landscapes he most desires for the Philippines. The comparison Bulosan offers between the white women who represent Carlos's ideals of democracy and Carlos's beloved mother and sisters situates the Philippines as central to his anti-imperialist and anticapitalist political vision.

The suffering of white women in *America Is in the Heart* recalls for Carlos the suffering of the Philippines and the suffering of his sisters and mother. Feeling empathy and love for certain white women, Carlos names them as part of his Filipino family, articulating their resemblance to his mother and sisters at home. Carlos witnesses the brutal gang rape of a young white girl on a boxcar, and the perpetrators knock him unconscious as he tries to protect her. Afterward, he says, "I struck a match and watched her face affectionately. She looked a little like my older sister, Francisca. There was a sudden rush of warm feeling in me, yearning to comfort her with the words I knew" (114). Carlos identifies with her. Her plight, "this ravished girl and this lonely night, in a freight train bound for an unknown city," inspires him to see her as a sister (114). He says, "I felt that there was a bond between us, a bond of fear and a common loneliness" (115). His experiences in the Philippines become the barometer by which he understands suffering and exploitation in the United States.

Carlos likewise incorporates into his family the prostitute Marian by naming her as both substitute sister and mother. She embodies for Carlos both a motherly affection and a sisterly love. Carlos says, "My heart ached, for this woman was like my little sisters in Binalonan" (211). In establishing Marian's similarity to his sisters, Carlos also proclaims her resemblance to the American sibling he has already adopted: "This Marian: she was small, quiet, and lovely with long brown hair. Her hair—where had I seen it before? The girl on the freight train! Could it be the same person?" (213). Given the biographical information he provides about both Marian and the girl on the train, it seems unlikely that they are the same person. Carlos connects them because of the similar brotherly affection they evoke in him.

Marian is a vulnerable character ravished by the world (like Carlos's sisters and the girl on the train) and also a maternal figure that protects Carlos and provides for him. In this way, she reminds Carlos of his mother: "I turned away from her, remembering how I had walked familiar roads with my mother" (211). Marian and his mother have similar hands, resulting from their work lives. Carlos describes Marian's hands as "rough; the fingers were stubby and flattened at the top" (211). Correspondingly his mother's hands are "big-veined, hard, and bleeding in spots" (22). Like his mother, "it was obvious that [Marian] had done manual work" (211). Marian works as a prostitute at night, while Carlos sleeps, to provide him with food and shelter. She sacrifices her physical health for Carlos and contracts syphilis; analogously, his mother starved herself to ensure that her children had enough to eat (218). Marian says, "What I would like is to have someone to care for, and it should be you who are young. I would be happier if I had something to care for—even if it were only a dog or a cat" (212). Marian's desire to care for something or someone is not sexual; it is parental and paternalistic (a cat or dog would be a substitute, and she specifically wants someone young). This care is not only physical. She provides the nurturing love that steers Carlos morally on the right path.

Like his Filipino family and his cultural roots back home, Marian serves to protect Carlos's humanity in the United States. As she is dying, she cries, "Promise me not to hate. But love—love everything good and clean. There is something in you that radiates like an inner light, and it affects others. Promise me to let it grow" (217). Marian, like Carlos's mother, is a guiding light who counters the abject and brutal treatment Carlos encounters in the United States. With Marian, Carlos continues to construct a mental map in which he categorizes the tragic and the beautiful in America as being like the Philippines. Rather than forge a new beginning and a new family in the United States, Carlos incorporates the women he meets into his existing Filipino family. The Philippines remains the location from which he understands and analyzes the United States, and the place in which he imagines his allies as he expands his network of political resistance.

While white women's sexual victimization and economic exploitation remind Carlos of his mother and sisters' suffering at home, the attractiveness of the US landscape recalls for Carlos his love for the land from which his family has been dispossessed. He recognizes the United States as beautiful because of its similarity to the Philippines: "The primitive beauty of Santa Fe reminded me of the calm and isolation of Baguio, the mountain city in Luzon where I had worked for Miss Mary Strandon. Morning was like a rose cupping its trembling dews, shattering and delicate, small but potent with miracles. But the nights were tranquil with millions of stars" (168). When he sits on the California coast at night, Carlos thinks, "The stars shone between the trees. It was like a long time ago in a land far away. Was it in Mangusmana that I had seen this same sky? And that lone star—had I seen it among the pine trees in Baguio?" (184). Later, after escaping a violent attack by vigilantes, Carlos and José "walked in the morning sun, smelling the orange blossoms and the clean air. I looked at the tall mountains on our right and stopped, remembering the mountains in my village" (197). The Philippines continuously emerge in the US landscape. The United States is never free from the Filipino presence. Bulosan writes the Philippines into the very mountains, flowers, and vistas of the United States. US western landscapes appeal to Carlos because they echo the resplendence of the Philippines. Just as the white women with whom Carlos associates remind him of his mother and sisters, the American earth conveys the allure of home. Despite Carlos's frenetic movement and frantic mobility in search of work and fleeing violence, these comparisons of women and land to the Philippines allow the Philippines to act as the geographic and narrative center of the text, the place to which Carlos's thoughts always return.

Carlos's remembrance of the Philippines fuels his struggle for life in the United States. His memories provide his anchor. When he "lost all hope" facing surefire death at the hands of yet another vigilante squad, it is the presence of the Philippines in the US landscape that inspires him (207). He states, "Looking swiftly to the east, I saw the big moon and below it, soon to move away, a mass of clouds that looked like a mountain of cotton balls. Suddenly I remembered that as a child I used to watch snow-white clouds sailing in the bright summer skies of Mangusmana. The memory of my village made my mind whirl, longing for flight and freedom again" (207). The warmth of Carlos's childhood drives this desire for survival. Carlos's love of the Philippines' landscape and familial comforts lies at the heart of his political identity, including his anticolonialist ideas. As Carlos puts it, "Thus it was that I began to rediscover my native land and the cultural roots there that had nourished me and I felt a great urge to identify myself with the social awakening of my people" (139). The Philippines' centrality to Carlos's developing political critique hints at the full-blown Filipino nationalism that would mark Bulosan's later years, as with his posthumously published novel, *The Cry and the Dedication.*[22]

Bulosan depicts the Philippines as the source of Carlos's spiritual sustenance and the fuel for his political aspirations. Carlos seeks to escape the poverty of home and yet also yearns to return to rectify the exploitation he could not address as a boy. Carlos says, "I was determined to leave that environment [the Philippines] and all its crushing forces, and if I were successful in escaping unscathed, I would go back someday to understand what it meant to be born of the peasantry. I would go back because I was a part of it, because I could not really escape from it no matter where I went or what became of me" (62). Carlos's struggle is animated and inspired by the aspiration to return triumphantly to the Philippines to bring justice to the peasantry. In his last visit home he promises his brother, "I will come back and buy that house [the family home]. . . . Wait and see!" (88). After surviving vigilante violence he proclaims, "Someday I will go back and climb these guavas [in my village] again. Someday I will make a crown of papaya blossoms" (198). Even after his brother and several friends leave to fight fascism in Spain, Carlos proclaims, "All right, go fight a war on another continent, like my brother Leon. But if I live I will go back to our country, and fight the enemy there" (240). This aspiration to return home is partly motivated by his desire to reclaim his father's land. Carlos explains, "I had not forgotten his [my father's] love for the earth" (76). In this way, Carlos privileges his relationship to the Philippines. His Filipino identity and emergent nationalism shape his political priorities. The landscape and his memory of the Philippines provide for his survival as well as the inspiration for the new world he seeks.

In positioning the Philippines as its narrative center, rather than setting it into the periphery, *America Is in the Heart* challenges imperialist geography. The fictionalized memoir encourages this anticolonialist cartography by casting the United States as Robinson Crusoe's island and Carlos as Crusoe. Before his journey to the United States, Carlos's brother "started reading the story of a man named Robinson Crusoe who had been ship-wrecked in some unknown sea and drifted to a little island far away. My brother patiently explained the struggle of this ingenious man who had lived alone for years in inclement weathers and had survived loneliness and returned safely to his native land" (32). As Carlos feels increasingly drawn to America, "a strong desire grew in me to see [Crusoe's] island" (32). Once in the United States, Carlos repeatedly refers to the country as an island. There he experiences the challenges of survival faced by Crusoe and is able to survive only because of his wits and the allies he nurtures. He says, "I died many deaths in these surroundings, where man was indistinguishable from beast" (135). Although he tries to escape from segregated impover-ished urban landscapes, Carlos says, "We were always driven back to this narrow island of despair" (134). Each challenge of his life in the United States becomes an island of its own: "Even when representative Vito Mar-cantonio introduced a bill in Congress proposing Filipino citizenship, even then I looked out the window of my room like a prisoner on some isolated island" (285). When Carlos declares that "it was a crime to be a Filipino in California," he describes this criminalization as the "narrowing of our life into an island" (121).

Through naming the United States as Crusoe's island, Bulosan chal-lenges the exoticization of colonized landscapes. He turns the tropicaliz-ing discourse of the Americas around, aiming it at the United States.[23] He highlights the expansive love, morality, and familiarity of the Philippines' landscape, while the United States evokes the primitive, barbaric, and can-nibalistic. Crusoe's eventual escape from the island suggests that Bulosan's own freedom will come only in his own escape from this "island." Freedom will require either his return home to the Philippines or his successful re-making of the United States as an extension of the Philippines.

Literary scholar Joseph Keith contends that the "islands" that Carlos finds himself on in the United States are those of marginalization, isola-tion, and alienation. As Keith beautifully articulates, "It is a geographic imaginary that animates, as such, the uneven incorporation of racialized subjects into the mainland of American citizenship, mapping a cartography of segregation in sharp contradiction to the inclusive national landscape of American pluralism."[24] He contrasts the alienation of the island with the boundlessness that Bulosan seeks. In this boundlessness, Keith asserts, Bulosan finds a cosmopolitan universalism, an alternative identity through which to root his politics.[25]

For the most part, I agree with Keith, but I would add that the politics around land captured in the spatial imaginary signify more than figurative claims. *America Is in the Heart* grapples with Carlos's desire for actual land, both as a claiming of the US landscape and as a reclaiming of land in the Philippines.[26] Throughout *America Is in the Heart*, nature's boundlessness cannot be separated from the bonds of kinship, community, and land for Carlos. At the book's start, Carlos states, "I knew that if there was one redeeming quality in our poverty, it was this boundless affinity for each other, this humanity that grew in each of us, as boundless as this green earth."[27] Carlos's ability to see beauty in the land and sky around him reflects this allegiance to land gained from his family and their agricultural roots. As Carlos says of his childhood, his brother Leon "had taught me to love the earth."[28]

In *America Is in the Heart*, justice requires a return to the land and a return of the land to its rightful owners. Carlos's descriptions of white US women and the US landscape as being like the Philippines is a narrative strategy to claim ownership over both. To mark the US land and women as part of the Philippines is a gendered way of claiming land for himself and the Philippine peasantry to which his parents belong. Carlos's brother Marcario explains that "America is not merely a land or an institution" but "a prophecy of a new society of men: of a system that knows no sorrow or strife or suffering."[29] This construction of America as being distinct from any particular place or nation becomes the political ideal that Carlos leverages to see land in both the United States and in the Philippines as the property of those who work on it. He takes ownership over American democratic ideals, defining them as being apart from the nation-state. In the final pages of the text, when Carlos describes "the American earth" as being "like a huge heart unfolding warmly to receive me," the American earth represents the idea of democracy rather than an assimilationist belonging to the US nation-state.[30] When Carlos claims intimacy with this earth, moreover, it is an earth that reminds him of the Philippines. The American earth restores him, in part, because of its similarity to the Philippines, similar to the way white women who remind him of his sisters and mother protect and guide him. His desire for the American earth is a desire for democracy and land in the Philippines.

STRANGERS IN A STRANGE LAND: GALARZA'S *STRANGERS IN OUR FIELDS*

While Bulosan renders the US agricultural landscape as familiar and familial, Galarza emphasizes its alienness and strangeness. In his muckraking exposé *Strangers in Our Fields*, he portrays the Bracero Program as a militarized space of industry outside of the regulatory agency of either the United States or Mexico. According to Galarza, the Bracero Program strips Mexican nationals of their masculinity, civil liberties, and national identity. The men leave Mexico to enter a militarized world of private industry from which US civil society is barred. The agricultural landscape of the Bracero Program, despite being territorially located in the United States, is outside of both nations. Galarza depicts braceros as denationalized subjects in a denationalized landscape. His solution is a renationalization of the US agricultural landscape and a return of the bracero subject to the status of Mexican national. Galarza's critique of the Bracero Program as encapsulating the economic imperialism between the United States and Mexico relies on his analysis of the subject positions that both nationalized and denationalized landscapes produce.

According to scholars Rodolfo Torres and Armando Ibarra, "Ernesto Galarza . . . was the most significant and prolific Mexican American social critic and public intellectual of the twentieth century."[31] Galarza's political and personal trajectory was remarkable.[32] He emigrated from Mexico as a child during the Mexican Revolution. According to Joan London and Henry Anderson in their compelling chronicle of the farmworkers' movement, "One of his earliest memories is of crouching on the floor of a train bearing [his family] north to the border as bullets spattered on the outside."[33] His family relocated to Sacramento, where Galarza spent his summers working in the Central Valley's fields.[34] Galarza excelled in the US educational system, receiving a bachelor's degree from Occidental College, a master's degree in Latin American studies from Stanford University, and a PhD in economics from Columbia University in 1944.[35] He initially sought employment in advocacy and policy rather than academia. After spending more than a decade at the Pan American Union in Washington, DC, he was appointed the director of research and education for the National Farm Labor Union (NFLU), which grew out of the Southern Tenant Farmers' Union and remained the predominant union for California agricultural laborers throughout the 1940s and 1950s.[36] Through his work in the fields with the NFLU, including supporting the DiGiorgio grape strike (1947–50), Galarza gained more knowledge of the Bracero Program's effects on California farm labor.[37] By 1955, he was actively researching the program under a grant from the Fund for the Republic. Galarza penned *Strangers* in 1956; it received national attention and sold out in two editions. He followed it up with a book-length exposé, *Merchants of Labor* (1964). He wrote *Spiders in the House and Workers in the Field* (1971) about the DiGiorgio strike (1947–50), and followed it with *Farm-workers and Agri-business in California, 1947–1960* (1978). *Barrio Boy* (1971), chronicling Galarza's childhood, is part of the Latina/o literary canon today. While writing these books, Galarza turned to teaching. He held faculty appointments at San Jose State University; the University of California, San Diego; and the University of California, Santa Cruz. He called himself a "professional intellectual migrant" as he re-engaged his life-long commitment to education, examining the shortcomings of the existent bilingual educational system and producing a series of children's books to be used in bilingual classrooms.[38]

Galarza is perhaps best known for his successful campaign against the Bracero Program. The Mexican and US governments positioned the Bracero Program as Mexico's contribution to World War II. It initially recruited Mexican men to meet perceived labor shortages in the United States for both railroads and agriculture. When the war ended, the railroad program was discontinued, while the agricultural program remained in effect until 1964.[39] The Bracero Program issued about 4.5 million contracts during its two decades. California consistently received the highest number of braceros among the twenty-six states in which the men labored.[40] Many progressives initially supported the program because of the labor protections it offered. As the majority of US labor safeguards did not apply to farmworkers, progressives believed the program might raise the standard for all workers.[41] Yet the Bracero Program operated in tandem with an underground market in undocumented labor, and the contracts' regulations were seldom enforced.[42] Over time, US labor advocates, including Galarza, came to believe that the Bracero Program lowered US wages, prevented legal workers from employment, and disrupted strikes through forced scab labor.[43]

Strangers appeared at a key moment in Galarza's political development. Scholars such as Stephen Pitti and Alicia Schmidt Camacho have heralded Galarza's transnational or migrant imaginary, highlighting his knowledge of Mexico's influence on the Bracero Program and his determination to oppose the Bracero Program without demonizing braceros.[44] However, Mireya Loza's exploration of Galarza's relationship to the Alianza de Braceros Nacionales en Los Estados Unidos, a transnational bracero organization, shows the ways in which Galarza's commitment to his Mexican colleagues and a transnational vision of labor organizing fell short as he increasingly viewed ending the Bracero Program and limiting unauthorized Mexican migration as necessary for Mexican American and Mexican advancement.[45] *Strangers* marked Galarza's strategic shift, his turn away from the Alianza, a turn fueled by Galarza's anger at both the Mexican and US governments' abdication of responsibility for the Bracero Program's promises.

This alteration in Galarza's efforts cohered to changes within the program's administration. Manuel García y Griego finds the period from 1947 to 1954, just before Galarza's publication, the moment that "almost all the significant changes" in the Bracero program occurred.[46] Galarza wrote *Strangers* directly following a major shift in the balance of power away from Mexico, and in the period immediately following Operation Wetback, an Immigration and Naturalization Service project in 1954 involving the mass deportation of Mexican immigrants.[47]

Galarza's research for the report included visiting several bracero work sites in Southern California as well as collecting surveys from members of the Alianza. Ironically, as Loza points out, in assisting Galarza with his research, the Alianza unknowingly contributed to its own demise.[48] Five thousand copies of the report were initially released, and its popularity led to a second run in 1957. Copies were distributed to leaders of Mexican American communities, the presidents and education directors of international unions, California's Farm Placement Services supervisors and representatives, and members of the California State Legislature.[49] Reviews appeared in publications such as the *Los Angeles Times*, the *Christian Science Monitor*, the *New Republic*, the *Catholic Worker*, and *Frontier*.⁵⁰ Leonard Nadel, who was well known for his stunning photographs of braceros, was inspired to embark on his bracero documentation efforts after reading *Strangers*.⁵¹ The California Farm Labor Association responded to the report by requesting that Secretary of Labor James Mitchell prevent its circulation, and Robert Goodwin, director of the Bureau of Employment Security, released a chapter-by-chapter rebuttal.⁵² *Strangers* not only contributed to the eventual termination of the Bracero Program but also generated immediate improvements in areas such as housing and transportation for both braceros and domestic farmworkers.⁵³

In *Strangers*, Galarza depicts the process through which the Mexican national becomes the bracero as one of denationalization. The Mexican national loses his identity and his humanity as he enters the program, a story Galarza tells through the composite figure of Pito Perez.⁵⁴ We are told, "Perez lives with his wife and four children in Rancho de la Mojerna, Michoacán" (Galarza, *Strangers*, 2). Galarza defines Perez in relationship to his family and his city of origin. When Perez decides to become a bracero, it is not his decision alone: "Perez talks to his wife and it is agreed that he should go" (1). Although the lack of economic opportunities open to Perez shapes his choice, ultimately he and his wife decide together. This image of Perez's agency contrasts with the powerlessness he faces within the system. Once he has decided to join the program, Perez disappears from the story. He is anonymous and lost in the system. Galarza captures this anonymity in the pamphlet's opening lines: "'In this camp,' one Mexican National told me, 'we have no names. We are called only by numbers'" (6). The bracero's anonymity contrasts with Perez's localized identity. No other Mexican nationals in *Strangers* are given names or background stories.

The Mexican nationals become the input for a product (the bracero) made in Mexico and sold in the United States. To describe this process, Galarza uses language reminiscent of boom-and-bust colonial economies, particularly the extractive mining of resources such as gold and coal. Claiming that "recruitment of workers below the border has been booming," Galarza positions the Mexican national as Mexico's latest natural resource to be extracted and transformed into a commodity (6). Statements such as "orders are placed by the United States representative at the recruiting center with the Mexican official of corresponding rank" emphasize braceros as a capitalist commodity purchase (4). Galarza writes, "The official machinery that has brought Perez up to this point has been moving long before his name was called" (3). Such descriptions evoke assembly lines or conveyor belts, depicting the Bracero Program as a transnational factory in which Mexican men are the raw material to be processed.

This production process transforms the men from Mexican nationals with recognized humanity into a new type of man, a denationalized commodity bought and sold on the international market. Galarza describes braceros as "new men [that] had to be trained for unfamiliar tasks in a delicate and sometimes tricky area of international relations" (10). This label "new" captures the men's transformation. In *Merchants of Labor*, Galarza elaborates, describing braceros as "the prototype of the production man of the future" and explaining that they were "an almost perfect model of an economic man, an 'input factor' stripped of the political and social attributes that liberal democracy likes to ascribe to all human beings ideally."[55] From Galarza's perspective, in stripping men of their national identities, the Bracero Program denies them their humanity.

As commodities rather than people, braceros are treated no differently than the crops they harvest. Galarza repeatedly emphasizes the similarity between the ways in which men and produce are transported. One bracero says, "We go to the fields in a truck that he uses for carrying tomato boxes" (51). In his field observations, Galarza notes, "In one tomato field 18 Nationals were loaded on a truck carrying a heap of empty lug boxes" (54). In three pages, Galarza reiterates the comparison between the men and the tomatoes five separate times: "'They take us to the fields in the same trucks they use to haul the tomato,' a bracero told me" (55). A photograph shows a line of identical trucks standing ready to transport either braceros or tomatoes (55). The two products—men and produce—appear interchangeable. The caption explains, "Sometimes we go in good buses, but other times we get into the same trucks they use for the tomatoes" (55). The picture depicts transportation through the aesthetics of mass production. Men and tomatoes are both commodities, objects to be bought and sold, ferried through the factory fields by truck.

It is not just men who are stripped of their national identities; the Bracero Program itself exists as a space outside the regulation of both the United States and Mexico. According to *Strangers*, when the Mexican national enters the Bracero Program, he leaves the official space of Mexico without entering the official space of the United States. Galarza writes, "Up to this point the bracero is still technically in Mexico" (4). In describing the bracero as only *technically* in Mexico, he implies that the Mexican state's citizenship rights have ceased to apply to the bracero. The bracero contract temporarily replaces the implicit contract between subject and government that constitutes citizenship. Similarly, Galarza's depiction of the bracero landscape suggests that the bracero is only *technically* in the United States. The privileges of citizenship and the protection of US civil society are denied to him.

The international agreement envisioned braceros as obtaining the protections of both US federal law and Mexican constitutional legislation. As Galarza writes, "When the recruitment program was originally begun, Mexico insisted, and the United States was glad to concede, that the affair should be conducted with close and scrupulous regard for the rights of the Mexicans to be transported to labor in the north" (10). Galarza makes clear that this vision is never achieved. The agreement is instead subject to the winds of capital production, and its implementation is constantly renegotiated based on profit-driven motives internal to the program. He says, "In the employment of Nationals, the restraints of Agreement and contract bend or break with the ease of spider webs. It is hardly surprising that the bracero cannot grasp what is happening to him and around him" (35). The program removes braceros from the national context of Mexico, trapping them between Mexico and the United States. They are in a new kind of space, in which they have no rights, and in which they are trapped like flies in a spiderweb. The disorientation produced by this new space is captured when one worker comments, "It seems we are lost even when we are right in the camp" (47). As flies trapped in Galarza's metaphorical spiderweb, workers cannot gain the perspective to see what is happening to them.

Galarza figures the transnational borderlands as outside of national sway, left in the hands of irrational capitalist development that privileges profit above individual liberties. The chapter "Records and Deductions"

highlights the absence of government regulation and accountability provided to the bracero. The spatial power relations of the system prevent the
bracero from accessing decision makers or power holders. Galarza writes,

> When the bracero asks questions about his insurance rights, he is likely
> to address himself to the nearest Spanish-speaking person of some rank
> or authority on the job or in camp. This person is usually a truck driver,
> a field foreman, a straw boss or a labor contractor. Here are some of the
> answers reported: "You'll have to see the bookkeeper, I didn't make out
> the paper"; "The extra nine cents is for the county"; "I took off the round
> dollar because I haven't time to make change for 200 men"; "I don't keep
> the money, I just send it to the consul." (57)

With such responses, the truck driver, the foreman, and the labor contractor divert authority onto some other invisible power holder. The bracero is
unable to advocate for himself because it is unclear from whom he would
seek protection or retribution. In Galarza's interpretation, the Bracero
Program's violations of citizenship rights, international agreements, and
human rights result from the lack of governmental jurisdiction and a transparent chain of command.

Galarza suggests that such an undemocratic system of rule will characterize any postwar economic model driven by this form of international
cooperation. Specifically, he says, "Since the contractor is the first person
in authority and for the most part the only person with whom the bracero
is in an immediate relationship, he becomes interpreter, administrator and
judge—law or no law" (61). The Bracero Program as a whole can be interpreted as a system of international privatization. The lack of accountability
ensures the denial of individual liberties and civil rights. Both the United
States and Mexico are displaced as the agricultural landscape is denationalized and agricultural labor recomposed through a set of spatially constituted power relationships.

The spatial relations within the reconstituted space of the Bracero Program emphasize flexible arrangements of labor. Galarza writes, "Some
growers have devised a system of loaning braceros back and forth. The informal transfer of small groups of braceros between different users within an

area of employment keeps the central labor pool flexible. . . . That labor force is considered best which most easily, quickly, and ungrudgingly responds to the caprices of weather and market." (65) Workers offset the instabilities of agricultural production, reducing the risks and increasing the profits of producers. The bracero's deportability contributes to this flexibility. One bracero explains to Galarza, "I can read the contract, and I know that several of the clauses are not observed. . . . But nobody would make a complaint for fear of being sent back to Mexico" (67). The braceros' inability to claim a right to the bracero landscape, risking deportation when challenging the system, results in silence. Jeffersonian democracy asserts that political independence requires an economic independence that can arise only from farming's rootedness to the land. Braceros' disconnection from the land defines their ultimate dependence on growers' whims. Because braceros lack a secure relationship to a nation and consequently a landscape on which their political and economic security may be built, they are inherently unfree.

Rather than create a space of cooperation between Mexico and the United States, the Bracero Program creates a space (or web) of national abdication for both countries. It erodes the individual rights and privileges of citizenship under economic conditions that displace the nation-state in favor of privatized denationalized economic development. The Bracero Program employs rural locations, trespassing ordinances, military protections, and fly-by-night transportation and housing to protect itself from the public eye. By situating the worker in a space that is neither in the United States nor in Mexico and is not subject to the protections of either nation's civil society, Galarza exposes the sociospatial relationships that prevent the braceros from receiving the rights guaranteed them in the international agreement.

Galarza suggests that the solution is to renationalize braceros as Mexican nationals under Mexican jurisdiction and renationalize US landscapes as being under American jurisdiction. Yet he insists that the US and Mexican governments will not do this of their own accord. Part of the reason that both nations have abdicated their responsibility is that they maintain their self-interest in the Bracero Program and the denationalized space in which it operates. This is exemplified in their opposition to labor unions' efforts to advocate for the braceros and bring them under the regulation of the international agreement, Mexican law, or US law. According to Galarza, increased government enforcement will fail as the solution to the bracero dilemma. Cancellation of the program is necessary.

Galarza positions US civil society as the party responsible for dismantling the Bracero Program. He reinforces this dynamic with the pamphlet's title, *Strangers in Our Fields*. "Our fields" emphasizes US ownership over the denationalized bracero landscape. It produces a community of readers, "us," and emphasizes Galarza's inclusion in that "us." The text calls on this collective "us" to reclaim "our" fields from the denationalized space of industry. Moreover, the text calls on us to remove braceros from this landscape by labeling them as strangers. As a stranger, the bracero is neither neighbor nor friend. He is neither visitor nor guest. He does not belong. "Stranger" (not one of us) contrasts with "our fields" (belonging to us). It emphasizes an us-them relationship also conveyed in chapter titles such as "Who They Are," "As They See It," and "What They Earn."[56] Galarza positions the readers as part of a community that ought to have ownership over and jurisdiction in the denationalized landscapes of the Bracero Program.

The report is set up as if it were evidence presented to a US jury testifying to the program's ills. Galarza includes ten photographs of the braceros' living and working conditions, along with eight photographs of documents such as pay stubs. None of the images depicts the braceros' perspectives.[57] For example, Galarza includes the photograph of a truck that transports workers from the angle of a viewer looking into the truck, inspecting it.[58] The picture's angle implies that the viewer is looking in from the outside, rather than peering out from inside the truck. Similarly, in an image of a medical exam, a man pulls back a patient's hairline to reveal a substantial head bump. The patient looks straight ahead, rather than at the examiner. He is on display for the viewer.[59] These images encourage the readers to see the braceros as victims and as strangers, outside of the "us" to which the readers belong.

This evidence presents the braceros as victims in need of assistance. Galarza quotes one bracero as saying, "These things [contract violations] have to be tolerated in silence because there is no one to defend our guarantees. In a strange country you feel timid—like a chicken in another rooster's yard."[60] Such a statement strips braceros of their masculinity while calling on members of the US public (as masculine roosters) to "defend" braceros by dismantling the program. US civil society is presented as the "rooster" that can protect the feminized braceros by safely returning them home to Mexico. In depicting the bracero as helpless, feminized, and in need of protection, Galarza reinforces the unequal relationships between nations.[61] He tasks US citizens with protecting braceros by dismantling the Bracero Program. Galarza states, "The common respect for legal obligations, as well as for civil and human rights, found in the general American community serves as a firm foundation for the protection of the individual. The Mexican national in the United States does not have the benefit of this powerful sanction."[62] With such statements, Galarza represents US society as the pinnacle of social responsibility and a role model for civil and human rights, an image the United States actively cultivated during the Cold War.

Galarza implicitly contends that a return to Mexico benefits braceros. In Mexico, the men regain their masculinity and political voice. No longer chickens in another rooster's yard, they can now be roosters in their own yard. As Galarza explains, "Once they are back in their own country, many Nationals regain enough self-confidence to express their discontent with what they encountered in the United States."[63] They protest the treatment they received in the United States and advocate through governmental channels to recover missing payments for their labor. Stripped of their political agency as braceros, they regain this status as Mexican nationals in Mexico. Just as Pito Perez loses his voice and identity when he enters the Bracero Program, Galarza portrays former braceros regaining their political voices when reentering Mexico.

The nation-state's primacy in human rights discourse in this period helps explain Galarza's move from transnational labor organizing to his focus on closing the Bracero Program and stopping unauthorized migration. In its 1948 "Universal Declaration of Human Rights," the United Nations defined human rights primarily in terms of national rights and national identities.[64] In the face of Mexican and US governmental abdication of responsibility, Galarza sought to bring agribusiness back under clear national jurisdiction. If the nation-state was responsible for the human rights of their citizens, renationalizing braceros became the most direct path Galarza saw for resisting the dehumanization that braceros experienced. In 1952,

Galarza "proposed that our union enlist the support of the labor movement with appropriate lobbying and political pressure to create an international zone extending one hundred miles south of the border and one hundred miles north of the border and that in this zone both countries join together to bring about changes, particularly in the matter of land tenure, so that these peasants and small town people in Mexico who were constantly trying to jump over the border could be stabilized."[65] Just a few years later, Galarza had little faith that the United States and Mexico were capable of such cooperation. Any shared space of governance between the nations was simply an expanded space for privatization and abdication of government authority. Galarza turned to a human rights model in which nations were responsible for ensuring the human rights of their own citizens, abandoning hope for a model in which transnational human and labor rights could be enforced and respected. In doing so, Galarza set the ideological and rhetorical stage for the civil rights rhetoric of the United Farm Workers, which was founded in 1965, just one year after the Bracero Program's termination.

CONCLUSION

Galarza and Bulosan most likely knew each other. They moved in similar social circles, and both struggled for the unionization of California's agricultural workers. In *Spiders in the House and Workers in the Fields*, Galarza references Filipino laborers' organizing activities in the 1940s and 1950s.[66] Likewise, *America Is in the Heart* denounces the Bracero Program, describing a scenario in which "the Filipino workers struck, but the companies imported Mexican laborers."[67] Both Bulosan and Galarza position interracial alliances as being essential for the success of farm labor unionization. When Carlos succeeds in uniting Mexican and Filipino workers, he proclaims, "I did not understand it then, did not realize that this was the one and only common thread that bound us together, white and black and brown, in America. I felt a great surge of happiness inside me!"[68] In their writing and organizing activities, Bulosan and Galarza attend to an interracial agricultural workforce even as they privilege the experience of distinct colonized labor groups (Filipino migrants and Mexican braceros).

In attending to colonized groups of laborers, Bulosan and Galarza place interracial alliances in the context of US colonialism, exposing the uneven relations between nations that shape the realities of US agricultural labor. Bulosan positions Filipino migrants' exploitation in the United States not only as the result of their marginalized positions as Filipinos in the United States but as a legacy of Spanish and American colonialism in the Philippines. He shifts the cartography of American imperialism to move Filipinos and the Philippines from the margin to the center, and opposes the abjection and alienage of Filipino workers by claiming the land and women of the United States for the Philippines. Galarza exposes how uneven relations between nations result in unregulated landscapes of transnational capital in which workers are denied their human rights and governments abdicate enforcement responsibilities. Through the metaphor of the spiderweb he showcases the danger of privatized spaces of industry and the abuses faced by workers trapped in such webs. Both Bulosan and Galarza expose the ways that uneven relationships between nations create the conditions for worker exploitation. They position US agriculture as the result of a historical palimpsest of colonialist and capitalist relations. In situating US agriculture in this context, they challenge the relationship between whiteness, land ownership, and citizenship that is foundational to the agrarianism that circulates in texts such as John Steinbeck's *The Grapes of Wrath*.

CHAPTER 6

"Elixirs of Death"

The United Farm Workers and the
Modern Environmental Movement

OST ENVIRONMENTAL HISTORIANS CITE RACHEL CAR-
son's *Silent Spring* (1962) as the modern environmental movement's birth announcement. They distinguish mid-twentieth-
century environmentalism from the conservationism and preservationism
of the Progressive Era in large part through its concern for toxins and other
forms of pollution. Many participants in the environmentalism of the 1960s
and 1970s expressed concern that human use of technology fundamentally
threatened the circle of ecological life and imperiled humanity's ability to
sustain itself. Carson echoed these themes, linking the death of songbirds
to the potential loss of human life. The popular concern for such issues
congealed with the first Earth Day in April 1970. Organizers billed Earth
Day as a national teach-in that included events at fifteen hundred colleges
and ten thousand schools.[1] As historian Adam Rome wrote, "The teach-ins
collectively involved more people than the biggest civil rights and antiwar
demonstrations in the 1960s."[2] Millions participated.[3]

The history of modern environmentalism is entangled with the remarkable story of the United Farm Workers, the first successful unionization effort for farmworkers. In 1962, the same year Carson published *Silent Spring*,
Cesar Chavez and Dolores Huerta resigned from the Community Service
Organization to focus on organizing farmworkers, and Chavez founded
the National Farm Workers Association (NFWA). In 1965, the largely Filipino farmworkers union, the Agricultural Workers Organizing Committee
(AWOC), began the famous grape strike, with Chavez's organization voting to strike in solidarity. In 1966, the National Farm Workers Association

(NFWA) and AWOC merged into the United Farm Workers Organizing Committee (UFWOC). On July 29, 1970, just three months after the first Earth Day, the United Farm Workers (UFW) achieved a major victory, signing 150 contracts with the major Delano grape growers, covering thirty thousand workers.[4] The success was short-lived, as the International Brotherhood of Teamsters began undermining the UFW by signing "sweetheart" deals with the growers. This controversy led to a renewal of the strike and boycott throughout the 1970s. The UFW never again had as many unionized workers.

For both the modern environmental movement and the United Farm Workers, 1962–70 was a key period of transformation and growing public awareness. Whereas previously the white American farmer was popularly perceived as an ideal authentic citizen, representations by and of the United Farm Workers depicted nonwhite peoples as being closer to nature, as natural environmentalists. Whiteness was no longer a requisite (and could be a hindrance) for an authentic relationship to the land. Simultaneously, the rise of a self-consciously environmentalist discourse (rather than one of conservation or preservation) reinforced the UFW's production of an environmental justice rhetoric. As the modern environmental movement changed popular understandings of nature and Americans' relation to it, the UFW expanded constructions of "environment" and "ecology" to capture the uneven exposure of farmworkers to pesticides while simultaneously positioning farmworkers as the new American environmental heroes, more capable than the federal government of protecting the broader American public from poisoning.

THE ENVIRONMENTALIST FASCINATION WITH THE UFW

California farmworker advocates often assert the national belonging of farmers and farmworkers by depicting their relationship to the landscape as "natural." They invoke Jeffersonian agrarian narratives in ways that legitimize farmers and farmworkers' experiences and critiques of injustice through reference to their status as ideal American citizens. Often these texts use a subject's relationship to the land or nature to articulate their racialized inclusion or exclusion from the nation. Many sympathetic commentators and advocates for the UFW invoked such a naturalization narrative, often through their depictions of Chavez, particularly authors who spoke from an environmentalist framework. Environmentalists' concerns from the 1960s shaped some UFW supporters' representations of Chavez. Their depictions of the Chicano leader reveal some of the latent racial ideologies that circulated in the support for both movements. They expose the changing racial politics of idealizing a natural relationship to the earth. Whereas earlier depictions of farmworkers often emphasized their whiteness or aspirational whiteness, representations of farmworkers in the 1960s and 1970s emphasized their "third world" status in ways that suggested that nonwhite workers had a more traditional relationship to nature.

The environmentalist fascination with the UFW drew on and reinforced a problematic understanding of Mexicans as being "natural" agrarian workers, closer to the land and to nature than their white counterparts. Such representations embraced Mexican farmworkers as a symbol of authenticity. By the 1960s and 1970s, nature had become, in part, a symbol of "the real" and "the authentic." Its embrace during this period constituted a reaction against the perceived artificiality of 1950s society.[5] Similarly, popular culture, political rhetoric, and even academic treatises from this period frequently presented Mexican American culture as being more "authentic" than mainstream white culture. A 1979 passage by literary critic Joseph Sommers illustrates this vein of thinking. Testa wrote, "Modern Anglo culture suffers from an *ersatz* quality deriving from loss of the past, urbanization, artificial and elitist sophistication, corruption by the manipulative mass media, and a voguish stress on the mental, the imaginary, and the irrational. The Chicano may live outside the mainstream, this critic would say, but his very exclusion has permitted the retention of traditional culture."[6] In this passage, Sommers offers a problematic opposition between artificial mainstream urban white culture and traditional authentic rural Mexican American culture. Similarly, in his April 22, 1970, Earth Day speech, Mexican American activist Arturo Sandoval proclaimed to a predominantly Chicano audience in Albuquerque, New Mexico, "And America—white America— has lost its ability to cry, and laugh and sing and love and live. And that is what we are addressing here today. Our humanity, our hope, and our determination to make this society—and all societies—human societies, livable societies. And to make those environments human, life-supporting kinds of environments."[7] For Sandoval, *la raza* was an inclusive term, "beyond skin color," for those who retained their humanity, a life he sees many white Americans as having forgotten. Both Sommers and Sandoval perceived Mexican Americans as experiencing and participating in a "real" life that white America had forsaken.

In incorporating Catholic and Mexican traditions in his organizing strategies and public relations efforts, Chavez challenged such countercultural visions of Mexican farmworkers. In drawing on traditions that resonated with Mexican and Mexican American farmworkers, Chavez did not present Mexican or Mexican American culture as being inherently timeless and unchanging. Rather, he transformed the meaning of the cultural events he depicted, endowing Mexican and Catholic culture with the possibility of social transformation. For example, the red and black of the UFW flag intentionally recalls the colors used for strikes in Mexico. References to the Mexican Revolution peppered Chavez's speeches.[8] Chavez frequently used traditional Mexican sayings, or *dichos*, as part of his outreach to farmworkers.[9] He scheduled the meeting during which his membership formally joined the Filipino farmworkers' grape strike for Mexican Independence Day. The UFW's *perigrancíon*, a 350-mile march from Delano to the Sacramento statehouse arriving on Easter Sunday 1966, consciously drew on Mexican Catholic traditions of pilgrimage, while Chavez's fasts recalled rituals of penance. Chavez's use of Catholic and Mexican American cultural icons and rituals countered popular stereotypes of Mexican American farmworkers as passive, ignorant, powerless, and lazy; instead, such icons and rituals empowered farmworkers.[10] In transforming the meanings associated with certain rituals, sayings, and symbols, the union leader demonstrated their adaptability. He proved that such traditions were not timeless and immutable. Indeed, Chavez critiqued the tendency of US counterculture participants to romanticize ethnic cultures. He stated, "It seems to me that one other reason that it was difficult to organize was that for some time back and more so today, people tend to romanticize the poor people. Or romanticize the Negro or the Mexican or anybody who was discriminated against. And we say that to help someone help themselves we have to look at him as a human being. And we cannot romanticize his race or his poverty if we are really going to deal with the problem and to help him as a human being."[11] This call from Chavez for his supporters to see farmworkers as full human beings with flaws suggests that his use of Catholic and Mexican traditions was not meant to further romanticize Mexican American culture or perpetuate stereotypes of it.

Despite Chavez's concerns about romanticization, many UFW supporters' embrace of both Mexican farmworkers and nature functioned as a declaration against mainstream society and an affirmation of the values of the 1960s and 1970s countercultural left, particularly this sense of authenticity, "the real," and traditional societies. These Chavez supporters celebrated the figure of the Mexican farmworker as Jeffersonian farmer, joining the concepts of "authentic nature," "authentic Mexican," and ideal American citizen. In writing about the liberal fascination with Chavez, Chicana/o Studies scholars Richard Griswold del Castillo and Richard A. Garcia highlighted Chavez's Jeffersonian appeal: "Mexican Americans, specifically, the farmworkers and Cesar Chavez, were existentially authentic, primarily because of their labor, their relationship to the land, their respect for their humanity, and their love of community. The Mexican farmworker was closer to the Jeffersonian ideal of the true 'common man.' As farmworkers, they were God's chosen children, threatened by industrial society."[12] The Jeffersonian ideal found new life when wrapped in the mantle of counterculture resistance to the perceived conformity and plasticity of middle-class Anglo-American consumer culture. Some UFW supporters romanticized Mexican American farmworkers' culture as an authentic alternative to the middle-class suburban white life, the perceived overcrowding and decay of increasingly black urban centers, and the industrialization of pesticide-dependent agriculture.

These concerns are evident in nature writer Peter Matthiessen's writing on Chavez. Matthiessen wrote *Sal Si Puedes*, one of the most frequently cited books on Chavez, from the position of an unabashed environmentalist.[13] His depiction of Chavez and the association he draws between farm labor and environmental degradation suggests the problematic assumptions underlying the rise of modern environmentalism in the 1960s and 1970s. Matthiessen's interest in the UFW stemmed from his concerns about pesticides. His friend Ann Israel asked him to copyedit an advertisement about pesticides that the UFW intended to publish in the *New York Times*.

This led Israel to introduce him to Chavez. After visiting Delano and spending time with Chavez and other key members of the UFW, Matthiessen convinced William Shawn, editor at the *New Yorker*, to run a profile of Chavez. The *New Yorker* published the piece in two parts, on June 21 and June 28, 1969. It was one of the first prominent published profiles of Chavez, and it was in the same magazine that had first published *Silent Spring*. From this profile, Matthiessen developed *Sal Si Puedes*, which Random House Press released in 1970.

When placed in the context of Matthiessen's previously published work, the *New Yorker* profiles and *Sal Si Puedes* appear as travel or nature narratives, the discovery of a rare, exotic, and threatened group in their natural environment. Matthiessen had previously published six books of nonfiction and four books of fiction. His first nonfiction book and most recognized work at the time, *Wildlife in America* (1959), focused on human-caused animal extinctions. This text "cultivate[d] Matthiessen's image as kind of a Thoreau-on-the-Road."[14] Matthiessen's brand of environmentalism and his travel narratives in the *New Yorker* shaped many readers' perception of Chavez. According to McKay Jenkins, the editor of Matthiessen's collected nonfiction works, "His many readers like to think of him as a kind of literary Indiana Jones searching the wilds of New Guinea or Africa or Nepal and bringing stories back alive."[15] Matthiessen's previous literary work encouraged his readers to encounter the *New Yorker* profiles and *Sal Si Puedes* through the same themes of authenticity, tradition, and loss that circulated in his other works.

Matthiessen's presentation of Chavez reflects the influence of population anxiety on midcentury environmentalism. Paul Ehrlich's *The Population Bomb* (1968) came out only a year before Matthiessen's profile. As with Ehrlich's work, fears about overpopulation are at the heart of Matthiessen's political analysis.[16] "Urban crowding and decay," according to Matthiessen, are among "America's most serious afflictions."[17] He lists these issues as being on par with racism and poverty, and explains that such concerns cannot be understood separately:

> In a damaged human habitat, all problems merge. For example, noise, crowding and smog poisoning are notorious causes of human irritability;

that crowded ghettos explode first in the worst smog areas of America is no coincidence at all. And although no connection has been established between overcrowding and the atmosphere of assassination, rat experiments leave little doubt that a connection could exist: even when ample food and shelter are provided, rats (which exhibit behavioral patterns disconcertingly similar to those of man) respond to crowding in strange and morbid ways, including neuter behavior, increased incidence of homosexuality, gang rape, killing, and consumption by the mothers of their young.[18]

Fears about population are at the heart of Matthiessen's political analysis. It is his root cause for the United States' social and political ills. Matthiessen's vision in *Sal Si Puedes* is of a nation threatened not by nuclear warfare but by proliferating metropolitan populations. The disturbing link between rats and the inhabitants of crowded ghettos unintentionally dehumanizes inhabitants of increasingly brown and black cities. He links urban uprisings to overcrowding rather than limited economic opportunities or racial oppression. For Matthiessen, the "symptoms of a damaged habitat are social." In *Sal Si Puedes*, the causes of this "damaged habitat" are repeatedly asserted to be overcrowding and overpopulation.

Matthiessen blames this damaged ecological and human habitat not only for overcrowding but also for homosexuality. He depicts homosexuality as a sort of unnatural and violent perversion alongside infanticide and gang rape. Matthiessen's homophobia is particularly illustrative of a problematic reasoning at work in some environmentalist ideologies. He draws upon a binary logic that affiliates heterosexuality with purity, normalcy, the nuclear family, and a pastoral natural environment, while associating homosexuality with pollution, perversity, a decayed urban environment, and a loss of fertility and reproductive capacity. His depiction of homosexuality reflects an environmentalist investment in images of limited heterosexual reproduction within the nuclear family and the protection of suburban childhood innocence.[19] By including homosexuality in his list of urban ills, Matthiessen conveys an implicit pastoral vision of the heterosexual nuclear family as normal and natural against which the unnaturalness of the dirty queer city is contrasted.

According to Matthiessen, the overcrowded city is the central cause of the poisoned countryside. He writes, "With the world population out of control, the use of pesticides has become necessary for efficient food production."[20] Pesticides, according to Matthiessen, would not be necessary if the human population were curtailed. Their application not only fosters the overabundance of people and perversity in urban centers but also results in the barren emptiness of the rural landscape. Matthiessen writes, "Hard-edged and monotonous as parking lots, the green fields are without life. The road we walked across the Valley floor was straight and rigid as a gun barrel, without rise or curve. Passing cars buffeted with hot wind the cornflowers that had gained a foothold between the asphalt and the dull man-poisoned crop, and pressed toads as dry as leaves gave evidence in death that a few wild things still clung to life in this realm of organophosphates and chlorinated hydrocarbons."[21] The landscape is reminiscent of a "gun barrel," suggesting violence directed not only against farmworkers but against nature itself. Words such as "dull" and "dry" and "straight" suggest the resulting lifelessness. Without curves or bright color, the land is monotonous and sterile. Without "wild things," the landscape lacks flavor, excitement, and joy. Only toads and cornflowers persist, but cars crush the toads dry and hot winds torment the cornflowers. In the same year that Joni Mitchell, in her song "Big Yellow Taxi," decried, "They paved paradise to put up a parking lot," Peter Matthiessen looked out at California's abundant fertile fields and thought only of lifeless parking lots.[22] In another passage, he writes, "Out here on the flat Valley floor there is nothing left of nature; even the mountains have retreated, east and west."[23] Nature abandoned the lifeless agricultural landscape in light of the poison sprayed across the land. The pesticides that Rachel Carson termed "elixirs of death" forced the withdrawal of timeless and monumental mountains.[24] Such language suggests the power of humans to radically alter their world, a common theme in 1960s environmentalist rhetoric, especially among scientists such as Carson and Barry Commoner.[25]

Matthiessen's image of death in the fields was fairly new in representations of farmworker oppression. Earlier works by authors such as John Steinbeck and Carey McWilliams emphasized the beauty of the landscape to contrast the bounty of the fields with the deprivation facing workers.

Steinbeck describes, for example, "a homeless hungry man, driving the roads with his wife beside him and his thin children in the back seat" who "saw the golden oranges hanging on the trees, the little golden oranges on the dark green trees; and guards with shotguns patrolling the lines so a man might not pick an orange for a thin child."[26] For Steinbeck, injustice emerged from the consolidated distribution of wealth and property. During the Great Depression, California was still a land of plenty, but the poor were denied access to the spoils of agricultural success. Children died of hunger while uneaten food rotted in the fields. For Matthiessen, writing in the 1960s, California's beauty and bounty were long lost. The fields were empty, barren, and vacant of life. McWilliams famously used the phrase "factories in the field" to counter the association of California agriculture with the pastoral. He emphasized the industrial nature of modern agriculture. For Matthiessen, industrialization had destroyed not only pastoral or Jeffersonian labor conditions but also the natural splendor of the earth itself. He saw not a factory in the field but a blighted and silent landscape without birds or other markers of wildlife.

In this poisoned landscape, Matthiessen represents Chavez as the possibility of life. Like the cornflowers and the pressed toads, Chavez is among the small signs of survival to which Matthiessen continually draws the readers' attention. Matthiessen describes those opposed to the UFW as barren, unsmiling, or, in the case of one character, as flavorless as grapes grown mostly for appearances.[27] In contrast, he depicts Chavez as jovial and lively. Matthiessen describes the union leader as smiling nearly two dozen times in the book.[28] Matthiessen writes, "Most of the people are jocular with Chavez, who has a warm humorous smile that makes them laugh, but after the joking, a few stood apart and stared at him with honest joy."[29] Chavez is gleeful and life-bringing.[30] Matthiessen largely reserves descriptions of joy and pleasure for Chavez. Occasionally, he also bestows them upon those who are interacting with Chavez; for example, "A Filipino in his sixties came up with a fine wordless smile and pumped Chavez's hand in both his own."[31] Later in the text Matthiessen describes a conversation with Danny Chavez (no relation to Cesar) about Danny's decision to join the UFW: "'I change!' he repeated gleefully, as if this were magic. 'And now I the Union man!'"[32] Chavez's magnetism enchants his followers. This association of the UFW with joy and glee participates in a trope that Rome identifies in late 1960s and 1970s environmentalism. Many counterculture participants and environmental thinkers of the period linked modern industrial society to death, in contrast to a fulfilling life close to nature.[33] Similarly, Matthiessen depicts farmworker resistance as a renewal of one's connection to the happiness environmentalists of the period associated with traditional and "natural" ways of living.

Matthiessen depicts Chavez as being exemplary of nature's best qualities, as many participants in the modern environmental movement understood nature. Chavez lacks the pretense and artificiality of monotone suburban consumerism. Matthiessen writes, "What emerges when Chavez talks seriously of his aim is simplicity, and what is striking in his gentle voice is its lack of mannerisms; it comes as naturally as a bird song."[34] In a world where pesticides and pollution threaten to silence all of the birds, Chavez warbles their song. He speaks a beautiful and melodic truth that could come only from an authentic and uncorrupted land. In another passage, Matthiessen grants Cesar the spiritual power that John Muir attributed to the Sierra Nevada mountain range. Matthiessen writes, "Cesar is so intensely present that talking to him is like going to a source, a mountain spring; one comes away refreshed."[35] In such moments, Chavez becomes a source of untarnished nature; his farmworkers' movement becomes a place like the wild mountains and the fresh streams to which white environmentalists journey to achieve a sort of spiritual cleansing. Through their work with Chavez, environmentalists can rediscover their true selves. Chavez and his farmworkers speak a truth that could come only from the land, and like birds and tracts of wilderness, they deserve protection from the threat of industrialization, in this case industrial farming.

Matthiessen's representations of Chavez blend the problematic image of the simple and traditional Mexican farmworker with the "ecological Indian" trope. The "ecological Indian" is that false and yet too common perception of Native Americans as living harmoniously with the earth. Such a perception homogenizes Native Americans by failing to recognize the diversity of Native American traditions and worldviews. Depicting Indians as romanticized environmental role models neglects the humanity and individuality of contemporary Native Americans. Such representations place Native

Americans outside of time and history rather than engage with the diversity and hybridity of contemporary Native cultures. This figure of the Indian as environmental hero appeared in the context of 1960s and 1970s environmentalism.[36] Nonnative environmentalists evoked the ecologically oriented Indian to convey an ancient wisdom that could address the contemporary environmental and spiritual crises. Most famously, a 1971 televised public service announcement for Earth Day depicted a Native American male guised in stereotypical garb paddling a canoe through a polluted American landscape. As a tear runs down the man's face, the audience is told, "Some people have a deep, abiding respect for the natural beauty that was once this country; some people don't. People start pollution. People can stop it." The ad juxtaposes the contemporary American lifestyle with a fantasy of an indigenous past. In such depictions, the "ecological Indian" appears as a Native elder from whose wisdom the rest of America can learn.[37] Native American activists in the Red Power movement used the counterculture's "ecological Indian" strategically to link sustainability and sovereignty. The visibility of Native activism and the central role environmental justice occupied in the story told by Native activists led many mainstream and countercultural Americans in the late 1960s and 1970s to conclude that contemporary Native Americans (not just their ancestors) had wisdom to offer the rest of America.[38]

Matthiessen grants Chavez the problematic power of this trope of indigenous environmentalism. He repeatedly emphasizes the Indianness of Chavez's appearance. For example, in what literary and cultural critic Ilan Stavans terms the "landmark" description of Chavez, Matthiessen explains that Chavez has "an Indian's bow nose and lank black hair."[39] Later in the text, Matthiessen describes Chavez's "seraphic Indian face with the dark, sad, soft eyes and delighted smile."[40] He associates Chavez's native countenance with childlike innocence and grace. At another point, he writes, "Alone in the shadows of the pew, the small Indian head bent on his chest and the toes of the small shoes tucked inward, he looked from behind like a boy of another time, at his prayers beside his bed."[41] Chavez's indigenous visage suggests timelessness and tradition. Matthiessen, through Chavez, collapses Mexican and indigenous identities, a rhetorical move some Chicano activists of the period would have embraced, although such activists would have emphasized a machismo rather than childlike grace as the outcome of this alchemy.[42] In granting Chavez an indigenous identity, Matthiessen deepens the connection between the UFW and a lost traditional relationship to the natural world.

Unlike Steinbeck, who in *In Dubious Battle* modeled his white characters after Mexican strikers and who professed a belief that white Americans would not stand for the treatment that Mexican, Filipino, Chinese, and Japanese immigrant workers experienced, Matthiessen perceives Chavez's racial difference as a strength rather than a weakness. Chavez, for Matthiessen, is both "ecological Indian" and American revolutionary. Matthiessen has no need to make Chavez white to render his Americanness, in part due to the discursive space the civil rights movement opened up. Indeed, Chavez sits at the heart of a "new American revolution" because of his difference from a traditional white citizenry standing for industrialization and progress.[43] Matthiessen's vision is clear in the closing statement of his text: "Chavez's cause had become a holding action for change that was inevitable, a clash of citizens versus consumers, quality versus quantity, freedom versus conformism and fear. And sooner or later the new citizens would win, for the same reason that other new Americans won, two centuries ago, because time and history are on their side, and passion."[44] Chavez, the indigenous American revolutionary, will win, standing on the side of citizens, quality, and freedom, facing down the conjoined evils of consumerism, conformism, and fear. An American revolution led by Chavez, Matthiessen suggests, will lead Americans back to rural, traditional ways in which simple people find joy in the land.

THE UFW'S ENVIRONMENTAL ETHIC

Matthiessen's romanticized depiction of Chavez as an indigenous eco-hero contrasts with the rhetoric in Chavez's speeches and the representations of nature in the plays of the UFW's theater troupe, El Teatro Campesino. While Matthiessen encourages population reduction, Chavez calls for land redistribution. While Matthiessen complains about the power of humans to radically change the earth, El Teatro Campesino suggests the power of farmworkers to change the world around them. Both Chavez and El Teatro Campesino assert that the hierarchies that farmworkers face are unnatural and reveal the power of farmworkers to change the conditions of their lives.

Whereas Matthiessen focuses on overpopulation and the resultant scarcity of resources as a key cause of injustice in the United States, Chavez emphasizes inequity of property ownership. According to Matthiessen, population was "the one thing we [Chavez and Matthiessen] do not agree on."[45] Chavez's critique of the population discourse resonates with what many environmental justice advocates might say today. He told "a cheering audience in Watts" that "the governments could take care of the population increase if resources were devoted to humanity instead of to such luxuries of power as wars and the moon."[46] The problem for Chavez was not the sheer number of people but the distribution of resources. According to Chavez, blaming poverty and pollution on population, which inevitably targets the poor, lets the rich off the hook. The contrast between the environmental ideologies of Matthiessen and Chavez is apparent when comparing *Sal Si Puedes* to a passage in Chavez's 1969 testimony to the Subcommittee of Labor of the Senate Committee on Labor and Public Welfare. The passage, which Matthiessen includes uncited in his book, is worth quoting at length:

> As one looks at the millions of acres in this country that have been taken out of agricultural production; and at the millions of additional acres that have never been cultivated; and at the millions of people who have moved off the farm to rot and decay in the ghettoes of our big cities; and at all the millions of hungry people at home and abroad; does it not seem that all these people and things were somehow made to come together and serve one another? If we could bring them together, we could stem the mass exodus of the rural poor to the big city ghettoes and start it going back the other way; teach them how to operate new farm equipment; and put them back to work on those now uncultivated acres to raise food for the hungry. If a way could be found to do this, there would be not only room but positive need for still more machinery and still more productivity increase. There would be enough employment, wages, profits, food and fiber for everybody. If we have any time left over after doing our basic union job, we would like to devote it to such purposes as these.[47]

Chavez idealizes reversing the worldwide trend toward urbanization. He envisions returning the urban poor to the country and providing them with land. It is Chavez at his most Jeffersonian, visualizing the future nation as being made up of small farmers. He pictures ghetto life as bleak, full of rot and decay. Yet he does not mention overcrowding nor does he blame urban denizens for social ills. Instead, he offers the US agricultural landscape as a place of renewal. Rather than the landscape of blight that Matthiessen describes, Chavez invokes agrarian landscapes as places of possibility, empty and waiting to be filled. While Matthiessen envisions a future in which there will be no space for any individual and land will become increasingly scarce, Chavez views the nation as full of tillable soil waiting to be filled with the yearning hands of America's urban poor.

It is on this question of land ownership that Chavez seems most like Steinbeck, McWilliams, and Sanora Babb. For Chavez, land ownership is at the center of the growers' consolidated power. In a spontaneous speech given at Solidarity House in Lansing Michigan, in 1967, Chavez stated, "Have you ever considered land—a lot of land—a lot of free water and a lot of cheap labor. Have you ever considered what this combination can do and is doing in the West? Because of the combination of these three elements, there are growers in California and the western part of this country that are not only rich but are very powerful."[48] The growers' vast accumulation of territory is central to their wealth and power. These sentiments appear elsewhere in Chavez's oeuvre, including an impromptu speech he gave at the Calvary Episcopal Church in Manhattan in 1968. There Chavez proclaimed, "We must turn our minds to the power of the land. . . . The interest can control not only the land but everything that moves, everyone that walks in the land."[49] By default, the workers become property controlled by the owners, much like the land on which they toil. Chavez implies that freeing the workers requires providing them with their own land. As Matthiessen rewords Chavez's argument, "If those in power were not so selfish, there would be room enough for all."[50] Consolidated land ownership results not only in the powerlessness of the worker but also the rise of the ghetto. There would be wealth (and room) for all, Chavez, implies, if land were equally distributed. This is the inverse of Matthiessen's argument. Matthiessen sees overcrowding as the fundamental cause of social ills within the city and also as the fundamental cause of the poisoning of the pastoral landscape. Chavez suggests, instead, that the unjust distribution of land is the root cause of both urban decay and blighted countryside. Whereas Matthiessen's argument is based in an ecological analysis of overpopulation and scarcity, Chavez grounds his analysis in the concentration of wealth. He suggests that the ownership of nature determines the perceived "natural order" of society. Thus, like Hisaye Yamamoto, Chavez concentrates not on naturalizing the workers' relationship to the land but on denaturalizing the racialized social hierarchy that governs agricultural labor conditions.

Los Actos, the plays of El Teatro Campesino (farmworkers' theater), similarly denaturalize the social hierarchies of agriculture. El Teatro Campesino, founded in 1965 by Luis Valdez, used improvisational political theater for organizing on the picket line, for education, and for fundraising.[51] El Teatro Campesino's play La Quinta Temporada ("The Fifth Season") disrupts the association between nature and farm hierarchies.[52] Written in 1966, La Quinta Temporada, emerged, like many of the company's plays, from collaborative improvisation that included Valdez and the farmworkers who supported the union.[53] As such, Valdez believed it represented farmworkers' social reality. He portrays the season of summer as an actor covered in dollar bills, saying, "This is the way farm workers look at summer."[54] Actos were often performed on the picket lines to encourage farmworkers to join the strike. They used humor to represent and transform the ways that farmworkers understood their lives. La Quinta Temporada features El Campesino (the farmworker), Don Coyote (a labor contractor), and Patrón (the boss) as they go through the four seasons of the year. In Summer and Fall, the farmworker earns money for his labor, but this money is stolen without his knowledge by Don Coyote and Patrón. When Winter, presented as a thug, arrives, Don Coyote and Patrón pay him off. Winter proclaims, "I am Winter and I want money. Money for gas, lights, telephone, rent."[55] To El Campesino, who has no money, Winter decrees, "Then suffer!" The stage instructions say, "WINTER drags the FARMWORKER D.S.C. [down stage center], kicking and beating him, then dumps snow on him from a small pouch. The FARMWORKER shivers helplessly."[56] Such a vision, in which the farmworker is a victim to both the seasons and to those higher in the agricultural hierarchy, suggests that the oppression of the farmworkers is as natural and inevitable as the passing of time.

However, the second half of the play challenges this interpretation of farmworker powerlessness. It transforms the farmworker perspective of nature and agriculture. When Spring arrives, she encourages the farmworker to fight for his rights. With Spring's encouragement, the farmworker strikes. Unions, La Raza, and the Churches appear onstage to protect the farmworker as Winter arrives. Due to the strike, Don Coyote and Patrón have no money and no protection. Patrón is forced to sign a union contract to protect himself from Winter. Once the union contract is signed, Winter is replaced by a new season, a fifth season of farmworker justice. Such a move suggests that the farmworkers have power not only over Patrón and Don Coyote but over nature as well. They are not trapped by the cycle of the seasons or the routines of their lives but can create a new season and a new way of life. Nature is entwined with socioeconomic structures in this *acto* and the farmworkers have the power to transform both. *La Quinta Temporada* asserts that the power relations of agribusiness are not as inevitable as the change in the seasons. Whereas environmentalists such as Matthiessen depict the human ability to transform nature as America's downfall, the play conveys that within human's power over nature resides the very possibility for a transformed socioeconomic reality for farmworkers.[57]

This distinction between Matthiessen's naturalization of the UFW's relationship to the landscape and the UFW's efforts to denaturalize the power relations of agricultural labor echoes the distinction between Rachel Carson's and the UFW's representations of pesticides. In both cases, the UFW emphasized the constructed nature of both nature and race, contesting both Matthiessen's ecological romanticization of farmworker struggles and Carson's vision of the "average citizen" that renders race invisible.

"A UNIVERSAL KILLER": RACHEL CARSON AND THE UFW'S PESTICIDE CAMPAIGN

Depending on the historian consulted, either Rachel Carson or Cesar Chavez can be granted primary credit for the 1972 federal ban on DDT. Carson and the UFW both influenced public perceptions of pesticides. Carson's *Silent Spring* highlighted the impact on wildlife and public health of the indiscriminate spraying of DDT and other chemicals. Many environmental organizations took up Carson's work in quite limited ways, as they were concerned primarily about the spraying of pesticides in national parks or federally designated wilderness areas. By connecting the health of farmworkers with American dinner tables, however, the UFW's campaign linking pesticides to consumer and worker health shaped public understanding of toxins more than did the activities of many environmentalists. The UFW capitalized on and expanded consumer interest in pesticide-free food.[58]

The UFW's pesticide outreach strategy differed significantly from Carson's representation of pesticides as poison. Carson and the UFW diverged in their depictions of the racialized body in the landscape. Carson portrays humans as a rather homogenous category with a particular ecosystem niche, similar to blackbirds or blue jays. She focuses on the "everyday person" or "average citizen," producing a kind of abstract universal citizenship in which white middle-class identity and legal citizenship status become an invisible norm. In contrast, the UFW highlights farmworkers' particular susceptibility to pesticides, depicting pesticides as a purposeful attack on unionized workers by growers. While Carson poses the need for an active educated citizenry to reduce indiscriminate spraying, the UFW places consumer safety in the hands of farmworkers, asking consumer citizens to move pesticide regulation away from the collaboration between state agents and farmers and instead trust the embodied expertise of farmworkers through the pesticide controls embedded in union contracts.

Silent Spring is popularly known as a book about DDT. Yet that label is a misnomer. Carson's work provides testimony of a variety of chemicals that damage human and ecosystem health, not just DDT. In her chapter detailing the types of poisons with which readers should be concerned, she makes clear that organophosphates such as parathion are as dangerous as chlorinated hydrocarbons such as DDT.[59] She links the two classes of poisons, which were both developed for use during World War II and gained popularity for domestic use after that war. Moreover, Carson suggests that to properly understand the consequences of such toxins for humanity, we need to shift our view of human inhabitation to a more ecological one. *Silent Spring* depicts humans as being embedded in a wider ecosystem, alongside other animals, plants, and nonliving matter. Carson portrays pesticide poisoning as a form of chemical trespass, a nonconsensual violation of humans and other beings. She replaces a modernist health framework that stipulates the separation of humans from the environment with a transcorporeal framework in which human and nonhuman bodies are not simply permeable but are connected to one another through their shared material environment.[60] *Silent Spring*'s ecological approach to public health is grounded in an assessment of chemical flows through nonhuman materials such as soil and water alongside a consideration of the ways in which those substances flow through the bodies of a variety of human and nonhuman species.

Carson additionally refutes a logic that renders animal life as other to human life and as less intrinsically valuable. She does not leave descriptions of suffering to the humans she discusses but also provides descriptions of small mammals' painful deaths. Carson quotes from a clinical description of dead ground squirrels: "The back was bowed, and the forelegs with toes of the feet tightly clenched were drawn close to the thorax. . . . The head and neck were outstretched and the mouth often contained din, suggesting that the dying animal had been biting at the ground" (Carson, *Silent Spring*, 99–100). Such descriptions establish nonhumans' capacity for suffering. Carson, moreover, describes the squirrel's body as "mute testimony," allowing it to speak to humans in death in ways in which it could not have in life (99). The testimony Carson provides is not merely a warning to humans that the same fate might befall us. The squirrel is not the canary in the coal mine but a tragedy in its own right: "By acquiescing in an act that can cause such suffering to a living creature, who among us is not diminished as a human being?" Carson asks (102). She presents ground squirrels and other dead animals as more than material evidence of the dangers that face humans. Nonhuman animals in *Silent Spring* have lives with value. Animal anguish and animal death are worthy of concern in their own right.

The spraying of pesticides in *Silent Spring* is indiscriminate, and its consequence is indiscriminate death. The targets of the spraying are often specific species, such as blackbirds or the Japanese beetle. Yet, as Carson repeatedly documents, the spraying never effects only the target species. "These insecticides are not selective poisons; they do not single out the one species of which we desire to be rid. Each of them is used for the simple reason that it is a deadly poison. It therefore poisons all life with which it comes in contact: the cat beloved of some family, the farmer's cattle, the rabbit in the field, and the horned lark of the sky" (99). Later she writes, "Parathion is not a specific for blackbirds: it is a universal killer" (126). The innocent and the guilty alike are killed. As Carson asserts of pesticides' many victims, "These creatures are innocent of any harm to man" (99). Carson uses the language of the courtroom to suggest the way that pesticides sentence animals to death without trial. She says, "Such rabbits or raccoons or opossums as may have roamed those bottomlands and perhaps never visited the farmers' cornfields were doomed by a judge and jury who neither knew of their existence nor cared" (126). She gives their death the gravity of murder. This is not neutral or natural death. Carson makes it clear that humans are to blame.

Indiscriminate death by universal killer conveys an equivalency between human and nonhuman life. It also suggests the universality of human exposure. Whereas environmental justice advocates point out the unevenness of human exposure to toxins, Carson, as part of her ecosystem approach, does not distinguish among the risks individuals face. Farmworkers, in Carson's depiction, are as equally at risk as homeowners and housewives. As Carson explains, the possible link between chemicals and cancer "concern such everyday people as farmers caught in the 'fallout' of their own spray rigs or of planes, a college student who sprayed his study for ants and remained in the room to study, a woman who had installed a portable lindane vaporizer in her home, a worker in a cotton field that had been sprayed with chlordane and toxaphene" (229). This list of humans caught by the spraying is similar to the list that Carson provides of animals in danger ("the cat beloved of some family, the farmer's cattle, the rabbit in the field, and the horned lark of the sky"; 99). Such a move elevates animals, suggesting the ways that Carson's concerns cross species boundaries, but also homogenizes the categories in which humans experience structural and symbolic violence. The farmer caught in his own spray is placed in the same category as farmworkers who have much less control over the conditions of their work. The conflation of a college student spraying for ants with farmworkers forced to enter a poisoned field is perhaps more egregious. The college student likely has access to education, medical care, and legal services that the farmworker does not. The college student has a high degree of choice over the conditions of his life compared to the farmworkers. The erasing of humans' differing chemical vulnerabilities based on factors such as race, citizenship status, and class produces the very invisibility that magnifies the violence facing certain groups of people.

While Carson does not distinguish among humans on the grounds of class or race, she does recognize gender as a significant category of analysis, often as a stand-in for the home. Women appear in *Silent Spring* primarily as housewives or mothers, whereas men appear as fathers, scientists, state agents, and a variety of workers. Men are exposed at work and at home, but women, like children, are exposed in or near the home. Indeed, the trespass of chemicals and dangers into the domestic sphere is one of Carson's recurring themes. In describing a spraying in Long Island, New York, Carson writes, "They sprayed the quarter-acre lots of suburbia, drenching a housewife making a desperate effort to cover her garden before the roaring plane reached her, and showering insecticide over children at play and commuters at railway stations" (158). Carson further points out the differences between the cheerful domestic scenes depicted on pesticide packaging and their poisonous reality. She explains that "the descriptive literature" on chemical sprays at hardware and garden stores "portrays a happy family scene, father and son, smilingly preparing to apply the chemical to the lawn, [and] small, children tumbling over the grass with a dog" (178). Chemical companies deploy images of domestic tranquility to sell their products, an image Carson replaces with the suffering of children, pets, and parents. Carson's depiction of domestic-sphere vulnerability resonated with Cold War cultural containment strategies. As historian Elaine Tyler May points out, the suburban fantasy of domestic bliss operated as a form of cultural containment alongside foreign policy goals of containing communism. Men and women sought security in the home in the face of the larger vulnerabilities they felt, such as the fear of nuclear attack.[61] Carson mobilizes such fears of nuclear fallout to depict the pesticide threat.[62] The threat of pesticides in the home suggests not the particular susceptibility of women or children to pesticides but rather that the home offers no refuge. Such depictions further Carson's argument that pesticides are an indiscriminate killer from which no one, no matter how innocent, is safe.

Silent Spring ignores the factors that increase the susceptibility of particular groups of people to pesticides. It is the power differential that distinguishes between farmers and farmworkers, even if both are exposed at work. Farmworkers do not have the same control over the conditions of their labor as farmers, nor are they given the same information about the chemicals they are using. They do not have the same access to medical facilities nor the same level of public concern and visibility. Individuals facing occupational exposure have compounded risks compared to those exposed solely in the domestic sphere. Whereas all consumers may be exposed through their meals, farmworkers are exposed when they pick the food and later again when they eat it.[63] Consequently, workers appear as peripheral to Carson's concerns about human exposure. In a book in which songbirds and fish each warrant their own chapter, farmworkers receive comparatively slim mention. Carson references farmworkers four times in a nearly four-hundred-page book. For the most part, they do not stand out in the text as a class of people that face an increased risk for pesticide exposure.

Carson instead relies on the character of the "everyday person" or "average citizen" as her primary subject.[64] The explicit inclusion of farmworkers in this category of "everyday person" is both problematic and progressive. It is significant that Carson includes farmworkers as equals to farmers and housewives. In the 1960s, the majority of farmworkers were perceived as being outside of the national norm. They were poor whites and poor African Americans in the South, and predominately Mexican Americans or Mexicans throughout the Southwest and West. The 1960 Edward Murrow documentary *Harvest of Shame* emphasizes the "otherness" of these farmworkers, sensationalizing their differences even as he argued for bettering their working and living conditions. Murrow represents farmworkers as if they constituted a nation within the nation. For example, the documentary opens with a shot of African American workers in Miami, Florida, as they wait to be hired, with the following narration: "This is not a place in the Congo. It has nothing to do with Johannesburg or Cape Town. It is not Nyasaland or Nigeria. These are citizens of the United States, 1960."[65] Murrow contends that these workers face third-world conditions that are out of place in the United States. The workers do not have access to the education or upward mobility that were seen as inherent to the American Dream. In a cultural moment in which farmworkers were depicted as being outside the nation or at least outside of national norms, Carson's decision to depict farmworkers as exemplary of the threats facing the "everyday" person and the "average citizen" asserts the national belonging of nonwhite and possibly undocumented farmworkers. In refusing to "other" such workers, Carson refuses to dehumanize them.

Yet it is problematic to ignore the specifics of farmworker vulnerability. To suggest that farmworkers face the same types of risks as other US residents ignores the significant structural constraints that farmworkers must navigate. Carson ignores the ways in which race, class, and legal status compound farmworkers' marginalization, implicitly arguing that race, class, and legal status do not multiply risk. This argument feeds into a myth of American equality of opportunity and contributes to a myth of shared risk. Carson's invention of the "everyday person" or "average citizen" produces a subjectivity akin to the concept of abstract or universal citizenship. As discussed in the introduction, abstract or universal citizenship represents formal citizenship before the law. It is not synonymous with substantive citizenship or with the lived experience of citizenship. As the ideal citizen is envisioned as being white, male, and heterosexual, the nonwhite, nonmale, or nonheterosexual body is often denied the privileges of ideal citizenship. Focusing on a so-called universal experience, as Carson does, exacerbates the power differential between those who can claim universal status because their differences are unmarked and those whose bodies register on the social order to prevent them from accessing substantive citizenship rights. Scholars from sociologists to historians have emphasized the problem of farmworker invisibility and described this invisibility as a key factor that allows and even exacerbates farmworker exploitation.[66] Neglecting the ways farmworkers are denied the full rights of universal citizenship exacerbates this social invisibility.

In contrast to Carson, the UFW's outreach strategy focused on the particular risks farmworkers faced. Outreach materials asserted that farmworkers were a special class of people, disproportionately exposed to pesticides, and therefore with disproportionate power to protect the broader

American public—which they envisioned as a nation of consumers—from
the harms of pesticides. Whereas Carson's book emphasized threats to the
everyday citizen and called for increased federal oversight, the UFW's depictions of DDT blamed growers' greed and emphasized workers' heroism.

The UFW expressed concern about pesticides, including DDT, early in
its organizational history.[67] The UFW filed a number of suits seeking public
disclosure of pesticide use in the fields; these suits were initially unsuccessful, as pesticide use was treated as a trade secret.[68] While the UFW
endorsed bans on DDT at the state and federal levels, their primary route
to limiting worker exposure to pesticides was through union contracts.
Worker safety regulations in union contracts explicitly included pesticides.
The UFW did not trust the state to enforce laws regarding farmworkers
or to effectively monitor for violations. Members of the UFW organizing
council, moreover, were well aware that banning any single pesticide would
have little impact on worker safety. Any particularly problematic pesticide,
such as DDT, could easily be replaced with a more heinous one, as in the
case with organophosphates. Organophosphates, such as parathion and
methyl, rapidly lose toxicity and thus have a lower environmental impact
than DDT. Yet, because organophosphates' toxicity is acute in the short
term, they are actually more harmful for farmworkers than chlorinated
hydrocarbon pesticides such as DDT.[69] Growers' use of organophosphates
increased after the 1970 ban on DDT went into effect.[70] Consequently, the
UFW sought to ensure that workers had some say in the pesticides to which
they were exposed and could respond more flexibly to new chemical threats
in the fields. UFW contracts required growers to keep extensive spraying
records to fully disclose their pesticide use to a health and safety oversight
committee; banned six of the pesticides most dangerous to farmworkers
(chlorinated hydrocarbon pesticides DDT, aldrin, dieldrin, and endrin, and
organophosphate pesticides parathion and TEPP); mandated the Health
and Safety Oversight Committee's approval prior to spraying organophosphates; and directed the growers to periodically test farmworkers for poisoning.[71] It is clear from the UFW contracts that they desired not just better
protections for farmworkers but a shift in the balance of power, increasing the control farmworkers had over the conditions shaping their lives.
Neither growers nor the state were deemed adequate to decide issues of

farmworkers' safety;[72] these were to be decided by the unions' health and safety oversight committees.

By writing protections for workers into union contracts, the UFW sent a clear message that union grapes would be safer for consumers. In doing so, they sought both to protect workers from pesticide exposure and to leverage the growing public concern about pesticides to increase support for their unionization efforts and deepen their grape boycott. The UFW consciously scared consumers away from grapes. Chavez publicly proclaimed, "I don't eat grapes because I know about these pesticides."[73] In 1968–69, the UFW engaged in an extensive public outreach campaign on pesticides to support the grape boycott. UFW organizer and nurse Marion Moses went on a tour in 1968 that included direct outreach to Ralph Nader, Charles Wurster of the Environmental Defense Fund, Tony Mazzocchi of the Oil, Chemical and Atomic Workers Union, and Barry Commoner's Scientists' Institute for Public Information.[74] Meanwhile, "the legal staff regularly disseminated pesticide updates. These information sheets included results of laboratory analyses of grape residues, how many pounds of various chemicals were used in a given year, strategies and tactics for pressuring markets to remove grapes, and articles and stories highlighting the dangers of pesticides to consumers and workers."[75] The UFW printed leaflets discussing pesticides and carried a significant numbers of stories for supporters and workers on pesticides in the union paper *El Malcriado*.

The UFW also reached out directly to the nascent environmental movement to gain support. They were one of twenty-four organizations and individuals signing on to the Environmental Action Coalition's press release announcing New York City's participation in the first Earth Day. The UFW's strategic planning document for the first Earth Day reveals their desire to include farmworkers as speakers at all of the major teach-ins and at Earth Day events to select political targets that would put pressure on growers.[76] As historian Robert Gordon details, the UFW attempted to further this environmentalist support for their boycott in 1972–73. The 150 contracts that the UFW signed in 1970 were set to expire in 1973, and the Teamsters had already started preemptively making sweetheart deals with the growers.[77] The alternative contracts with the Teamsters removed the UFW's pesticide protections, encouraging Chavez to seek allies in the environmental move-

Cover of the United Farm Workers' newspaper *El Malcriado*, January 15, 1969. © by United Farm Workers.

Cover of the United Farm Workers' newspaper *El Malcriado*, June 1–30, 1969. © by United Farm Workers.

ment. Smaller groups more representative of burgeoning tendencies of midcentury environmentalism, such as Environmental Action and Friends of the Earth, responded positively to Chavez's call to endorse the boycott. Larger old-guard organizations such as the Sierra Club and the Audubon Society declined to entangle themselves in what appeared to be a labor conflict between the Teamsters and the UFW. They also did not wish to endorse new social movements that not all in the conservation movement sanctioned.[78] Thus, the UFW's relationship to the environmental movement reveals in part the rifts and changing strategies of an environmental movement itself in flux and suggests the limits of Matthiessen's environmentalist depiction of Chavez. Matthiessen's vision of eco-warrior Chavez would have appealed only to certain segments of environmentalists; it would not have been particularly compelling to conservationists focused on protecting large tracts of undeveloped land from resource extraction.

The distinction between the more established environmental movement and the UFW emerged in the latter's portrayal of pesticide danger. Many major conservationist groups were concerned only when pesticides threatened national parks or wilderness areas. In contrast, the threat to wildlife was not important to the UFW. The UFW referenced the effect of pesticides on nonhuman creatures only on rare occasions, such as briefly when Chavez testified before Congress.[79] The UFW's rhetoric around pesticides also differed from that of environmentalists concerned primarily with public health. Whereas Rachel Carson spoke of the "everyday person" or "average citizen," the UFW consistently emphasized the unique threats facing farmworkers. In the opening page of their longest and most polished pamphlet on pesticides, the UFW stated, "In California, the agricultural industry experiences the highest occupational disease rate—over 50% higher than the second place industry."[80] In other materials, they asserted that farmworkers had three times the amount of pesticides in their bodies as the average person.[81] The UFW considered farmworker mothers and farmworker children as groups with increased vulnerability. Handwritten notes on such newspaper articles encouraged boycotters to reprint headlines such as "Pesticides Poison Farm Children."[82] Chavez was quoted in one such article stating, "These farmworker children are suffering from high levels of DDT in their blood and from low cholinesterase levels in their blood plasma."[83] Another article explained that the children were exposed when they both worked and played alongside their parents. This article quoted a rural physician, who said, "Some parents said, 'Well, this is something farmworkers just have to suffer with."[84] Such statements emphasize the regularity with which farmworkers were exposed. Indeed, in one of the newspaper articles the UFW reproduced for distribution, a rural physician claimed that over 50 percent of farmworker children had chronic pesticide poisoning.[85] In their press relations and public outreach work, the UFW did not present workers as being ignorant of the dangers of pesticide use. Rather, they suggested that without a union, workers felt they must simply suffer as a particular class of oppressed people.

The UFW connected the vulnerability of farmworker children to the uncertain future of farmworkers as a whole. As one article in *El Malcriado* stated, "Since many farm worker mothers breast feed their babies, the danger of poisoning the babies, or giving them cancer or some unknown disease, is even greater. Time may be running out for us and our children."[86] Such language suggested the discourse of endangered and threatened species. Farmworkers were particularly vulnerable, and farmworker children even more so. While environmentalists spoke broadly about the need to protect the environment for future generations and for children, the UFW specifically outlined the hazards farmworker children faced and raised the possibility that farmworkers as a group faced a perilous and indeterminate future. The UFW may have been one of the first organizations to apply such endangered species rhetoric to oppressed minority groups, but it later became a popular rhetorical tactic in environmental justice campaigns.[87]

While Rachel Carson wrote of indiscriminate spraying having unintended consequences, the UFW portrayed pesticide spraying as a deliberate and knowing act of violence against farmworkers. The cartoon cover to *El Malcriado* from February 15, 1969, shows a sneering and almost smiling grower spraying pesticides on scurrying workers.[88] The workers flee while looking up in terror. In the background, a man wearing a protective mask pushes dead workers into graves. A line of crosses mark more graves in the background. There are no crops in the image. The workers are not accidentally sprayed but purposefully massacred. The growers' pests are not the bugs that threaten grape production but farmworkers favoring unioniza-

Cover of the United Farm Workers' newspaper *El Malcriado*, February 15, 1969. © by United Farm Workers.

tion. El Teatro Campesino's play *Vietnam Campesino* offers a more explicit version of the visual rhetoric of the *El Malcriado* cartoon. In this play, the grower sends his son with a crop duster to dump pesticides on workers to break a strike or *huelga*. He says, "Go to it, son, give 'em hell!" followed by the aside "That'll fix their huelga."[89] Such representations contend that the poisoning of farmworkers is not merely a harmful and unintentional side effect of food production but an explicit attempt to murder farmworkers and exterminate the farmworkers' movement. It becomes one of the ways in which the UFW exposes the growers' dehumanizing and violent treatment of farmworkers.

The UFW represented pesticides as being a weapon against the union, implying that growers had launched a war on farmworkers. When the UFW discussed organophosphates, particularly parathion, the organophosphate most likely to be used on grapes, they emphasized their message that pesticides were a weapon of war. In their communications, parathion was almost always described as a nerve gas developed by Nazis during World War II.[90] Such phrasing linked growers with Nazis and farmworkers with holocaust victims. The Vietnam War provided an even more direct connection for the UFW between war and pesticide use. *Vietnam Campesino* renders this link explicit when the character General Deliverance drops scab lettuce covered with DDT on Vietnam as the latest weapon of the war.[91] The pesticide-laden lettuce is delivered by the same character that earlier in the play had purposefully sprayed Mexican workers in the field. The play repeatedly asserts the similarity between Vietnamese campesinos and California farmworkers as a way to encourage farmworker opposition to the Vietnam War. It does so in part by suggesting that the pesticides sprayed on farmworkers are as much a weapon against them as the bombs dropped on the North Vietnamese. As General Deliverance tells the grower, "Well, Butt, there you are: mission accomplished. You spray pesticides, and I bomb Vietnam."[92] In the play, the ignorance of the public allows the growers to launch chemical weapons. When Butt objects to General Deliverance's plan by saying, "Yeah, but I still say the American public will never buy it," the general responds, "Never buy it? Hell, who do you think has bought it for the last ten years?"[93] When Butt's son returns to spray pesticides on striking workers a second time, Dolores Huerta stops him by threatening a public outreach campaign on pesticides.[94] The play portrays the public as the union's secret weapon against the chemicals that the growers deploy against the UFW.

The UFW painted a picture of growers attacking agricultural laborers with pesticides and simultaneously positioned farmworkers on the front lines of a battle to defend the American public from these same pesticides. One UFW flyer explained to concerned consumers, "The only way to get regulation of pesticides like parathion, a nerve gas developed by the Nazis in WW II, so that we can be assured of safe food, is through the workers."[95] Another UFW pamphlet emphasized this message: "Because of the total inadequacies of federal and local agencies to control pesticide spraying, because of the criminal negligence of the growers and pesticide-producing companies, because of the dangers of unchecked and unregulated pesticide use, the United Farm Workers believe that ONLY through a strong farm workers union can both the farm worker and consumer be protected."[96] The UFW needed consumers to fear pesticides in grapes in order to gather broad public support for the boycott.

The UFW organizers also wanted the American public to trust farmworkers to regulate pesticides more than they trusted the state, so that the union rather than federal regulation would appear as the solution to the pesticide contamination crisis. The UFW consistently messaged that farmworkers were looking out not only for themselves but for all Americans. Consequently, the UFW emphasized that negotiations with growers in January 1969 broke down because farmworkers would not compromise on consumer health. UFW representatives repeatedly declared UFW's willingness to compromise on wages but not on pesticides. Speaking at Iona College in New York, UFW representative Jose Guevara stated, "We know pesticides hurt farmworkers, so they hurt consumers too. . . . We could have come to terms on money, but we would not give in on pesticides."[97] While the UFW repeatedly asserted that the growers put profit above human welfare, the UFW made clear that they were willing to sacrifice their own wages to protect the well-being of the American public.

The UFW used their stance on pesticides to reframe their mission from one of labor struggle to one of consumer advocacy. A messaging memo from the UFW's general counsel Jerry Cohen to organizers stated, "The growers wanted us to quit talking about the problems of poisons; they wanted to muzzle the union in return for a contract with ten growers. We would not be muzzled because we feel we have a moral obligation to tell consumers of the harms that can be caused by DDT, Amino trizole, and other poisons."[98] Through this language of moral obligation, the UFW positioned themselves as the best protectors of consumer health. Neither the state nor the growers could be trusted to safeguard consumers over their own interests. Only the UFW would prioritize their ethics, putting concern for consumer health above workers' desire for a contract. Such messaging was part of the UFW's larger strategy to create an alliance between the self-interest of farmworkers and that of consumers, an alliance in which the farmworkers would receive not only sympathy from consumers but trust. As one outreach flyer proclaimed, "It's a matter of good health for you to support the grape boycott," as "already the farm workers union is paying off in the interest of the public health."[99]

Yet the extent to which the general public's and farmworkers' interests actually aligned was less than the UFW rhetoric presumed. Consumers' and producers' needs were distinct. They were exposed to different parts of the plants at different times. A food item could be determined safe for human consumption while posing a danger to farmworkers. Toxicology studies of pesticides in the 1950s and 1960s generally focused on the residues left on the parts of plants that consumers would ingest, rather than the parts of plants with which workers came into contact.[100] A significant contention in the UFW's 1969 negotiations arose because of the growers' primary concern with consumer food residues and negative publicity and the UFW's focus on worker health.[101] The growers were concerned about the effect of the UFW's pesticide messaging even if a contract were signed, since the contract would prohibit pesticides that had already been applied to the fall crop.[102] Yet the UFW was willing to declare all union grapes free of pesticides, even if this would not be true for grapes picked the year of the first contract. UFW's negotiators appear to have considered securing a contract with long-term pesticide protections worth misleading consumers for a year.[103] The UFW's stance on pesticides in these negotiations is particularly striking since it was these very same 1969 negotiations that the UFW messaged as failing precisely because of the union's concern for consumer health. Their belief was that one season of mislabeled crops was worth the long-term benefit of the contract and its pesticide protections for the future.

This strategy fit with the UFW's larger goal of shifting power to the union and to workers. Sociologist Ulrich Beck argues that modern society is a "risk society," a social order structured around risk. In this risk society, relations of definition are relations of domination; those who are dominant in society are those able to define risk.[104] With pesticides, farmworkers engaged in a Gramscian war of position, attempting to transform power relationships by claiming their right to define risk in their own terms. The UFW sought to situate themselves, not growers or state regulators, as the true experts about pesticide risks. In doing so the UFW deployed as much scientific evidence as they could find. Pamphlets and speeches relied heavily on the testimony of experts and scientific studies, engaging in a strategy that Stacy Alaimo sees as common to groups struggling to make visible the too-often invisible consequences of trans-corporeality.[105] However, UFW testimony of pesticide danger also depended on farmworkers' embodied knowledge, their direct knowledge of the consequences of pesticide exposure.[106] UFW materials show farmworkers combatting the powerful legitimacy of state and grower expertise with their own combination of science and bodily knowledge. The UFW emphasized not just the need for pesticide regulation but for the participation of workers in the decisions that growers made about pesticides.[107] The UFW contracts may not have promised transparency for consumers, but they did substantially increase transparency for workers. The union sought to recognize the uneven landscape of risk farmworkers faced and to shift the power of the social structure toward farmworkers. Federal regulation of pesticides alone, especially given UFW fears of lax enforcement, had the potential to weaken consumer concern without significantly reducing worker exposure or increasing worker power.

What were the consequences of the UFW's strategy of aligning consumer and worker self-interest? Sociologist Jill Harrison has critiqued the UFW's approach, arguing that coding protections for workers into union contracts renders such safeguards vulnerable if the union falters. Indeed, the UFW succeeded in gaining a significant number of contracts only in the 1970s and only in California. Harrison contends that urging consumers to purchase union grapes to protect themselves from pesticides detracted from a focus on federal regulation, a particularly problematic development given the simultaneous growth of an organics market. According to Harrison, the rise of an organic consumers' market emerged from a 1960s libertarian ethos that problematically dovetailed with the rise of neoliberal economics strategies that privatized environmental goods as privileges to be purchased. Organic produce allows safe food to be an environmental good that some can afford, while others must consume toxins. Harrison challenges this focus on elective certification rather than regulation; she presents certifications such as organic as being unable to protect workers and consumers equally. What if, she asks, regulations outlawed the worst of all pesticides for all food production, protecting everyone?[108]

Stronger federal pesticide regulations and more pesticide bans would offer both consumers and workers protections we currently lack. Yet pesticide regulation at the federal level, such as the purchasing of organic products by a pesticide-wary public, does nothing to protect workers from other abuses. Moreover, neither federal regulation of pesticides alone nor the production of a powerful and popular organics market redresses the power imbalance between farm owners and farm laborers on a national level. How can we envision a solution to environmental injustice that redresses and transforms power relations between workers and growers? Is there a way to develop a regulatory process that allows farmworkers to develop and enforce pesticide regulations?

One of the core demands of the environmental justice movement has been to create transparent governmental processes through which those most affected by environmental or occupational toxins could have increased control over the conditions in which they live, work, and play. The UFW complicates Carson's exposure of environmental toxicity by showing that pesticides, rather than being an indiscriminate and universal killer, violated humanity in uneven ways. Structural and symbolic violence renders some populations, specifically farmworkers, more vulnerable to pesticide poisoning than others. The UFW's campaign against pesticides makes clear that federal regulation alone is not enough. Farmworkers must be central to discussions of which pesticides they should be required to apply. The UFW's demands and Harrison's recommendations need not be mutually exclusive. Farmworkers and other consumers would benefit both from stronger unions and stronger federal regulations.

The modern environmental movement's and the UFW's concern with pesticides contributed to the rise of "a coherent set of alternative food beliefs, practices, and institutions" that food studies scholar Walter Belasco has termed the "countercuisine."[109] This countercuisine has been central to the alternative food movement in the twenty-first century.[110] Yet, as the next chapter addresses, the alternative food movement replaces Carson's vision of the "everyday person" with a problematic consumer citizenship that continues to marginalize the producer-centered vision of farmworker organizations and resists those organizations' attempts to shift food systems' power relations. Moreover, the alternative food movement disregards the power bestowed upon the farmworker as environmental hero by the UFW and its environmentalist supporters, and instead restores the American farmer to his privileged place as nature's steward.

CHAPTER 7

Fit Citizens and Poisoned Farmworkers

Consumer Citizenship in the Alternative Food Movement

I N 2004, FOOD STUDIES SCHOLAR PATRICIA ALLEN WROTE, "Everywhere you look these days there are signs that people are beginning to take charge of their food system."[1] She describes a multifaceted alternative food movement that aims "to reconstruct the agrifood system to become more environmentally sound, economically viable, and socially just."[2] A decade later, the alternative food movement has expanded, and its internal ideological rifts have also grown.[3] This chapter examines the incommensurable cultural logic at play within two ideological clusters of the alternative food movement: consumer-focused and worker-focused. The consumer-focused branch of the alternative food movement celebrates the self-sufficiency of the American farmer alongside the conscious consumerism of the neoliberal citizen. It renders responsible citizenship visible in the maintenance of bodily norms, linking anxiety over obesity to concerns about individual and national security. It operates in tandem with a worker-centered branch that prioritizes the perspectives of food systems workers, including farmworkers. The worker-centered branch focuses on the injustices inherent in the neoliberal structure of many food systems, a racialized and gendered structure that produces profit by exploiting vulnerable populations, including unauthorized migrants. It humanizes food systems workers and seeks to increase their power by recognizing food systems' dependence on their labor. Examining these two tendencies within the alternative food movement side by side reveals the persistence into the twenty-first century of the racial script that establishes the farmer as proper citizen and the farmworker as abject alien.[4] It exposes the set of assumptions about neoliberal citizenship, fitness and health, and social injustice that promotes, for example, aerobic fitness classes as the solution to farmworker suffering, and reveals how these assumptions reinforce rather than challenge the causes of farm worker suffering.

VISIBLE FARMERS/INVISIBLE WORKERS

While environmentalists and the United Farm Workers (UFW) positioned farmworkers as being closer to nature than the average American in the 1960s and 1970s, alternative food movement participants in the early twenty-first century considered farmers as the true environmentalist practitioners of Jeffersonian ideals. In doing so, they shifted the focus away from Mexican and Filipino farmworkers and back to the iconic white American farmer-citizen. This farmer-citizen is heralded as environmental hero in the neoagrarian writings of Wendell Berry and Wes Jackson, as well as in Michael Pollan's salute to farmer Joel Salatin in his best-selling book *The Omnivore's Dilemma* (2006).[5] Following Salatin's appearance in Pollan's work, the *Washington Post* declared him "America's Most Famous Farmer" and *Time* called him a "sage" and "celebrity" of the sustainable food movement. Books, articles, and documentaries have bestowed upon Salatin a celebrity status akin to that which the emergent environmental movement granted Cesar Chavez in the early 1970s (see chapter 6).[6]

This nostalgic embrace of the small-scale farmer marginalizes farmworkers, as is evident in *The Omnivore's Dilemma,* one of the best-selling books of the alternative food movement.[7] Pollan's book is commendable for its attention to the ecological ills of industrial farming and the environmental and political importance of food. However, in a book in which the cows, chickens, and farmers have names, Pollan does not name a single slaughterhouse worker or worker at a food processing plant. Workers' invisibility is particularly problematic given the politics of sight operating in the work. Pollan contends that we need to reckon with "the full karmic price" of our meals.[8] He proclaims, "The more I'd learned about the food chain, the more obligated I felt to take a good hard look at all of its parts."[9] He invokes "the right to look," but he does not look for farmworkers.[10] When Pollan mentions workers (only twice in the book), they function as indictments of industrial agriculture rather than as individual humans whose perspectives should be considered and whose humanity should be embraced.[11]

Mainstream celebrations of local and organic produce often privilege a relationship between land ownership and white citizenship through romanticizing the family farm, ignoring the labor needs of such farms and their frequent reliance on the same racialized hierarchies that mark industrial agriculture. As Margaret Gray's *Labor and the Locavore* makes clear, buying local offers no assurance of fair labor treatment.[12] The environmental and social injustice that runs to the core of modern US food production cannot be fixed by adjusting the scale of agriculture.[13] Rather, as food studies scholar Julie Guthman asserts, it is the process of agriculture that must be transformed.[14] This transformation must prioritize the perspectives of food systems workers. The energy that workers contribute and the experiences they have as food producers should be recognized as key components of the moral calculus that determines what Pollan terms our meals' karmic price.

Some in the alternative food movement do privilege the voices and perspectives of food systems workers. From his book *Fast Food Nation* to his film *Food Chains*, Eric Schlosser continues to impress upon audiences that food systems are labor systems.[15] Mark Bittman in his *New York Times* column has repeatedly called for justice for food systems workers. In "Can We Finally Treat Food Workers Fairly?" Bittman pointedly asks, "And what does it say that you can buy a can of tuna guaranteed to be dolphin-safe but can't guarantee that its human producers—fishers, processors, transporters, packers, sales representatives—haven't been abused?"[16] The Food Chain Workers Alliance likewise insists on labor issues' centrality to the food movement and position food systems workers as food movement leaders.[17] In presenting the concerns of the labor movement and the immigrant rights movement as food systems concerns, such organizations and individuals provide an ideological alternative to the nostalgic embrace of the farmer.[18]

VOTE WITH YOUR DOLLAR

Despite these clear differences, both wings of the alternative food movement mobilize consumer citizenship as one of the primary strategies for socioeconomic change. Eric Schlosser ends *Fast Food Nation* with a call to transform production through our consumption habits. By choosing establishments to patronize, he asserts, you "can still have it your way," a reference to Burger King's famous slogan.[19] Similarly, the documentary *Food, Inc.* concludes with a call to vote with your dollars.[20] The majority of organizations and public intellectuals engaged in the alternative food movement have consistently encouraged us to see eating as a moral, political, and ecological act.

In asking participants to change food systems through their purchases, the alternative food movement engages a strategy common to US social movements from the American Revolution to the present. While abolitionists urged consumers to avoid slave-made goods, supporters of slavery called for consumers to prioritize purchases of plantation-made products.[21] Throughout the twentieth century, black communities in the United States mobilized consumer protests against racial discrimination. This included boycotts against Jim Crow street cars in over twenty-five cities between 1900 and 1906, "Don't Buy Where You Can't Work" campaigns in the 1930s, and the Montgomery Bus Boycott of 1955–56.[22] Black Lives Matter continued this activism in the twenty-first century with its call for consumers to Blackout Black Friday with a boycott on November 28, 2014.[23] Boycotts and buycotts (purchasing to support a cause) historically have given consumers a mode of power outside of electoral politics.[24] Consumer activism offers a productive avenue of protest for those either excluded from or marginalized by other forms of political action, and it supplements other social movement strategies.

Lawrence Glickman, a historian focused on consumer politics, usefully distinguishes between consumer activism and consumer movements, the latter of which perceives conscious consumerism as proper citizenship. According to Glickman, a consumer movement did not emerge until the Progressive Era and was not named as such until the Great Depression. Many Progressive Era activists believed a consumer identity was the proper way to reconcile citizenship with industrialization, urbanization, and increasing distance between production and consumption. Glickman writes, "Progressives so closely identified the practices of consumption and citizenship that they often described the two in overlapping terms."[25] Progressive Era intellectuals perceived all consumption as a moral and political act. Consumers, like citizens, had responsibilities and rights.[26] The consumer movement urged consumers, like citizens, to be informed and make ethical decisions. This notion of responsible consumerism expanded political participation to include those denied full participation in electoral politics. It also positioned consumers as a broad interest group with rights that the state needed to protect.[27] The consumer movement replaced a Jeffersonian narrative in which farmers provided the backbone of a nation of self-sufficient and politically independent producers with the notion of a "consumers' republic" in which consumer citizens saw themselves connected to markets around the world.[28] These consumer citizens felt responsible for making informed decisions because their purchases had ethical and economic consequences in locations they would never personally see.[29] Their influence can be seen in the alternative food movement, especially in its claims to read all acts of consumption as political and ethical quandaries. Older forms of consumer activism, such as boycott and buycott strategies, persist in the alternative food movement alongside consumer movement ideology.

The diversity of ways in which the alternative food movement engages with consumers is consistent with divisions long present in American consumer politics. Glickman describes the two primary strains in US consumer politics: "one stressed expertise, individualism, and the products which consumers bought; the other emphasized collective action, a social conception of consumption, and the labor which made such products."[30] Some food movement organizations embrace a politics of consumption focused on collective action and social good. For example, Real Food Challenge (RFC) is a student-based organization less interested in the morality of the decisions made by any individual consumer than in shifting the choices available to consumers within constrained systems. As RFC explains, "Our primary campaign is to shift $1 billion of existing university food budgets away from industrial farms and junk food and towards local/community-based, fair, ecologically sound and humane food sources—what we call 'real food'—by 2020."[31] Similarly, the Coalition of Immokalee Workers (CIW), a worker-based human rights organization focused on tomato workers in Florida, uses a model of consumer politics developed from the UFW's produce boycotts. Through their Fair Food Program, the CIW increases wages for workers by generating agreements directly with the corporations that consumers encounter—fast-food restaurants such as McDonald's, food service providers such as Sodexo, and supermarket chains such as Trader Joe's. Here, it is not the grower that is tasked with coming up with a penny extra per pound of tomatoes picked but the multinational corporations from which the consumers ultimately purchase their tomatoes. Consumers in the CIW model act as conscientious allies with producers.[32]

Other segments of the food movement are more focused on individual purchasing decisions. As Slow Food USA suggests, "A better, cleaner and fairer world begins with what we put on our plates—and our daily choices determine the future of the environment, economy and society."[33] Companies such as the supermarket Whole Foods Market and the fast-food chain Chipotle have capitalized on calls for consumers to spend more dollars at farmers markets and less money on processed industrial food. In its "Values Matters" advertising campaign, Whole Foods Market states, "We want people and animals and the places our food comes from to be treated fairly. The time is ripe to champion the way food is grown and raised and caught. So it is good for us and for the greater good, too."[34] Whole Foods Market urges consumers to show that values matter to them in selecting where to shop. According to their campaign, the issue is not what you buy but where you buy it.

Whole Foods Market's "Values Matters" campaign exemplifies a tendency within the individualized consumption wing of the food movement to promote a win-win-win among the greater good, better quality food, and personal well-being. As Chipotle says, "We're committed because we understand the connection between how food is raised and prepared and how it tastes."[35] Whereas CIW mobilizes consumers with the rhetoric of solidarity and social justice with food systems workers, Chipotle and Whole Foods argue that it is in the consumer's self-interest to purchase the products they promote. Like Slow Food USA, they implicitly proclaim pleasure as "politically productive and morally legitimate."[36] In much of the environmental movement, consumers are told to buy less. In the alternative food movement, consumers are urged to buy differently. Thus, the food movement capitalizes on what Glickman calls "virtuous pleasure" in an environmental movement that has often been characterized by its focus on "virtuous sacrifice."[37] Rather than tell consumers to reduce, reuse, and recycle, food movement activists tell consumers to purchase high-cost, high-quality food, and to slow down and savor the sensuous pleasure of the meal.[38] They share the message that socially just and environmentally sustainable food tastes better and is better for you.

Nowhere is the focus on personal health more closely linked with sustainability and social justice than in the individualized consumer wing of the food movement, which has joined forces with the antiobesity movement, using the medicalized concept of an obesity epidemic to motivate changes in consumer purchasing habits.[39] In *Jamie Oliver's Food Revolution*, a reality television series, and in his public appearances, chef Jamie Oliver presents individual purchasing habits as the primary problem. His focus on individual, rather than governmental, responsibility resonates with a libertarian discourse of environmentalism. As he told the *Los Angeles Times*, "I've given up on governments . . . once people have a few skills and confidence, they make different choices in the grocery store. Once they make different choices in the grocery store—and on the Main Street fast-food restaurants—then companies will be forced to serve a higher quality offer. That's when the real change happens."[40] According to Oliver, obesity is primarily caused by consumer ignorance and can be solved by educating consumers to change the purchases they make. Oliver thus positions the solution to a perceived public health crisis as being within the realm of consumer choices.

While the inclusionary nature of consumer citizenship is appealing in that it incorporates those denied meaningful electoral participation, it is particularly problematic in terms of individual purchases, especially when the goal is public health. Focusing on individual purchasing power as a means to address public health issues that have emerged as a result of the industrial food supply contributes to what environmental justice and civil rights activist Van Jones has called "eco-apartheid."[41] Those who can afford to provide their families with pesticide-free produce do so. Others are left to purchase pesticide-laden produce for their loved ones. Pollan and others insist that the poor change their priorities and spend more money on food, and less on everything else. When Pollan calls the public's failure to purchase local and organic "less a matter of ability than priority," he ignores the economic realities that many face.[42] He also ignores the constraints endured by many communities due to residential segregation and the lack of investment in poor communities and communities of color. Food access can be limited by local availability, including lack of transportation to stores and markets, creating such geographical constraints as "food deserts."[43] Moreover, Pollan increasingly positions home cooking as the key to a good diet.[44] For many families, time to prepare food from scratch is limited, and families in substandard housing may lack access to a working kitchen altogether. Expecting fresh cooking from families is a burden that continues to fall primarily on women, adding to the labor of their second (or third) shift at home. According to sociologists Sarah Bowen, Sinikka Elliott, and Joslyn Brenton, for working class women, "cooking is at times joyful, but it is also filled with time pressures, tradeoffs designed to save money, and the burden of pleasing others."[45] The food movement's increasing focus on home cooking exacerbates inequalities that families and individuals face in terms of time as well as money. The focus on working families' poorly ranked priorities, according to Pollan, or ignorance, according to Oliver, suggests an individual (or group-based) moral failing.

In reducing the solution to food systems inequalities to individual purchasing practices and food-preparation techniques, the alternative food movement participates in a problematic history of dietary reform movements that, as food studies and American studies scholar Charlotte Biltekoff argues, produces "good" and "bad" eaters. As she puts it, "Dietary ideals primarily convey two interlocking sets of social ideals: one communicates emerging cultural notions of good citizenship and prepares people for new social and political realities; the other expresses the social concerns of the middle class and attempts to distinguish its character and identity."[46] That is, on one hand dietary reform movements have attempted to teach moral characteristics and knowledge that are seen as important for citizenship in particular eras. On the other hand, the failure of some groups to live up to these dietary ideals has functioned to establish the identity of the middle class as distinct from the working class, particularly in moments in which the line between such class identities seemed threatened. By the late nineteenth century, a concern with health itself became a marker of middle-class authority, identity, and responsibility.[47] From the Progressive Era onward, nutrition emerged as "an ideology that governs not just how we think about food, but also how we think about ourselves and other people."[48]

As Biltekoff and Guthman argue, the focus on health as a consequence of food choices resonates within a twenty-first-century neoliberal framework.[49] Whereas the welfare state sees a social contract in which the state protects its citizens in return for productivity, the neoliberal state sees the ideal citizen as a "minimal consumer of state health and welfare services."[50] Making healthy choices becomes a marker of proper neoliberal citizenship. In this neoliberal model, state regulation is outsourced to consumer self-regulation. Citizen health is not the state's responsibility. Rather, it is the responsibly of the informed, educated, moral citizen making proper choices and exercising self-control and self-discipline. Unhealthy people, in this model, fail to live up to dietary ideals and thus fail to live up to citizenship ideals.[51] In claiming that eating sustainably, locally, and with justice in mind is also healthier, the food movement unintentionally aligns itself with neoliberal cultural values of willpower, self-control, discipline, and personal responsibility. It suggests that attentive food consumers are being good neoliberal citizens by consuming morally for others and the earth (food movement values) while also consuming morally for themselves (healthy eating). In taking personal responsibility for their own ethical and personal well-being, they contribute to national well-being by avoiding the use of state resources.

The focus on obesity rather than broader notions of health makes one's body a visible sign of citizenship fitness. It is the body, rather than one's purchasing habits or food preparation, that manifests as visibly healthy or unhealthy.[52] The body becomes a visible corporeal marker of one's proper or improper citizenship.[53] Fat bodies, in obesity epidemic and food movement discourse, serve as a sign of ill health that imperil the nation's future. Oliver exemplifies this logic when he states, "Our kids are growing up overweight and malnourished from a diet of processed foods, and today's children will be the first generation ever to live shorter lives than their parents."[54] The nation is threatened by the poor choices individuals make in failing to take care of their children and themselves. As Biltekoff points out, fatness even became a security threat in the post-9/11 nation. The war on terror and the war on obesity were declared only two months apart, contributing to "a pervasive sense of endangerment that served important political purposes on the terror 'home front.'"[55] The documentary *Fed Up* makes explicit this connection between obesity and terror. In the opening minutes of the film, stock footage of American suburbs intermingles with familiar voices of newscasters speaking of an "emerging epidemic" that serves as "a threat to national security." As the on-screen image switches to a global map, a voice says, "It is a terror from within."[56] Overweight bodies are made to bear the burden of fear of failed security, self-surveillance, and self-discipline, even in a film such as *Fed Up* that repeatedly asserts that obesity is not caused by a failure of willpower or self-control.

The alternative food movement not only suggests proper consumption as one way that individuals can properly protect their families, but also positions farmers as necessary for national security. In an essay opposing President George W. Bush's national security strategy, Wendell Berry describes agriculture as "the economic activity most clearly and directly related to national security." He considers the US food system particularly vulnerable to terrorist "disruption" because of its dependence on "genetically impoverished monocultures, cheap petroleum, cheap long-distance transportation, and cheap farm labor," and implicitly offers his own brand of Jeffersonian farming as a security solution.[57] In 2008, Pollan addressed then president-elect Barak Obama as "Farmer-in-Chief." Pollan's choice of moniker likewise positions farming as important to national security, linking Jeffersonian ideals to national defense.[58] He raises similar concerns to Berry's about food systems vulnerability: "When a single factory is grinding 20 million hamburger patties in a week or washing 25 million servings of salad, a single terrorist armed with a canister of toxins can, at a stroke, poison millions. . . . The best way to protect our food system against such threats is obvious: decentralize it."[59] Both Berry and Pollan position farmers, rather than military might, as central to national well-being.

With its focus on the family farmer as America's proper defender and the consumer as the nation's proper citizen, the alternative food movement naturalizes neoliberal forms of consumer citizenship through its connections with older narratives about the independent farmer-citizen. According to Glickman, in Progressive Era consumer movements, the ethical consumer replaced the independent Jeffersonian producer as the ideal citizen. Instead of celebrating the self-sufficiency and independence of the family farmer, the consumer movement celebrated the power that the consumer wielded in an increasingly interdependent world.[60] In the twenty-first century, the alternative food movement has found a way to bring the ethical consumer and the independent farmer-citizen back together again.

Through proper food purchases and preparation techniques, the neoliberal consumer citizen regains the self-sufficiency and independence that the modern globalized world seems to threaten. In *Cooked*, Pollan poses a question to which cooking from scratch at home is the answer: "How can people living in a highly specialized consumer economy reduce their sense of dependency and achieve a greater degree of self-sufficiency?"[61] Whereas ethical consumers of the twentieth-century consumer movement found their power in their interdependent world, ethical twenty-first-century consumers seek independence, resisting complicity in systems that seem morally ambiguous at best. Pollan's focus on reducing consumers' "sense of dependency" tempers anxieties about middle-class white American identities in a world of transnational market integration where debates about the future and the meaning of the nation-state proliferate. The US economy, we are reminded daily, is deeply reliant on a global economy and not isolated from political, economic, or environmental turmoil across the planet. In this moment in which US consumers are constantly reminded of global interdependence, the alternative food movement offers them the opportunity to regain the perceived independence of the Jeffersonian farmer. If, as Glickman suggests, consumer politics often provides a way for Americans to articulate a model of citizenship appropriate for the social, economic, and political changes around them, the alternative food movement provides the nostalgic reassurance of the American farmer at the same time as it suggests the personal power of an independent neoliberal citizen.

"THEIR BONES": LOCATING FARMWORKER HEALTH

Yet where does this concern with self-sufficiency, personal responsibility, and individual health leave food systems workers, including farmworkers? The food movement's dietary ideal emphasizes fresh fruits and vegetables. To eat fresh fruits and vegetables in the United States is, by and large, to eat products harvested by farmworkers. As medical anthropologist Seth Holmes explains, migrant farmworkers' experience is one of suffering, and by suffering he means "not only physical sickness, but also mental, existential, and interpersonal anguish."[62] Yet this anguish and suffering fails to register as a problem implicit in calls to eat more fresh fruits and vegetables. In the contrast between the unhealthy processed prepared food and the fresh brightly colored virtuous vegetable, the human that picked that vegetable somehow vanishes, once again, from the moral equation at play.

The embrace of antiobesity rhetoric by some in the alternative food movement is part of the process that naturalizes farmworker suffering. According to Holmes, "The perception of inequalities as normal, deserved, and natural permits the reproduction of such destructive social formations as well as indifference to them."[63] He argues, "It is vitally important . . . to understand how the ongoing mistreatment and suffering of migrant laborers has become taken for granted, normalized, and naturalized by all involved."[64] The antiobesity movement's contribution to the naturalization of farmworker suffering is apparent in discussions of farmworker obesity. The University of California, Davis, for example, launched a three-million-dollar study of farmworker obesity in which it offered nutritional education and exercise classes. The press release explained that Zumba classes were "an ideal way to help farmworkers combat obesity, one of their most serious health hazards."[65] The use of Zumba, a fitness program incorporating various forms of Latin American music and dance, is particularly ironic, as the study appropriates Latin American cultural expressions into a project of racial discipline. The study's proposed solutions position obesity rates as evidence of farmworker failure to engage in proper restraint (food restriction) and self-discipline (exercise). It blames farmworkers' obesity rates on farmworkers. It also legitimizes farmworkers' position on the outskirts of the nation, as abject aliens rather than proper consumers, by implicitly suggesting that farmworkers' broader suffering is caused by the same ignorance and inactivity that result in their obesity, ignoring the structural causes of both.

The causes and consequences of farmworker suffering appear very differently when farmworker perspectives are privileged. Helena María Viramontes's novel *Under the Feet of Jesus* (1995) unveils the processes that mask farmworkers' visibility in both US food systems and society. It counteracts the invisibility it reveals through the coming-of-age narrative of Estrella, a thirteen-year-old Chicana farmworker. Estrella's budding romance with fifteen-year-old Alejo is disrupted when he is sprayed with pesticides. He becomes deathly ill and Estrella must find him medical help. At the novel's end, Estrella has managed to get him to an emergency room and must leave him there, possibly to die. These events develop Estrella's political consciousness. As literary critic Paula Moya notes, Estrella's political transformation occurs as she confronts a nurse with a crowbar to secure the money the family needs for gas to drive Alejo to the hospital.[66] She justifies her actions by referencing the exploitation of her labor rather than the denial of her US citizenship rights or society's refusal to recognize her national identity. Unlike the consumer citizenship that texts such as Pollan's *The Omnivore's Dilemma* promote, Viramontes's novel places producers at its political center. Viramontes sees food systems workers and imagines their lives and desires in a way that Pollan does not. Consequently, her novel opens up political possibilities that remain unseen in the writings of many obesity-concerned alternative food movement writers such as Pollan.

Farm labor fundamentally shapes Viramontes's characters' lives. Her detailed description of this work disrupts pastoral images of farming by emphasizing the physical difficulty of the work. The novel introduces the work lives of farm laborers through a comparison of Estrella's experiences with advertisers' depictions of the Sun-Maid raisin girl. Viramontes writes, "Carrying the full basket to the paper was not like the picture on the red raisin boxes Estrella saw in the markets, not like the woman wearing a fluffy bonnet, holding out the grapes with her smile, ruby lips, the sun a flat orange behind her. The sun was white and it made Estrella's eyes sting like an onion, and the baskets of grapes resisted her muscles, pulling their magnetic weight back to the earth."[67] The pastoral image of the farm girl captured on the Sun-Maid raisin box obfuscates the physical difficulty of farmworkers' work and the economic insecurity and immobility of their migrant lives. The woman on the raisin box is not a farmworker. She does not labor. She instead holds out her grapes like a gift. She shares the bounty of nature with the consumer. As geographer Don Mitchell asserts, the popular image of the California countryside erases the labor that creates the countryside.[68] Images of the blessed bounty of fertile fields, of oranges and peaches hanging from trees, ignores the workers who maintain the landscape. Viramontes's insistence on the painful repetitiveness of

Estrella's tasks places workers' bodies at the center of California's harvest. Viramontes writes, "Morning, noon, or night, four or fourteen or forty it was all the same. She stepped forward, her body never knowing how tired it was until she moved once again. Don't cry."[69] Farm labor is not associated with glowing beauty or youth in Viramontes's novel. Rather the strenuous, tedious work ages bodies. Descriptions of muscles "coiled like barbed wire," an aching back and knees, and a "sore hip" indicate that Estrella's body is strained beyond her thirteen years.[70]

Consequently, there is no innocent idyll at work in the text. There is no nostalgic longing for a lost youth.[71] Agricultural labor strips the characters of their youth: "The nature of their lives had a way of putting twenty years on a face" (Viramontes, Under the Feet of Jesus, 111). The repetitiveness of the tasks Viramontes describes conveys workers' lack of freedom and limited socioeconomic mobility. Varicose veins shackle Estrella's mother Petra like "vines choking the movement of her legs" (61). The painful ailments that limit Petra's physical agility echo the economic constraints that have shaped and limited the possibilities of her life. The economic factors that mold the characters' bodies, constraining their freedom of movement, also determine the contours of the characters' lives and the possibilities open to them. When Estrella's love interest Alejo asks Estrella, "You always gonna work in the fields?" Petra thinks, "What a stupid boy!" (117). Alejo's ambitions, picking peaches to save money for school supplies, result in his pesticide poisoning and possible death. The mobility and uncertainty inherent in their jobs as migrant farmworkers prevents the socioeconomic mobility to which characters such as Alejo aspire. The novel refutes the pastoral images available to consumers by depicting the difficulties and limitations of producers' lives.

Viramontes's contrast of the Sun-Maid raisin box with Estrella's daily work signals the text's prioritization of production over consumption and its critique of consumer citizenship. The text moves between Estrella's labor in the fields and her encounter with the Sun-Maid box in a grocery store aisle. Estrella occupies subject positions simultaneously as both the producer and the consumer. In positioning Estrella this way, the text resists a clear separation of the categories of producer and consumer. Petra too later appears as both producer and consumer as she shops for food with her children in tow (108–12). Such scenes describe the family's food insecurity. The store offers only unappetizing remnants of fresh fruit and vegetables, "squished old tomatoes spilled over onto the bruised apples" (110). In asserting that not all consumers have the same experiences or opportunities, the novel complicates any turn toward consumer purchasing as the solution to the problem of unjust working conditions.

The novel privileges knowledge that emerges from production over an "imitation" knowledge that emerges from an isolated consumption-oriented identity. Viramontes writes, "The woman with the red bonnet did not know this. Her knees did not sink in the hot white soil, and she did not know how to pour the baskets of grapes inside the frame gently and spread the bunches evenly on top of the newsprint paper" (50). The Sun-Maid raisin woman who "did not know" suggests a typical consumer who is uninformed about the processes of production. In addition to highlighting consumers' ignorance of the production process, the description conveys Estrella's knowledge. The labor that Estrella performs requires mastery of a certain set of skills. It is for this reason that Estrella can reprimand her brother, *"You don't know how to work with the sun yet"* (53). Estrella's knowledge contrasts with the ignorance of the nurse who refuses to treat Alejo. Viramontes describes the nurse, like the woman on the raisin box, as a fake. The nurse "wore too much red lipstick too much perfume and asked too many questions and seemed too clean, too white just like the imitation cotton" (141). With such a depiction, Viramontes suggests that the nurse lacks the knowledge that would truly help Alejo.

Estrella's political consciousness transforms in this scene as she realizes that her labor allows the nurse's security. The nurse indirectly consumes Estrella's farmwork as she benefits from the system that exploits Estrella and her family. Outraged by the nurse's thoughtlessness, Estrella applies Alejo's geography lesson to understand her exploitation:

> She remembered the tar pits. Energy money, the fossilized bones of energy matter. How bones made oil and oil made gasoline. The oil was made from their bones, and it was their bones that kept the nurse's car from not halting on some highway, kept her on her way to Daisyfield to pick up her boys at six. It was their bones that kept the air conditioning in

> the cars humming, that kept them moving on the long dotted line on the map. Their bones. Why couldn't the nurse see that? Estrella had figured it out: the nurse owed *them* as much as they owed her. (148)

Etrella's energy, her labor, is foundational to the system. Just as fossils create the oil upon which an unsustainable society functions, the labors of Estrella and her family produce the cheap produce and other commodities that "kept [the nurse] on her way to Daisyfield" (148). The system could not function without her energy, her work. The nurse's consumer lifestyle depends on Estrella's producer lifestyle. Estrella's sacrifices allow the nurse certain luxuries.

Notably, oil proves a powerful symbol for Pollan as well. In *Omnivore's Dilemma*, Pollan repeatedly asserts that industrial agriculture problematically produces food from petroleum rather than the energy of the sun.[72] Viramontes extends Pollan's analysis through Estrella's realization that this oil metaphorically includes her life and labor. Estrella's realization is an articulation of a producer politics often lost in the alternative food movement's focus on consumer citizenship. Viramontes's novel replaces consumer politics with a producer politics as Estrella's analysis of her own labor provides the moral imperative for her actions. The crucial dilemma in *Under the Feet of Jesus* is not consumers' ignorance of the ways in which food moves from farm to fork. Rather, the issue is that workers lack control over the conditions of their labor.

This concern with workers' power distinguishes the types of consumer politics that the Coalition of Immokalee Workers offers from the mode of consumer citizenship and self-sufficiency promoted by some in the alternative food movement. The consumer citizenship developing out of the nexus of the antiobesity and alternative food movements positions consumers as the single most important subject position in food systems. It reduces the consequences of the industrial food system to consumers' visible bodily health (or fit citizenship). In this way, it further marginalizes and erases the physical and emotional harm that food systems workers experience. Moreover, it reduces farmworkers' well-being to concerns over obesity presumably caused by inactivity and nutritional ignorance. What would the alternative food movement look like if workers' bodies, rather than consumers' bodies, became the visible marker of health to which we turned to assess our food systems? What if the alternative food movement's definition of health was broadened beyond visible bodily norms? What if it focused less on imagining food systems that did not require workers and more on imagining food systems that offered just, fair, and dignified sites of work? What if the twenty-first-century alternative food movement concentrated on shifting relationships of domination and definition so that farmworkers had more control over their lives?

US fields have been the site of extensive violence to farmworkers' bodies and minds. Farmworkers are disproportionately exposed to pesticide poisonings. They have lower life expectancies and higher infant mortality rates than the average American.[73] They have among the highest rate of occupational injury in the nation and increased mortality from multiple forms of cancer.[74] The contemporary US food system is far from healthy. Yet the focus on obesity marginalizes the corporeal experiences of those most exploited by food systems and naturalizes their suffering. It has reified rather than rectified farmworkers' abject status. It is the twenty-first-century migrant rights movement, not the alternative foods movement, that has most successfully countered the abject status assigned to farmworkers, rejecting the racial logic of Jeffersonianism that remains inherent in the alternative food movement. Instead, the migrant rights movement mobilizes depictions of nature and the natural to suggest an alternative form of political belonging which I term "denizenship." It is to the cultural politics of the migrant rights movement that *The Nature of California* now turns.

"Tienes una Madre Aquí"

Environmentalism and Migration in
the Twenty-First Century

T HROUGHOUT THE TWENTIETH CENTURY, ARTISTS, ADVO-
cates, authors, and other cultural producers have turned to stories
about farmers and farmworkers to sort out who belongs to the nation and who is alien to it. Some have mobilized ideas about nature and land
ownership to exclude groups from the nation, and others to write groups
into the nation. Nature and land ownership have been central pivots on
which the racial gate keeping of the nation have turned. These depictions
of race, nature, and nation have not been limited to representations of
farming. The national identity attributed to landscapes and to people in
those landscapes continues to shape our ideas about border control and
border crossers. It shapes the emotional response people have when they
hear about hundreds of thousands of unaccompanied children crossing
into the United States from Central American homelands and the reactions
they have when Liberian immigrant communities in the United States are
shunned due to fears of Ebola. It shapes the political response of nation-
states to such crises. Addressing the process through which particular people are rendered abject to the nation is a necessary step in our work toward
achieving full and substantive human rights for all people, regardless of
citizenship status, racial or ethnic identity, or national origin.

Weaving new stories of relationships among people, between people and
places, and between humans and the more-than-human world is equally essential, and it is to these stories that this conclusion turns. Migrant rights
art, literature, and other cultural production is at the forefront of a new
ecological politics that re-conceptualizes the relationship between people

and place. Helena María Viramontes's novel *Under the Feet of Jesus* (1995) and Favianna Rodriguez's poster "Migration Is Natural" (2012) suggest the importance of shifting our understanding of the relationship between humans and the more-than-human world. Their art offers a model for thinking through the intertwining of ecological, social, political, and economic systems without universalizing the uneven and unequal experiences of humans. Their creative work articulates a politics that does not rely on the racial construction of citizenship and land ownership. Instead, it recognizes both inhabitation and migration as forms of belonging and rewrites the politics of nature at play in dominant culture discourses.

DENIZENSHIP

In a pivotal moment of Viramontes's *Under the Feet of Jesus*, Petra confronts her daughter Estrella's fear of La Migra, or border patrol. In this scene, Petra articulates an extralegal and terrestrial form of belonging for Estrella by naming the earth as Estrella's mother. She says, "Tell them que tienes una madre aquí. You are not an orphan, and she pointed a red finger to the earth. Aquí."[1] This is a particularly powerful moment in the text because Estrella possesses legal citizenship. She was born in the United States. Her birth certificate is under the feet of her mother's statue of Jesus. Yet Petra does not rely solely on Estrella's legal citizenship to assert her belonging. She instead articulates what I call a politics of denizenship.[2] Viramontes refutes the racialized binary between white citizen and nonwhite criminalized immigrant by naming Estrella as a denizen. Linking her place of belonging to her place of being, Petra emphasizes Estrella's inhabitation rather than her documentation. In doing so, she repudiates the abjection of alienage without attempting to claim the property of white citizenship. Instead, Estrella's belonging emerges from her participation in social, economic, and ecological systems.

The novel emphasizes ecological systems' inextricable imbrication with social and economic systems through the metaphor of fossil fuels. As discussed in chapter 7, Estrella's political consciousness transforms when she situates herself within a larger socioeconomic system:

> She remembered the tar pits. Energy money, the fossilized bones of energy matter. How bones made oil and oil made gasoline. The oil was made

from their bones, and it was their bones that kept the nurse's car from not halting on some highway, kept her on her way to Daisyfield to pick up her boys at six. It was their bones that kept the air conditioning in the cars humming, that kept them moving on the long dotted line on the map. Their bones. Why couldn't the nurse see that? Estrella had figured it out: the nurse owed *them* as much as they owed her.[3]

In this passage, Viramontes mobilizes a concept that Lisa Park and David Pellow have labeled "environmental privilege."[4] The nurse who refuses to provide Estrella's love interest Alejo with adequate health care fails to recognize that her own relative economic stability and physical comfort depends on the political powerlessness of exploited workers such as Alejo. Estrella invokes a story Alejo has told her about the woman found in the La Brea Tar Pits to figure her own bones as the fossils that allow the system to run. Her energy output, her physical and emotional sacrifice as a farmworker, is not easily separated from the gasoline that allows society's cars to function.

In using oil as a metaphor for the exploitative structure on which late-twentieth-century US society relies, Viramontes prefigures contemporary scholarly conversations about oil culture and infrastructure, or the ways in which everyday lives in the United States have been organized around the consumption of fossil fuels.[5] She also presents a vision of intertwined materiality through the merging of human and fossil energy that resonates with the work of environmental scholars such as Nancy Tuana and Stacy Alaimo, who offer new conceptual models for the relation between human and more-than-human nature. Nancy Tuana uses the phrase "viscous porosity" to describe this new relationship, while Stacy Alaimo employs the term "trans-corporeality."[6] Both concepts dissolve strict boundaries between humans and nonhumans by emphasizing bodily permeability. As Tuana writes, "The viscous porosity of our bodies and that of PVC allow for an exchange of molecules, where PVC and phthalates pass through the porosity of skin and flesh, particularly the mucosal linings of our intestines and our lungs. Plastic becomes flesh."[7] Alaimo and Tuana draw on an interactionist model that not only troubles the stability of bodies and objects but also asserts the inseparability of matter and meaning. They build on Karen Barad's conception of interaction in which objects and subjects emerge from the interactions of phenomena both social and material rather than exist independent of them.[8]

Seen through such an interactionist lens, Estrella's relationship to the earth and to fossil fuels appears more than metaphorical. Estrella's assertion that the fossils are "their bones" alters the meaning of Petra's proclamation that Estrella's belonging emerges from the earth. Her belonging is rooted not in a biologically or divinely determined stable natural order but in the complex relations among social practices, economic structures, ecological systems, and contested ideologies that shape Estrella's bodily reality. Estrella can locate her parentage in the soil because her bones are buried in the earth. It is the sacrifice of her bodily well-being, the grinding up of her bones, that provides the fuel that keeps the system in motion. Her body, her bones, and the gasoline are not a priori objects with an independent existence. Rather, they are produced from the interaction of social, physical, political, economic, and ecological forces. Estrella's political identity and ecological belonging, her denizenship, emerges simultaneously from the material and the ideological. In her refusal to legitimize Estrella's political status through her relationship to a nationalized nature, Viramontes disrupts the Jeffersonian assumptions and racial logic at work in texts such as Steinbeck's *The Grapes of Wrath*, offering instead an earth-based belonging rooted in an interactionist model of humans' relationships to the more-than-human world.

MIGRATION IS NATURAL

The twenty-first-century migrant rights movement in the United States has embraced the understanding of ecological belonging that Viramontes articulates in *Under the Feet of Jesus*. Through the work of artists such as Favianna Rodriguez, the movement draws heavily on monarch butterfly imagery to proclaim migration as natural and beautiful. Through the butterfly motif, migrant rights artwork disrupts the naturalization of the nation-state as the arbiter of rights and suggests a form of political belonging rooted in mobility and transformation rather than stasis and assimilation.[9] In its intertwining of butterfly and human futures, this artwork also revises relationships between humans and ecological systems, challenging the "politics of the natural" that underwrite the racialized depictions of nature in agricultural discourses. It offers instead a vision of the relationships between humans and nonhuman species similar to what Donna Haraway terms "naturecultures," an inseparable entanglement of the biological and the cultural that troubles distinctions between human and nonhuman.[10] Like Viramontes's tar pits metaphor, migrant rights butterfly artwork suggests the imbrication of political, cultural, economic, and ecological systems in ways that challenge the very process of naturalization at work in the dominant cultural discourse.

Monarch butterflies became a prominent part of the US migrant rights movement as a result of their adoption by the UndocuBus Project and the solidarity actions it inspired. The UndocuBus was a large bus painted aqua blue and covered with orange images of monarch butterflies. Filled with undocumented riders, it traveled from Arizona to the Democratic National Convention (DNC) in Charlotte, North Carolina, over a six-week period in the summer of 2012. The ride went through ten states and sixteen cities in the US South, self-consciously evoking the freedom riders. Outside of the DNC, ten individuals participated in an act of civil disobedience, risking deportation as well as arrest. The monarch butterflies were not only painted on the bus—they adorned the riders' T-shirts, appeared on signs carried at UndocuBus protest stops, and they featured in murals painted at the UndocuBus launch in Tucson.[11] Supporters were encouraged to post images of themselves on Tumblr making butterflies with their hands in solidarity with migrants threatened by the hostile anti-immigrant policies of many states and the US federal government. Following the protest, the organizers, No Papers, No Fear, put out a call urging migrant rights groups globally to adopt the butterfly as their symbol and asking artists to produce work with the butterfly at its center.[12]

Rodriguez is one of the cultural workers responsible for the UndocuBus butterflies. A printmaker and digital artist born to immigrant parents and raised in the Bay Area, Rodriguez is well-known for her political posters. While she is a catalyzing force for monarch art, she is not the first or the only artist to use butterfly imagery. As Rodriguez points out, "It was not my idea; it was an idea that's been circulating throughout Latin America for a number of years now."[13] Other US artists embracing this motif include Melanie Cervantes, Cesar Maxit, Jesus Barraza, Ernesto Yerena, Hector Duarte, and Julio Salgado. Rodriguez explains that she uses the monarch butterfly because it "symbolizes the right that living beings have to freely move. . . . Like the monarch butterfly, human beings cross borders in order to survive."[14] Rodriguez and other migrant rights artists draw on the monarch butterfly's migration to subvert the naturalized and racialized relationship between nation and identity.

To better understand the connection that migrant rights butterfly art draws between human and butterfly migration, it is useful to examine one of Rodriguez's many evocative pieces of art, "Migration Is Natural."[15] This composition, in the shape and color of a yellow border patrol sign, implicitly references the infamous "running immigrant" caution signs that started populating Southern California freeways in the 1990s.[16] It contains the image of a monarch butterfly and the phrases "Butterfly Crossing" and "Migration Is Natural." Each butterfly wing contains a human face in profile, a butterfly image that also appears in Rodriguez's work "Migration Is Beautiful." Rodriguez created the image as six-feet-tall street art exhibits that were placed around Tucson, and also sells the image as stickers on her website in packs of five, ten, or fifty.[17] This piece aligns human and butterfly migrants to contend that human migration should be as acceptable as butterfly migration. Whereas Barbara Kingsolver's novel *Flight Behavior* parallels human and monarch migration, Rodriguez integrates human faces into her butterfly wings. In doing so, she counters a clear separation of people and nature by depicting butterflies and humans as materially embedded in the same ecological, political, and economic systems.

Whereas yellow diamond signs typically signal drivers to be cautious, Rodriguez's butterfly caution signs do not warn viewers about the dangers of immigrants. They instead ask audiences to be protective of migrants, ensuring that they are not harmed, intentionally or unintentionally. With the butterfly, Rodriguez counters images of immigrants as individuals to be feared, as threatening racial others. Butterflies replace the fright-invoking image of unnamed faceless men scaling the border wall with a brightly colored celebration of rebirth. Rather than the hordes of locusts that right-wing propaganda often predicts, butterflies are a welcome addition to the garden. Conservationists, moreover, consider butterflies an indicator species, able to give advance warning of broader ecological decline.[18] The proc-

Favianna Rodriguez,
"Migration Is Natural,"
http://favianna.tumblr.com/.

lamation that humans are akin to butterflies suggests the possibility that
they act as indicators of the human-rights and social-justice conditions of
the places through which they migrate.

Butterflies' cross-cultural connotations serve in Rodriguez's art to hu-
manize unauthorized border crossers. Butterflies have long been linked
to the human soul. Monarch butterflies return each year to one of their
wintering sites in Angangueo, Mexico, around the Day of the Dead. It is
said that they are the returning souls of lost and deceased children, an
idea perhaps tracing back to the Aztec beliefs that humans would return
as hummingbirds and butterflies. The association is similar in Greek mythology; the Greek word for "butterfly" is "psyche," or "soul." To imagine
the migrants as souls is to emphasize their humanity in a reality that too
often denies the humanness of their experience. Simultaneously, by evok-

ing these stories, Rodriguez's art encourages us to see the butterflies, too, as having souls. In humanizing migrants and monarchs, Rodriguez imbues both butterfly and human migrants with nonmonetary intrinsic worth.

"Migration Is Natural" articulates a justification for migrant belonging that does not rely on unauthorized immigrants' economic contributions.[19] Throughout *The Nature of California*, labor has been central to ways in which individuals denied legal or substantive citizenship rights claim belonging to the nation and to the earth. In contrast, the butterfly is more aesthetic than productive. In this way, it offers an alternate argument to deportations to that of the United Farm Workers' "Take Our Jobs" campaign. The "Take Our Jobs" campaign contends that unauthorized migrants are necessary for the nation because of their labor; they do jobs that legal citizens will not. In contrast, migrant butterflies assert migrant belonging outside of the category of work or national necessity. The art suggests that monarchs and migrants are inherently entitled to migration and belonging regardless of their economic productivity. Rodriguez's butterfly art thus presents a politically transformative argument for migrants' rights that resists the fungibility of human and nonhuman life.

Through the use of the monarch butterfly Rodriguez undercuts the legitimacy of the nation-state, as monarch butterfly life cycles are incompatible with place-based models of citizenship and assimilation-based understandings of immigration. Monarch butterflies have an incredible range and impressive migration capabilities. Populations are found on continents and islands including but not limited to North America, Central and South America, Europe, Northwest Africa, Hawaii, the Galápagos Islands, the Solomon Islands, the Philippines and Taiwan, New Zealand, Australia, New Guinea, India, the Azores, and the Canary Islands.[20] While monarch butterflies usually make it to Europe from the United States by catching transport on ships, they have been reported to fly from one continent to the other. Butterflies are one of the only insects capable of transatlantic migration. Within North America, monarch butterflies are known for their annual seasonal migration. Their migration patterns resemble those of many birds instead of those of other insects or even other butterflies. The North American eastern population winters in Mexico, flies through the United States and Canada, and then returns to Mexico through the United States. A western population that is not fully isolated from the eastern population winters in Southern California rather than Mexico.[21] Notably, the butterflies migrate as individuals, rather than in preformed aggregate groups.[22] While this is an annual migration, it is not a migration that occurs within the life of a single butterfly. Some monarch butterflies live for only two months. Eggs are deposited along the trip. The butterfly's annual migration occurs over three to four generations; occasionally a fifth generation is found.[23] The monarch butterfly thus counters earlier models of immigration that focus on transplantation and assimilation by instead emphasizing the multigenerational movement of people across places.

By proclaiming the multigenerational migration of humans to be natural, Rodriguez engages in a process that cultural studies scholars term "naturalization." Following Noël Sturgeon, I define naturalization as the use of representations of nature to suggest that particular social or economic relations, social identities, or behaviors are natural. As Sturgeon points out, the power of calling something "natural" lies in the way that we imagine nature itself. To call an act, a relationship, or an identity natural is to suggest it is pure, morally good, outside of human control, innate, and of either biological or divine origin—all ideas derived from the dominant Western imagination of nature.[24] Consequently, if something is natural it cannot be questioned. It has political and moral legitimacy, hence the power of the debate over the naturalness or unnaturalness of heterosexuality and homosexuality.[25]

The butterfly imagery replaces the logic that the nation is natural with the idea that migration is natural. Migration, like nature, is seen as pure, pristine, unquestionable, and an innate human capacity. This counters the cultural logic that depicts undocumented immigrants as criminals and the act of trespassing borders as perverse, selfish, and outside of social norms. To call migration natural is to call it normal, to place it well within the accepted realms of human behavior. It is also marks it as outside of the regulatory authority of the nation-state. Against a regime that dehumanizes and criminalizes migrants, it declares the act of migrating as quintessentially human, as natural a behavior as the nurturing of one's own young.

The use of the monarch butterfly in UndocuBus artwork opens up new possibilities for disputing the nationalist discourse of nature used by anti-immigrant activists and parts of the mainstream environmental movement. The monarch butterfly is a call not for rights of inclusion within the nation but for the rights of all human beings to cross borders. It disrupts the regime that sanctifies nations as the distributor of rights and national belonging as necessary for the distribution of rights. In this model, one need not belong to a particular nation to be guaranteed rights and equal protection within that nation. Moreover, one need not belong to *any* nation to be guaranteed rights and equal protection; stateless people are as deserving of rights as naturalized citizens. Rodriguez's claim that migration is natural dissociates belonging from national citizenship or membership in a national community. This is a crucial issue as the numbers of stateless people or people who do not hold citizenship to any nation grow worldwide. This is an issue of particular concern to many climate justice activists, who believe that as resources become scarcer and certain locales become uninhabitable, stateless populations will dramatically increase. The rewriting of migration as an issue not of national security but of natural rights suggests a mode of political belonging situated outside of the nation-state.

Yet Rodriguez's art does more than simply deploy the politics of the natural. It also alters the vision of nature written into the cultural politics at play, queering relations between humans and nonhumans. The butterfly in "Migration Is Natural" has two human faces in its wings. Rodriguez's website includes instructions on printing out your own butterfly wings to attach to your back at the next migrant rights rally you attend. She envisions a butterfly that is human and a human who is butterfly. Similarly, in one of Julio Salgado's pieces, "Queer Butterfly," a man sprouts butterfly wings from his back. The text on one wing reads, "Joteria Migrante Amor Familia Unidad Paz," while the other wing contains the English equivalent, "Migrant Queerness Love Family Unity Peace." Salgado inscribes the words "I Exist. Yo Existo" on the man's torso.[26] Salgado's art makes apparent the queerness of both Rodriguez's and Salgado's human claim to the natural, resting on the slang use of *mariposa* (butterfly) for "queer." In declaring queer migrants to be natural and embracing *la mariposa* as the iconic migrant activist, Salgado pays homage to the central role that undocumented queer youth have played in the migrant rights movement, an intersectional politics captured in the undocuQueer identity.[27] Moreover, Salgado's and Rodriguez's merging of the human and the nonhuman, this human-butterfly hybridity, suggests the inseparability of the human from the butterfly. It creates a queer world in which the independence and autonomy of humans and butterflies cannot be assured, but in which neither is reduced to a mere product of the other.[28] That is, it suggests, an interactionist model of human and more-than-human relations similar to that operating in Viramontes's novel.

In depicting the intertwined bodies and souls of humans and butterflies, Rodriguez and Salgado not only cast the identities of butterflies and humans as interdependent but their survival possibilities as well. While migrant rights butterfly artwork naturalizes queer migrant identities, it also engages with the plight of monarch butterflies. North American monarch butterflies' migration has been termed an "endangered phenomenon." Their survival faces a number of obstacles, including the deforestation of their wintering habitats in Mexico and Southern California, the habitat fragmentation and loss of their spring breeding grounds, and a variety of threats to milkweed, including herbicide exposure. Monarch butterflies face mortality at all stages of life from pesticides, including those used to control gypsy moth and mosquito populations, and millions of monarchs die annually from automobile mortality. Climate change will likely shift the range of milkweed that migrating butterflies depend on, while temperature variation could alter the timing of the migration. An increase of extreme weather events may devastate wintering populations that rely on a delicate balance between temperatures cool enough to keep them at rest and warm enough to keep them alive.[29] Understanding the threats to monarch butterflies requires both bioregional (local) and eco-cosmopolitan knowledge.[30] Monarch butterflies' survival relies on a complex mix of habitat restoration and preservation, both at winter roosting sites and throughout the multinational breeding grounds in which monarchs travel and live. It also requires the butterflies to adapt to the variations in temperature and milkweed range that climate change brings. While monarch butterflies are often depicted as fragile, to survive they will need to be resilient and adaptable.

These threats cannot be separated from those facing many human communities, including transnational migrant communities. The devastation of butterfly habitat emerges from the same global economic forces that have contributed to the unsustainability of migrants' lives in their home countries, contributing to unauthorized human migration. The obstacles that butterfly migrants face on their journey echo the risks that human migrants face in their dangerous trek across militarized Southwest borderlands. The threats facing monarchs, like those facing humans, exist at the nexus of ecological, economic, political, and cultural forces.

In choosing to depict monarch butterflies, Rodriguez and other artists have chosen to align themselves with a creature whose fate is uncertain because it is bound up in economic choices and ecological changes that are already under way. In doing so, they emphasize the agency of both human and butterfly migrants. As No Papers, No Fear expresses it, "As we set out to change the world, each of us were changed ourselves. We had to lose our fear. To take control of our destiny we had to embark on a hard path. . . . As individuals and as a community, we took steps to fly free like the monarch; free from fear, free from intimidation."[31] The organization replaces a discourse of vulnerability and fear with one of freedom, agency, and transformation. They depict human and butterfly migrants as capable of taking control of their own futures.

The butterfly has a history as a symbol of resistance to structures of neoliberal global capitalism. During the 1999 World Trade Organization (WTO) protests in Seattle, protestors on stilts danced in monarch butterfly costumes. Protest signs shaped like butterflies proclaimed, "The WTO kills butterflies." The concern about monarch butterflies at the time was genetically modified (GM) corn. A Cornell University study, performed in a laboratory, showed that monarch butterfly larvae exposed to GM Bt corn could die. This study was of grave concern because of the proximity of corn plants and milkweed, the food of monarch butterfly larvae. Activists worried that if the GM corn was released, the pollen could transfer to milkweed plants and butterflies would die.[32] Today, GM corn evokes not only fears of butterfly death but also anxieties about Mexican cultural survival. As anthropologist Elizabeth Fitting writes, "A longtime symbol of lo mexicano, or Mexicanness, maize has recently come to represent rural and even national culture threatened by neoliberal policies and corporate-led globalization in debates about genetically modified (gm) corn."[33] The North American Free Trade Agreement altered Mexico's relationship to corn. Mexico now imports most of its corn. With fewer economic opportunities in the countryside, Mexican laborers have become the country's primary export.[34] The unauthorized arrival of GM corn in the Mexican countryside is figured in social movement discourse as a threat to both butterflies and indigenous rural Mexicans, whose complicated relationship to industrial agriculture,

unauthorized migration, and remittances is at the heart of the corn debate. Depictions of butterflies and corn thus evoke the forces of neoliberal
globalization that both imperil butterfly migration and compel indigenous
Mexicans to rely on migration for survival. They also conjure resistance to
neoliberalism.

Such associations were cemented by migrant rights groups' participation in the People's Climate March, which attracted around four hundred
thousand demonstrators to New York City in September 2014. The People's
Climate March offered a different view of the communities concerned about
climate justice than that often portrayed by the media. Indigenous peoples'
organizations, including Idle No More, led the march. Organizations from
communities most affected by climate change were highly visible, including El Puente, the National Network for Immigration and Refugee Rights,
and the New York City Environmental Justice Alliance. The National Domestic Workers Alliance marched with signs that read, "Migrant Women
Workers Are a Force of Nature" and "Clean Up the Climate Mess," while
Brown and Green: South Asians for Climate Justice carried a banner reading, "Decolonize the Climate."[35] The march placed racial justice, migration,
colonialism, and indigenous sovereignty front and center. Rodriguez committed significant time on the ground in New York preparing artwork to
be used in the march.[36] She explained her presence to the *New Yorker* by
saying, "'Migration is an effect of ecological destruction,' which is caused,
in large part, by fossil fuel extraction and combustion, which drives climate
change."[37] In such a context, migrant rights activists' use of the monarch
butterfly becomes simultaneously an act of ecological solidarity and of self-
preservation.

At the People's Climate March, members of the migrant rights contingent marched under a large blue parachute banner designed by Rosario
Gonzalez. An ear of corn formed the stalk of a butterfly body covering the
banner.[38] Human faces appear in the butterfly's wings. The banner reads,
"Climate Change Affects Us All; El Cambio Climatico Afecta Todos." This
image communicates the fate of the butterfly as being inseparable from the
fates of corn and campesinos. Transnational migrants, corn, and butterflies
are intermeshed both ideologically and corporeally. Replacing the butterfly's head, abdomen, and thorax with a stalk of corn communicates the
threats facing butterflies and human migrants as being bound up with is-

CultureStrike, Photograph of People's Climate March Banner,
http://www.culturestrike.org/.

sues of national identity, indigeneity, neoliberal economics, climate change,
technology, and ecological change. It depicts a climate politics enmeshed in
larger migrant rights and human rights agendas and suggests human and
more-than-human struggles to survive as intertwined. From this banner's
message, and from the migrant rights contingent that marched beneath
it, emerges a new ecological politics, one that situates political belonging
outside of land ownership and racial citizenship and instead embraces a
queerness, and a queer migration, that breaks down distinctions between
farmer and farmworker, citizen and alien, and human and nonhuman.

Notes

1 "Ag 101," US Environmental Protection Agency, accessed May 6, 2015, http://www.epa.gov/agriculture/ag101/; Carolyn Dimitri, Anne Effland, and Neilson Conklin, "The Twentieth-Century Transformation of US Agriculture and Farm Policy," United States Department of Agriculture, *Economic Information Bulletin* 3 (2005), available at http://www.ers.usda.gov/publications/eib-economic-information-bulletin/eib3.aspx.

2 "Take Our Jobs," United Farm Workers, accessed September 25, 2010, http://www.ufw.org/toj_play/TOJNEW_12_JAL.html.

3 "Migrant Worker, Part 1," *The Colbert Report*, Comedy Central, video 5.08, September 22, 2010, accessed September 23, 2010, http://www.cc.com/video-clips/xr7q4y/the-colbert-report-fallback-position---migrant-worker-pt--1; "Migrant Worker, Part 2," *The Colbert Report*, Comedy Central, video 6.11, September 23, 2010, accessed September 24, 2010, http://www.cc.com/video-clips/puxqvp/the-colbert-report-fallback-position---migrant-worker-pt--2.

4 The "abject alien" draws from McClintock's application of Kristeva's concept of the abject to empire. McClintock asserts, "Certain groups are expelled and obliged to inhabit the impossible edges of modernity: the slum, the ghetto . . . and so on. Abject peoples are those whom industrial imperialism rejects but cannot do without: slaves, prostitutes, the colonized, domestic workers." I use "abject alien" instead of "abject person" because farmworkers' perceived status as "alien" cannot be disconnected from their status as "abject." McClintock, *Imperial Leather* 72.

5 My thinking here is influenced by Cheryl Harris's "Whiteness as Property." In looking to citizenship and alienage to understand each other, I also draw on the work of Mae Ngai, Linda Bosniak, and Joseph Keith.

6 My thinking here develops from Toni Morrison's reading of the central role blackness has played in US literature in producing whiteness.

7 Jefferson, *Notes on the State of Virginia*, 164–65.

8 Ibid, 165.

9 Myers may be one of the first scholars to point out the connection between Jefferson's approach to land and to race. Myers argues that Jefferson situated both people of color

and the land as that which must be benevolently conquered by the white farmer. Native Americans and African Americans, according to Jefferson, lacked the appropriate way of looking at land to lay claim to the Lockean property and political rights central to his agrarianism. Myers, *Converging Stories*, 24, 33.

10   Molina, *How Race Is Made*, 6–10, 32–33.

11   Glenn, *Unequal Freedom*, 35, 53; Berlant, *Queen of America Goes to Washington DC*, 18.

12   Hector St. John Crévecoeur, *Letters from an American Farmer*, 44.

13   Ibid., 45.

14   The common etymologies of the terms "native," "nature," and "nation" (from the Latin *natio*, or "birth") suggest the fascination with natural history and taxonomy that arose along with modern forms of political power. P. Wald, "Naturalization," 171.

15   P. Wald, "Naturalization," 171.

16   Sturgeon, *Environmentalism in Popular Culture*, 21.

17   Ibid., 20, 24–26.

18   Ngai, *Impossible Subjects*, 7.

19   E. Lee, *At America's Gate*, 4.

20   Ibid.'

21   Daniels, *Politics of Prejudice*, 16, 68–70.

22   Lopez, *White by Law*, 47–77.

23   Ngai, *Impossible Subjects*, 6. European Jews were not treated in substantial ways as white until after World War II. Brodkin, *How Jews Became White Folks*.

24   Ngai, *Impossible Subjects*; Molina, *How Race Is Made*, 1.

25   Ngai, *Impossible Subjects*, 6–7.

26   Ibid, 8.

27   Almaguer, *Racial Fault Lines*, 72, 193–204; Gonzalez, *Labor and Community*, 135–60; Ruíz, *Cannery Women*, 72–98; Vargas, *Labor Rights*; Weber, *Dark Sweat*, 12.

28   Ngai, *Impossible Subjects*; Molina, *How Race Is Made*.

29   Ngai, *Impossible Subjects*; Molina, *How Race Is Made*.

30   Reed, "Toward an Environmental Justice Ecocritism," 145–62; Arnold et al., "Forum on Literature and the Environment."

31   Buell, *Future of Ecocriticism*.

32   Gottlieb, *Forcing the Spring*, 34; Sze, "From Environmental Justice Literature," 165.

33   Di Chiro, "Nature as Community," 298–320; Bullard, "Environmental Justice," 19–42; Gottlieb, *Forcing the Spring*.

34   Works that exemplify second-wave ecocriticism include Adamson, *American Indian Literature*; Adamson, Evans, and Stein, *Environmental Justice Reader*; R. Stein, *Shifting the Ground*; Armbruster and Wallace, *Beyond Nature Writing*; Murphy, *Farther Afield*; Bennett and Teague, *Nature of Cities*; Stein, *Perspectives on Environmental Justice*.

35   Adamson and Slovic, "Guest Editors' Introduction," 6.

36   For postcolonial ecocriticism, see Huggan and Tiffin, *Postcolonial Ecocritism*; DeLoughrey and Handley, *Postcolonial Ecologies*; Nixon, *Slow Violence*; Caminero-Santangelo, *Different Shades of Green*; Roos and Hunt, *Postcolonial Green*; and Wright, *Wilderness into Civilized Shapes*. For ecocriticism and queer theory, see Mortimer-Sandilands and Erickson, *Queer Ecologies*; and Seymour, *Strange Natures*. For ecocriticism and materialist feminist theory,

see Alaimo, *Bodily Natures*. Works on race and ecocriticism include Schweninger, *Listening to the Land*; Myers, *Converging Stories*; Outka, *Race and Nature*; Finseth, *Shades of Green*; Gamber, *Positive Pollutions*; and Hayashi, *Haunted by Waters*. Such subfields do not of course encapsulate the entirety of current ecocritical scholarship, which ranges from animal studies to ecomedia studies to object-oriented ontology. Moreover, early ecocritical scholarship is more diverse than the "wave" model suggests, as questions of gender, indigeneity, and the postcolonial were also present among scholarship published alongside "first wave" ecocriticism.

37 Bederman, *Manliness and Civilization*; Haraway, *Primate Visions*, 26–58.

38 Cronon, "Trouble with Wilderness," 69–90. See also Spence, *Dispossessing the Wilderness*; and Jacoby, *Crimes Against Nature*. For a more recent history of the wilderness movement, see J. M. Turner, *Promise of Wilderness*.

39 Ross, "Social Claim on Urban Ecology," 15–16, 19; Gottlieb, *Forcing the Spring*, 63–64.

40 Ray, *Ecological Other*.

41 Gamber, *Positive Pollutions*, 7–9.

42 Kosek, *Understories*, 142–82; Stern, *Eugenic Nation*, 115–49; Coates, *American Perceptions*.

43 Bederman, *Manliness and Civilization*; Coates, *American Perceptions*; Kosek, *Understories*; Ray, *Ecological Other*.

44 Gottlieb, *Forcing the Spring*, 47–52.

45 Dunaway, *Natural Visions*, 134–42; Gottlieb, *Forcing the Spring*, 330–32; Rome, *Bulldozer in the Countryside*, 141–46.

46 This critique, which has gained traction among contemporary environmental cultural studies scholars, was made during the 1960s by the New Left. Gottlieb, *Forcing the Spring*, 139.

47 Gottlieb, *Forcing the Spring*, 333; Stern, *Eugenic Nation*, 127.

48 Park and Pellow, *Slums of Aspen*, 131.

49 Gottlieb, *Forcing the Spring*, 333–35; Park and Pellow, *Slums of Aspen*, 140–43, 150–51.

50 Coates explicitly compares the Lacey Act of 1901, a "'sparrow exclusion act' of sorts," to the Chinese Exclusion Act. Shinozuka points out that the Plant Quarantine Number 37 was put in place just a year after the Asiatic Barred Zone, and its supporters explicitly used anti-Asian rhetoric and imagery. Coates, *American Perceptions*, 44; Shinozuka, "Deadly Perils," 833–34.

51 Coates, *American Perceptions*, 37, 47, 50; Shinozuka, "Deadly Perils," 839.

52 Coates, *American Perceptions*, 51.

53 Ibid., 10, 50–51.

54 See also Robert Gottlieb's description of nativist environmentalism's roots in Progressive Era anti-immigrant sentiment, Kosek's consideration of the Sierra Club's immigration debates in the late 1990s, and Park and Pellow's exploration of contemporary nativist environmentalism. Gottlieb, *Forcing the Spring*, 333–35; Kosek, *Understories*, 160–63; Park and Pellow, *Slums of Aspen*, 128–61.

55 "Ad Campaigns," Californians for Population Stabilization, March 17, 2009, http://www.capsweb.org/press/our-tv-ads; FAIR: Federation for American Immigration Reform, accessed December 17, 2008, http://www.fairus.org/.

56 Julia Wong, "California's Farmworkers Hung Out to Dry," *In These Times*, August 8,

2014, accessed May 21, 2015, http://inthesetimes.com/working/entry/17060/california
_drought_hangs_farmworkers_out_to_dry; "Drought and Farmworkers in California,"
National Public Radio, December 12, 2014, accessed May 21, 2015, http://www.npr
.org/2014/12/12/370406728/drought-and-farmworkers-in-california.

57 Adamson, *American Indian Literature*; Ybarra, "Erasure by U.S. Legislation," 135–47;
Hayashi, "Beyond Walden Pond," 58–79; K. Smith, *African American Environmental
Thought*; Finney, *Black Faces*; Peña, *Mexican Americans*; Outka, *Race and Nature*; Myers,
Converging Stories; Schweninger, *Listening to the Land*; Vázquez, "They Don't Understand";
Finseth, *Shades of Green*; Ruffin, *Black on Earth*. See also Deming and Savoy, *Colors of
Nature*.

58 The most sustained discussion of race and the georgic is in William Conlogue's *Working
the Garden*. Myers addresses the role of race in Jeffersonian agrarianism, and Outka
considers the racial implications of the pastoral in relationship to plantation agriculture.
However, no sustained discussion of the role of race in the American pastoral is found in
Terry Gifford's definitive work *Pastoral*, Stephanie Sarver's *Uneven Land*, or the texts and
introduction in Hagenstein, Gregg, and Donahue's *American Georgics*. Myers, *Converging
Stories*, 24, 33; Outka, *Race and Nature*, 29–49.

59 White, "Are You an Environmentalist," 171–85.

60 D. Mitchell, *Lie of the Land*.

61 Gray, *Labor and the Locavore*; Guthman, *Agrarian Dreams*.

62 Sackman, *Orange Empire*, 18–19, 22–24, 46–47, 84–87, 120–22, 181–84.

63 D. Mitchell, *Lie of the Land*, 8.

64 Almaguer, *Racial Fault Lines*; Daniel, *Bitter Harvest*.

65 Molina, *How Race Is Made*, 3.

66 Ibid., 6–11, 22.

67 California agriculture has a long history of representation prior to the Great Depression, such as Helen Hunt Jackson's *Ramona* (1884). For representations of California
agricultural landscapes and workers before the Great Depression, see Street, *Beasts of
the Field*; and Henderson, *California*.

68 Edward Murrow, *The Harvest of Shame*, CBS, November 24, 1960; Boyle, *Tortilla Curtain*;
Consumers League of New York, *Joads in New York*; Bruce Springsteen, "The Ghost of Tom
Joad," Sony, 1995, compact disc. Susan Shillinglaw makes a similar point, noting, "Over
the years, Tom Joad's name and that speech have become shorthand for engagement."
Shillinglaw, *On Reading "The Grapes of Wrath,"* 39.

69 Sackman has termed this group of white progressives, including Dorothea Lange, Paul
Taylor, John Steinbeck, and Carey McWilliams, the "agrarian partisans." Sackman, *Orange Empire*, 11.

70 Lye, *America's Asia*.

71 Ngai, *Impossible Subjects*, 100, 103, 106, 119–20, 129, 137–38; Gonzalez, *Guest Workers*.

72 Ngai, *Impossible Subjects*, 139; M. Garcia, *World of Its Own Race*, 175.

73 D. Mitchell, *They Saved the Crops*, 66, 211, 219, 241–42, 249, 291, 293, 294, 368, 425, 517–18.

74 For a discussion of Filipinos' roles in the formation of the UFW, see Vera Cruz, *Personal
History*; Bardacke, *Trampling Out the Vintage*; Ganz, *Why David Sometimes Wins*; M. Garcia, *From the Jaws of Victory*; Pawel, *Union of Their Dreams*.

75 Gottlieb and Joshi, *Food Justice*, 20.

76 US Department of Labor, "Findings from the National Agricultural Workers Survey (NAWS) 2001–2002," Report 9, March 2005.

77 Allen, *Together at the Table*, 27; Brown and Getz, "Farmworker Food Insecurity," 131; Liu and Apollon, "Color of Food," 3.

78 Liu and Apollon, "The Color of Food," 3; Hansen and Donohoe, "Health Issues," 157.

79 Gottlieb and Joshi, *Food Justice*, 20.

80 Allen, *Together at the Table*, 27; Sasha Khokha, "Female Farmworkers Speak Up about Sexual Harassment," National Public Radio, January 4, 2014, accessed June 7, 2015, http://www.npr.org/2014/01/04/259646787/female-farmworkers-speak-up-about-sexual-harassment; "Rape in the Fields," Center for Investigative Reporting, June 25, 2013, accessed June 7, 2015, http://www.pbs.org/wgbh/pages/frontline/rape-in-the-fields/.

81 Hansen and Donohoe, "Health Issues," 158.

82 US Department of Labor, "Findings." For contemporary experiences of migrant farmworkers, see Holmes, *Fresh Fruit*.

83 David Bacon links workplace deportation raids directly to union organizing. Bacon, *Illegal People*, 1–23.

1. "SETTLERS GALORE, BUT NO FREE LAND"

1   For the strikes of 1933–34, see Daniel, *Bitter Harvest*, 141–66; Guerin-Gonzales, *Mexican Workers*, 116–38; McWilliams, *Factories*, 211–29; D. Mitchell, *Lie of the Land*, 130–55; Taylor, *On the Ground*, 17–158; Weber, *Dark Sweat*, 79–112.

2   Starr situates the struggles between migrant farmworkers and the Associated Farmers during the Great Depression as an expression of the growing contest between the Far Right (fascism) and the Far Left (communism), domestically mirroring conflicts on the world stage. The Right was not incorrect that many of the strikes were communist-led. Neither was the Left wrong to see a fascist influence at work in the Associated Farmers. Starr, *Endangered Dreams*, 61–83, 156–96.

3   Lye, *America's Asia*, 153.

4   Chan, *This Bittersweet Soil*, 301–40.

5   Lye notes that McWilliams's initial support for internment might be understood as "potentially permanent sites of voluntary colonization," in line with the types of colonization he sought for white workers in *Factories in the Field*. Lye, *America's Asia*, 155.

6   For an etymology of the epithet "Agricultural Pest No. 1.," see Sachs, "Civil Rights in the Field," 217–18; McWilliams, *Education of Carey McWilliams*, 77. Douglas Sackman coined the term "agrarian partisans" in reference to the artists and intellectuals who advocated on the behalf of California's agricultural workers in the 1930s, specifically Dorothea Lange, Paul Taylor, Carey McWilliams, and John Steinbeck. Sackman, *Orange Empire*, 11.

7   Loftis, *Witness to the Struggle*, 171–73; McWilliams, *Education of Carey McWilliams*, 78; Benson, *True Adventures*, 371–72; Parini, *John Steinbeck*, 199–200.

8   Davis, "Optimism of the Will"; Denning, *Cultural Front*, 18.

9   Scholarship on McWilliams has generated one biography, a handful of articles, and a

small collection of dissertations. See Canelo, "Carey McWilliams"; Corman, "Teaching"; Critser, "Making of a Cultural Rebel"; Critser, "Political Rebellion of Carey McWilliams"; Davis, "Optimism of the Will"; Donald Gantner, "Regional Imagination"; Geary, "Carey McWilliams and Antifascism"; Klein, *Apocalypse Noir*; Meyer, "Great Exception"; Navarro, "Contributions of Carey McWilliams"; Robinson, "Remembering Carey McWilliams"; Richardson, *American Prophet*; Sachs, "Civil Rights in the Field"; and Starr, "Light and the Dark." Noteworthy discussions of McWilliams are also found in Pagan, *Murder at the Sleepy Lagoon*, 7, 12, 276, 307–9, 315, 324, 337, 351, 402; M. Garcia, *World of Its Own*, 18, 46–49; Starr, *Endangered Dreams*, 162, 174, 175, 212, 262–68; W. Stein, *California and the Dustbowl Migration*, 20–21, 117–25, 128–29, 134–36; Vaught, *Cultivating California*, 1–10; Vaught "Factories in the Field Revisited," 149–84; and Weber, *Dark Sweat*, 177, 186–87, 192, 206.

10 Loftis, *Witness to the Struggle*, 62–76; Richardson, *American Prophet*, 55–92; Critser, "The Making of a Cultural Rebel"; and Critser, "The Political Rebellion of Carey McWilliams."

11 For public reception of *Factories in the Field*, see Richardson, *American Prophet*, 91–92.

12 McWilliams, *Education of Carey McWilliams*, 64–112.

13 For McWilliams's political activities, see Richardson, *American Prophet*; and McWilliams, *Education of Carey McWilliams*.

14 McWilliams also served as editor of the *Nation* for twenty years (1955–75), where he encouraged and published progressive public intellectuals, including Ralph Nader and Howard Zinn. See Davis, "Optimism of the Will"; and Robinson, "Remembering Carey McWilliams."

15 Chan, *This Bittersweet Soil*, 280–84.

16 McWilliams, *Factories*, 12–13.

17 Ibid., 15.

18 Ibid., 103.

19 Ibid., 28.

20 Ibid., 22. Vaught contests the accuracy of McWilliams's claims about land monopolization of California. Vaught, *Cultivating California*, 165–66.

21 McWilliams, *Factories*, 39.

22 For more on Lux and Miller, see Igler, *Industrial Cowboys*.

23 On Boas's and Margaret Mead's influence on McWilliams, see Robinson, "Remembering Carey McWilliams," 421.

24 McWilliams, *Factories*, 78.

25 Ibid., 110.

26 Weiss, "Ethnicity and Reform," 566–85.

27 In keeping with national trends, many of California's antifascists, including McWilliams, used broad definitions of fascism encompassing racism and antiunionism. As Daniel Geary asserts, "Under the rubric of fascism, McWilliams described such American phenomena as union busting, anti-Semitism, nativism, militarism, capitalist exploitation, scapegoating, lynching, red-baiting, and vigilante justice. Antifascism, as a political posture that called for radical reforms toward economic reconstruction and racial equality in a democratic constitutional order, provided McWilliams with a basic continuity of political instinct." Geary, "Carey McWilliams and Antifascism," 912.

28 McWilliams, *Factories*, 104.

29 Ibid., 306.

30 Ibid., 309.

31 Ibid., 306.

32 Ibid., 129.

33 Mae Ngai identifies the repatriation number as four hundred thousand. Lopez uses five hundred thousand. Balderrama and Rodriguez put the number closer to one million. Ngai, *Impossible Subjects*, 8; Lopez, *White by Law*, 27; Balderrama and Rodriguez, *Decade of Betrayal*, 121–22.

34 McWilliams, "Getting Rid of the Mexican," 322–29.

35 Not all migrant workers were transient. The citrus industry relied more on a model of fixed communities of family. See M. Garcia, *World of Its Own*, 88; Gonzalez, *Labor and Community*, 7–11.

36 McWilliams, *Factories*, 108.

37 Cott, *Public Vows*, 175–79; Coontz, *Way We Never Were*, 137–38.

38 McWilliams, *Factories*, 308.

39 Ibid., 309.

40 The *Nation* provides a particularly coherent almost weekly record of McWilliams's writings during this period. These changes are also documented in the books McWilliams published during the 1940s.

41 As Ngai points out, the 1924 legislation was adopted in part to prevent a flood of Eastern European WWI refugees; its solidification of whiteness was merely coincidental. Ngai, *Impossible Subjects*, 17. Others have argued that this solidification of whiteness occurred in the post–civil war period, or during the period of Asian exclusion. E. Lee, *At America's Gate*; Takaki, *Iron Cages*; Roediger, *Wages of Whiteness*.

42 Both before and after the 1930 census, Mexicans were classified as legally white. Ngai, *Impossible Subjects*, 54. On repatriation campaigns, see Balderrama and Rodriguez, *Decade of Betrayal*; Guerin-Gonzales, *Mexican Workers*; A. Hoffman, *Unwanted Mexican Americans*; and Sanchez, *Becoming Mexican American*, 12, 122–23, 209–26.

43 Allmendinger, *Imagining the African American West*, xi; Arax, "Lost Tribe's Journey"; McBroome, "Harvests of Gold."

44 McWilliams, *Factories*, 195, 224.

45 Not all black workers descended from US slaves. By World War I, there was significant black immigration from the Caribbean and West Indies. These newer immigrants were not part of mainstream consciousness during this period.

46 In 1949, McWilliams refers to the "peculiar institution" of farm labor in California. He moves away from a citizen-noncitizen dichotomy to an understanding of slavery as the fundamental relationship between owner and worker in California agriculture. McWilliams, *California*, 150.

47 McWilliams, *Factories*, 102.

48 Almaguer, *Racial Fault Lines*, 179–82; Lye, *America's Asia*; Saxton, *Indispensable Enemy*.

49 McWilliams, *Factories*, 306.

50 Ibid., 114.

51 Ibid., 102.

52   Ibid., 130.

53   Ibid., 133. Numerous historians have documented nonwhite workers' participation in unionization efforts. Almaguer, *Racial Fault Lines*, 72, 183–204; Gonzalez, *Labor and Community*, 135–60; Ruíz, *Cannery Women*, 72–98; Weber, *Dark Sweat*; Vargas, *Labor Rights*.

54   McWilliams's other writings from the 1930s demonstrate this awareness as well. Throughout this period, he asserted nonwhite labor's militancy in the *Nation*, *American Mercury*, and *Pacific Weekly*. McWilliams's focus on a particularly mythic American relationship to land through farming appears to shift the presentation of his ideas, with troubling implications.

55   McWilliams, *Factories*, 134.

56   Ibid., 139.

57   Ibid., 323.

58   Ibid., 306.

59   By 1946, McWilliams referred to this contention as naive. According to Weber, Mexican workers leaned more toward militant action than white "American" workers. This may have resulted from white migrants' faith in voting, which Mexican workers did not share. McWilliams, "Poverty Follows the Crops"; Weber, *Dark Sweat*, 12.

60   McWilliams, *Factories*, 9. For a discussion of McWilliams's antifascist writings, see Geary, "Carey McWilliams and Antifacism"; Richardson, *American Prophet*, 73–83.

61   Herbert Klein's influence can be seen here. Klein, who coauthored several articles with McWilliams, occasionally under the pseudonym Clive Belmont, lived in Berlin from 1930 to 1934 as a correspondent for the *Chicago Tribune*. Klein's perspective on the role that the entrenched landed elite played in the rise of German fascism influenced McWilliams's perceptions of the Associated Farmers. See Geary, "Carey McWilliams and Antifascism," 923. McWilliams's suspicions are backed up by a recent book on the influence of fascist ideas on the Associated Farmers during the New Deal. Almanzar and Kulik, *American Fascism*.

62   Sucheng Chan finds McWilliams's contention that the Chinese provided the cheap labor that allowed for land monopolies both offensive and inaccurate. Chan, *This Bittersweet Soil*, 301–40.

63   McWilliams, *Factories*, 103.

64   Each section of the chapter "Land Monopolization" includes explicit discussion of the ways in which settlers were excluded from those lands, such as "Railroad Grants" and "Land Speculation."

65   McWilliams, *Factories*, 15.

66   Ibid., 19.

67   McWilliams, "Exit the Filipino."

68   Geary, "Carey McWilliams and Antifascism," 919.

69   Later works such as *North from Mexico* that explicitly include nonwhite workers in the American nation reflect McWilliams's changing political ideologies.

70   "Factories in the Field: Doho's Book Review," *Doho*, October 5, 1939; "McWilliams Raps Anti-Alien Bills as UnAmerican," *Doho*, June 15, 1940; "Committee Takes Steps to Help California Aliens," *Doho*, August 1, 1940; "Carey McWilliams' Talk Slated by the JACL, Demos," *Kashu Mainichi*, April 18, 1940 (2984); "McWilliams Praises Issei for Developing

California," *Kashu Mainichi*, April 20, 1940 (2986), 1; "McWilliams Will Call Meeting, Acquaint Aliens on Registration," *Kashu Mainichi*, June 20, 1940 (3046), 1; "Alien Protection Group Formation Pushed Here," *Kashu Mainichi*, July 16, 1940 (3071), 1. *Rafu Shimpo* also reported on McWilliams's efforts to support Japanese immigrants and Japanese Americans, but with more hesitation, in "JACL to Hear McWilliams," *Rafu Shimpo*, January 21, 1940 (11,874), 3; "Alien Registry Unconstitutional Says McWilliams," June 11, 1940.

71 For the conservative response to *Factories in the Field*, see McWilliams, *Honorable in All Things*, 93; Shillinglaw, "California Answers *The Grapes of Wrath*," 183–201.

72 Mitchell's novel has been underanalyzed. Sackman and Loftis each dedicate a paragraph to *Of Human Kindness*. Sackman, *Orange Empire*, 280–81; Loftis, *Witness to the Struggle*, 170. Shillinglaw provides a more sustained discussion in "California Answers *The Grapes of Wrath*." Conlogue's *Working the Garden* provides the only extensive analysis of the work.

73 Steinbeck, *Harvest Gypsies*, 25.

74 For racial representations of poor white farmers, see Foley, *White Scourge*.

75 R. C. Mitchell, *Of Human Kindness*, 81.

76 Ibid., 64

77 Ibid., 68.

78 Ibid., 95.

79 Ibid., 150.

80 Higham, *Strangers in the Land*, 234–63.

81 R. C. Mitchell, *Of Human Kindness*, 345.

82 Lye, *America's Asia*, 153.

83 Hartranft, *Grapes of Gladness*, 58.

2. FROM FARMER TO FARMWORKER

1 Migrations to California during the Great Depression were fewer than migrations during the decades both preceding and following the 1930s. W. Stein, *California*, 3.

2 Gregory, *American Exodus*, 9–10.

3 Gregory points out that between 250,000 and 300,000 southwestern migrants moved to California in the 1920s without gaining attention. He also reveals that the majority of southwestern migrants to California during this time were not displaced Dust Bowl farmers. Only 6 percent of southwestern migrants to California were from the Dust Bowl proper, and only 36 percent of southwestern migrants between 1935 and 1940 were farmers. Nearly half of southwestern migrants were from cities. Gregory, *American Exodus*, 10, 11, 15.

4 Lange and Taylor, *American Exodus*, 35.

5 Sackman, *Orange Empire*.

6 Thank you to Brill for permission to reprint S. Wald, "We Ain't Foreign."

7 For California as America's Eden, see Sackman, *Orange Empire*, 18, 28, 229; and Loftis, *Witness to the Struggle*, 7.

8 For the popularity of the Great Depression migration narrative, see Denning, *Cultural Front*, 260, 265–67; and Battat, *Ain't Got No Home*, 9–11.

9   D. Mitchell, *Lie of the Land*, 13–17; Sackman, *Orange Empire*, 18, 28, 54, 229.

10 Beegel, Shillinglaw, and Tiffney Jr., *Steinbeck and the Environment*.

11 Denning's reading of race in the novel has been challenged. Charles Cunningham believes Steinbeck replaces his focus on deserving white poor in *The Harvest Gypsies* with a class-based solidarity in *Grapes of Wrath*. More compellingly, Erin Battat suggests the novel's inclusiveness comes "on the level of form and genre." I find her argument that Steinbeck presents Tom as a combination of mythic western and fugitive slave, and that the novel itself draws its narrative patterns from fugitive slave narratives, quite convincing, even as I differ with her assessment that the novel's engagement with "discourses of ethnicity and race in California" is not racially exclusive. Battat, "Okie Outlaws and Dust Bowl Fugitives," 453–80; Cunningham, "Rethinking the Politics"; Denning, *Cultural Front*, 267; Saxton, "In Dubious Battle," 252.

12 In 1997, Peter Lisca could write, "With the exception of one chapter on the figure of the Indian in Louis Owens's monograph, *The Grapes of Wrath* has not been especially fertile territory for ethnic studies." Little on race in the novel has been published since then. See Lisca, "*Editors' Introduction*" 559; Owens, *Promised Land*, 58–64; and Lancaster, "Subverting Eugenic Discourse."

13 Ngai, *Impossible Subjects*, 27.

14 Steinbeck, *Grapes of Wrath*, 233.

15 For the figure of the mythic western, see Kolodny, *Lay of the Land*, 89–115; Slotkin, *Gunfighter Nation*; Slotkin, *Regeneration through Violence*; Slotkin, *Fatal Environment*; H. N. Smith, *Virgin Land*; and F. Turner, *Frontier in American History*.

16 Steinbeck, *Grapes of Wrath*, 36.

17 Brown, *Good Wives*, 42–74; Cronon, *Changes in the Land*, 53, 56–57.

18 M. Johnson, *Black Masculinity*, 30, 75, 108; Smith, *Virgin Land*.

19 Kolodny, *Lay of the Land*.

20 M. Johnson, *Black Masculinity*, 25, 55; Kolodny, *Land of the Land*, 4–6, 67.

21 Steinbeck, *Grapes of Wrath*, 25.

22 Bederman, *Manliness and Civilization*, 173, 176; Deloria, *Playing Indian*, 5; Huhndorf, *Going Native*, 19–78; Slotkin, *Regeneration through Violence*, 14–16.

23 Jule, who is one half Cherokee, states, "Wisht I was a full-blood. I'd have my lan' on the reservation. Them full-bloods got it pretty nice, some of 'em." Steinbeck, *Grapes of Wrath*, 339.

24 Steinbeck, *Grapes of Wrath*, 325.

25 Ibid., 339.

26 Owens, *Promised Land*, 61.

27 Ibid., 60–61. Steinbeck, *Grapes of Wrath*, 323.

28 Steinbeck did not originally intend to establish the Joads' whiteness in this manner. As Susan Shillinglaw points out, "In manuscript, Tom Joad has Indian blood: his eyes were 'very dark brown and there was a hint of brown pigment on his eyeballs that usually means some Indian blood.' Steinbeck crossed out the last phrase. Although it seems that he briefly intended to link Tom's history more forcefully with the Cherokee saga, he didn't do so. In this novel, Steinbeck's warp was clearly the story of white southwestern migrants because whiteness was the gauntlet he threw down to the Associated Farmers." Shillinglaw, *On Reading "The Grapes of Wrath*," 109.

29 Cott, *Public Vows*, 33; Lopez, *White by Law*, 40; Stanley, *From Bondage to Contract*, x–xi, 2–10.

30 For critical race theory on the "possessive investment in whiteness," see Ignatiev, *How the Irish Became White*; Lipsitz, *Possessive Investment in Whiteness*; Roediger, *Wages of Whiteness*.

31 Steinbeck, *Grapes of Wrath*, 11.

32 Ibid., 13, 20,

33 Ibid., 406–7.

34 Lye, *America's Asia*.

35 For racial scripts, see Molina, *How Race Is Made*, 6–11.

36 Steinbeck, *Grapes of Wrath*, 236.

37 Ibid., 221.

38 Ibid., 235.

39 Ibid., 233.

40 Ibid., 232.

41 In *The Harvest Gypsies*, Steinbeck stated, "Recently, led by the example of the workers in Mexico, the Mexicans in California have begun to organize." As Weber and Stein both argue, Mexican and Mexican American workers proved far more militant than white workers, despite McWilliams's and Steinbeck's predictions to the contrary. Steinbeck, *Harvest Gypsies*, 54; W. Stein, *California*, 256–74; Weber, *Dark Sweat*, 12.

42 Ngai, *Impossible Subjects*, 8. Lopez states that five hundred thousand were repatriated. Balderrama and Rodriguez put the number of repatriates at closer to one million. Balderrama and Rodriguez, *Decade of Betrayal*, 121–22; Lopez, *White by Law*, 27.

43 Benson and Loftis, "John Steinbeck," 194–223.

44 Saxton sees Steinbeck's decision as strategic and also as arising out of a radical history of slippage between racial and radical egalitarianism. Saxton, "In Dubious Battle," 249–62.

45 For the 1933–34 strikes, see Daniel, *Bitter Harvest*, 141–66; Guerin-Gonzales, *Mexican Workers*, 116–38; McWilliams, *Factories*, 211–29; D. Mitchell, *Lie of the Land*, 130–55; Taylor, *On the Ground*, 17–158; and Weber, *Dark Sweat*, 79–112.

46 Steinbeck, *Grapes of Wrath*, 232.

47 Ibid., 349.

48 Ibid., 232.

49 Ibid., 334.

50 Ibid., 232.

51 For Steinbeck's invocation of Jeffersonian democracy, see Eisinger, "Jeffersonian Agrarianism," 143–50; Owens, *Promised Land*, 51–55.

52 Steinbeck, *Grapes of Wrath*, 89.

53 Ibid., 90.

54 Ibid., 49.

55 Timmerman, "Squatter's Circle," 137–47.

56 Steinbeck, *Grapes of Wrath*, 37.

57 Timmerman, "Squatter's Circle," 142.

58 Timmerman argues that Pa's role as patriarch of an individual family is replaced over the course of the novel by Ma's role as the center of the "fambly" of man. Timmerman, "Squatter's Circle," 140, 145.

59   Steinbeck, *Grapes of Wrath*, 194–95.

60   Ibid., 244.

61   Ibid., 282.

62   Ibid., 287.

63   Ibid., 307.

64   Denning, *Cultural Front*, 266–67.

65   For a sampling of the numerous biblical readings, see Ditsky, "End of *The Grapes of Wrath*";
     Lisca, "Dynamics of Community."

66   See Ditsky, "The Ending of *The Grapes of Wrath*"; French, "Education of the Heart," 24–25;
     Lisca, "Dynamics of Community"; and Owens, "Culpable Joads," 108–16.

67   Slotkin, *Regeneration through Violence*, 12, 14.

68   Steinbeck, *Grapes of Wrath*, 419.

69   Szalay, *New Deal Modernism*, 162–83.

70   Steinbeck, *Grapes of Wrath*, 153.

71   The possible exception here is Jule, the half-Indian character. He plays a significant role
     in the collective "we" as he first spots the instigators at Government Camp. Why did
     Steinbeck include a Native American figure when there were more Mexican workers at
     the camps? Building on Huhndorf and Deloria, I suggest that Jule functions in the novel
     to demonstrate that the Joads and other migrants "naturally" belonged to the American
     nation, and were somehow indigenous to it, without threatening Steinbeck's racial con-
     struction of the migrants as white. See Deloria, *Playing Indian*, 5; and Huhndorf, *Going
     Native*, 5.

72   Babb, *Names*, xiii.

73   Battat, *Ain't Got No Home*, 46, 66.

74   A. Wald, "Introduction," ix–xv; Rodgers, "Foreword," vii–xii; Battat, *Ain't Got No Home*,
     44–47; Wixson, *Dirty Plate Trail*, 5, 154.

75   Wixson, *Dirty Plate Trail*, 35.

76   Rodgers, "Foreword," ix–xi; Battat, *Ain't Got No Home*, 49.

77   A. Wald, "Introduction," x.

78   Women writers' landscape representations are a topic of considerable scholarship. An-
     nette Kolodny and Vera Norwood highlight the domestic language some women writers
     use to claim a space in nature, while Stacy Alaimo considers the way some women writers
     seek out nature as an escape from the domestic and as an "untamed" model for "insur-
     gency," what she terms "undomesticated ground." Yet Babb's rewriting of the working
     agricultural landscape marks her terrain as outside both the domesticated language
     Kolodny and Norwood discuss and the undomesticated or "wild" lands Alaimo considers.
     Alaimo, *Undomesticated Ground*, 14–18.

79   Babb, *Names*, xiii. This echoes Pare Lorentz's *The Plow That Broke the Plains* (1936).

80   Ibid., 97–98.

81   Ibid., 97.

82   For more on equitable gender relations in the novel, see Battat, *Ain't Got No Home*, 41–70.

83   Ibid., 61.

84   Babb, *Names*, 104–5.

85   Ibid., 164.

86   Ibid., 171.

87 Ibid., 154.

88 Ibid., 156.

89 Babb, *Names*, 180. Garrison's name recalls white abolitionist William Lloyd Garrison, editor of the *Liberator*, thus referencing an earlier cross-racial movement.

90 Ibid., 185.

91 Babb's depiction of Dust Bowl migrants' antiracist education counters the knowledge that historians have of white migrants' culture and of black Californians' perceptions of the new workers. Los Angeles' black community perceived white Dust Bowl migrants as bringing the corrupting influence of Southern racism into the potentially free land of the far West. The Los Angeles black community's perceptions of white Southerners may have been correct. Dust Bowl migrants were disturbed by their perception that California had looser attitudes toward racial mixing than their home states. Flamming, *Bound for Freedom*, 310, 312; Gregory, *American Exodus*, 166–69; Weber, *Dark Sweat*, 149.

92 Battat, *Ain't Got no Home*, 65.

93 Babb, *Names*, 187.

94 While hundreds of thousands of white migrants moved to California during the Depression years, available statistics show it is possible that tens of thousands of black farmers also migrated. Allmendinger, *Imagining the African American West*, xi. Lange and Taylor report that 90 percent of three hundred thousand migrants were "native white Americans." This would imply that 10 percent (no small number) were likely African Americans and Mexican workers. Lange and Taylor, *American Exodus*, 146. See also Arax, "Lost Tribe's Journey"; and LeSeur, *Not All Okies*. For African Americans in the West more generally, also see Broussard, *Black San Francisco*; De Graf, Mulroy, and Taylor, *Seeking El Dorado*; Flamming, *Bound for Freedom*; Moore, *To Place Our Deeds*; Sides, *L.A. City Limits*; and Weber, *Dark Sweat*, 6–7, 149, 182–83, 194, 290, 294.

95 Battat, *Ain't Got No Home*, 66; Wixson, *Dirty Plate Trail*, 87; Weber, *Dark Sweat*, 290, 294.

96 For one of Lange's photos of African American farmworkers in California, see Street, *Photographing Farmworkers*, 114.

97 Wixson, *Dirty Plate Trail*, 163.

98 Babb, *Names*, 49.

99 Ibid., 99.

100 Ibid., 203.

101 Ibid., 221.

102 Ibid., 222.

3. THE "CLOUDED CITIZENSHIP" OF ROOTED FAMILIES

1 Grodzins, *Americans Betrayed* 27; tenBroek et al., *Prejudice*, 80. The Grower-Shipper Association effectively acted as a subsidiary of the dominant Western Growers Protective Association, whose membership controlled 85 percent of the market on California row-crop vegetables. Grodzins, *Americans Betrayed*, 25–30, 61, 175, 219, 276.

2 "The Specter of the Japanese Farmer" comes from Lye, *America's Asia*, 102. Japanese Americans' rural experience has been relatively neglected in the field of Asian American studies, an absence historian Gary Y. Okihiro pointed out in 1989. Only a handful of

scholars have taken up Okihiro's exhortation to focus on rural Asian American history, including Lye, *America's Asia*; Matsumoto, *Farming the Home Place*; Niewert, *Strawberry Days*; Azuma, *Between Two Empires*; Fujita-Rony, "Shared Pacific Arena"; and Tsu, *Garden of the World*.

3   Lye, *America's Asia*, 109.

4   Thomas and Nishimoto site a forty-five/fifty-five split between agricultural and nonagricultural production in the population. As Lye explains, "The unreliability of the data is at least partly the result of conditions of economic informality characterizing Japanese farm operation that, with the passage of the 1920 Alien Land initiative, were only exacerbated." Thomas and Nishimoto, *Spoilage*, 4; Lye, *America's Asia*, 112.

5   TenBroek et al., *Prejudice*, 23–25, 62; Daniels, *Politics of Prejudice*, 16, 68–70. On differences between the anti-Chinese and the anti-Japanese movements see Daniels, *Asian America*, 118.

6   See tenBroek et al., *Prejudice*, 25–26; Daniels, *Politics of Prejudice*, 70–72.

7   See tenBroek et al., *Prejudice*, 50–53; 78.

8   For the agricultural ladder, see Foley, *White Scourge*, 9–11; Jamieson, *Labor Unionism*, 5.

9   Grodzins, *Americans Betrayed*, 9.

10 Matsumoto, *Farming the Home Place*, 46; Tsu, *Garden of the World*, 7.

11 All western states in the continental United States, except Colorado, eventually passed some version of the Alien Land Law. Walz, "From Kumamoto to Idaho," 416.

12 Azuma, *Between Two Empires*, 14, 65–66; Lye, *America's Asia*, 111; Daniels, *Asian America*, 143–44; and Ichioka, "Japanese Immigrant Response," 157–78.

13 Daniels, *Politics of Prejudice*, 87; Daniels, *Asian America*, 163.

14 Daniels, *Asian America*, 134, 144; Modell, *Economics*, 94–95; McWilliams, *Prejudice*, 80.

15 P. Smith, *Democracy on Trial*, 65.

16 Daniels, *Asian America*, 163; P. Smith, *Democracy on Trial*, 65; Iwata, "Japanese Immigrants," 32.

17 Neiwert, *Strawberry Days*, 48–49.

18 The range of 30 to 35 percent is widely used in discussing the prewar era. Thomas and Nishimoto, *Spoilage*, 4.

19 Iwata, "Japanese Immigrants," 33; Grodzins, *Americans Betrayed*, 168; McWilliams, *Prejudice*, 87; Modell, *Economics*, 8, 96, 104, 106–07; and P. Smith, *Democracy on Trial*, 66. Iwata states that Japanese Americans grew nearly thirty thousand acres of grapes, and nineteen thousand acres of fruits and nuts, including plums, peaches, prunes, apricots, apples, almonds, walnuts, and cherries. They grew three thousand acres of nursery crops, and provided 65 percent of the flower industry. Iwata, "Japanese Immigrants," 33. Azuma and Neiwert point out that these crops tended to be the most labor intensive and so were less desirable for white farmers to plant. Azuma, *Between Two Empires*, 64; Neiwert, *Strawberry Days*, 48–49.

20 Part of their success here resulted from cities' increasing demands for fresh produce. M. Garcia, *World of Its Own*, 56; Neiwert, *Strawberry*, 48–49.

21 Daniels, *Asian America*, 164; Iwata, "Japanese Immigrants," 25; Matsumoto, *Farming the Home Place*, 89; Thomas and Nishimoto, *Spoilage*, 4. For specific information on Los Angeles, see Modell, *Economics*, 99.

22 Grodzins, *Americans Betrayed*, 36–37; Weglyn, *Years of Infamy*, 93–97.

23 Chiang, "Imprisoned Nature," 241.

24 Daniels, *Asian America*, 244–46.

25 P. Smith, *Democracy on Trial*, 221; Weglyn, *Years of Infamy*, 97–99; Thomas and Nishimoto, *Spoilage*, 54.

26 New Deal officials staffed and administered the camps, working toward New Deal aims of racial assimilation through cultural erasure. Drinnon, *Keeper of Concentration Camps*, 4; Lye, *America's Asia*, 141–203; P. Smith, *Democracy on Trial*, 170–80.

27 Creef, *Imagining Japanese America*, 34.

28 Ibid., 36.

29 Ibid., 37–39.

30 Larry Tajiri, "Tomorrow's Farms," *Rafu Shimpo*, July 21, 1935 (10270).

31 I read the English section of each paper from 1930 through 1941; publication ceased following Pearl Harbor. The examples given are representative, as listing dozens of key trends that appeared daily over the period of a decade was impractical. I also consulted the Communist Party's *Western Worker* from 1930 to 1941 and the progressive Japanese American *Doho* from its first issue in 1938 through the end of its run in 1941.

32 For ethnic newspapers, see Park, *Immigrant Press*; Miller, *Ethnic Press*; Bonus, *Locating Filipino Americans*, 128–63.

33 For the Japanese American press, see Daniels, *Asian America*, 167; Yoo, *Growing Up Nisei*, 68–92.

34 The papers should be considered neither an objective record of events nor a reflection of Japanese American opinion as a whole. They represent the viewpoints of writers, editors, and owners. While similar in their depictions of agriculture, the two papers differed slightly in their political slants. *Doho* found *Kashu Mainichi* to be more militaristic and pro-Japan than *Rafu Shimpo*. From my reading, *Kashu Mainichi* also appeared to be more sympathetic to the Democrats, liberals, and unions than *Rafu Shimpo*.

35 Larry Tarjiri, "Tomorrow's Farms."

36 Azuma, *Between Two Empires*, 91.

37 "Nisei Agriculture," editorial, *Kashu Mainichi*, February 4, 1934 (777), literature page.

38 "Southland Farmers Await New Era in Agriculture," *Rafu Shimpo*, October 11, 1933 (9630).

39 "Nisei Urged to Take Up Agriculture at JACL Banquet," *Kashu Mainichi*, March 16, 1938; "Time Too Short for Mooting on Farms," *Rafu Shimpo*, December 17, 1935 (10417), 8.

40 "A New Era in the Farm Industry," editorial, *Rafu Shimpo*, November 5, 1933 (9665), 2; "Agriculture Is Seen as Best Vocation to Attain Recognition by American [sic]," *Rafu Shimpo*, November 18, 1935 (10389), 6. See also "Farm Board Asked to Aid for Sake of Nisei Future," *Rafu Shimpo*, December 16, 1933 (9705), 8.

41 "Stay, Pioneers Stay!" *Kashu Mainichi*, February 14, 1934 (777).

42 George H. Nakamoto, "Must We All Be Farmers/What Do the Elders Want of the Nisei? Are There Any Other Avenues of Enterprise for Them?" *Rafu Shimpo*, December 1, 1935 (10401).

43 M. M. Horii, "Farm Life Seen as Ideal Basis for Nisei Livelihood," *Rafu Shimpo*, December 8, 1935 (10408), 4.

44 "Agriculture Is Seen as Best Vocation."

45 Azuma, *Between Two Empires*, 114.

46 Nisei farmer, "See Future of Nisei in Farming," *Rafu Shimpo*, December 24, 1936, 6. See also "Nisei Farmers Take Over Growers Confab," *Kashu Mainichi*, April 26, 1940 (2992).

47 Kamata Ota, "Warning Sounded on Farming Crisis," *Rafu Shimpo*, December 1, 1935 (10401).

48 "Farm Crisis in Urgent Need of Rehabilitation by Capable Nisei Hands," *Rafu Shimpo*, November 12, 1935 (10383), 6.

49 Daniel, *Bitter Harvest*, 141–66; McWilliams, *Factories in the Field*, 211–29; Jamieson, *Labor Unionism*, 90–92; Daniels, *Asian America*, 17–158.

50 "Crisis Reached in Farm Labor Problem; See End as Concessions Offered," *Kashu Mainichi*, July 2, 1933 (570), 1. Other examples include "To Stabilize Farm Labor in South Land," *Kashu Mainichi*, February 8, 1934 (781); "Ranchers, Laborers Deadlock," *Kashu Mainichi*, June 10, 1933 (548); "Ranchers to Refuse Demands," *Kashu Mainichi*, June 14, 1933 (552); and "Gardeners Pledge to Stand Pat," *Kashu Maincihi*, June 15, 1933 (553).

51 "Editorial," *Kashu Mainichi*, August 13, 1933; "L.A. Strike Ends with Japanese Leaders and Mexican Union Workers," *Kashu Maincihi*, July 10, 1936; "Japanese Growers Spurn Mexican Strikers' Demand for Special Privileges," *Rafu Shimpo*, June 23, 1935 (9537).

52 Daniels, *Asian America*, 158–59.

53 "Man Hunt Follows Gun Play," *Kashu Mainichi*, October 5, 1933 (663).

54 The *Western Worker* was the Community Party paper in California. On the red-baiting of the Japanese Farm Laborers' Association, see Daniels, *Asian America*, 159.

55 "Lodi Japanese Involved in Grape Pickers' Strike; Frenzied Mobs in Lodi Streets," *Kashu Mainichi*, October 8, 1933 (666). Other examples include "Red Elements within Our Japanese Community," *Kashu Mainchi*, November 5, 1941 (3537); "Red Agitators Threaten Japanese Farms in Move to Force Wage Increase," *Rafu Shimpo*, January 13, 1935 (10083).

56 Red-baiting is apparent in *Rafu Shimpo*'s coverage of the 1936 celery strike. "Japanese Farm Workers Move to Join Mexicans to Boost Wage Claims," *Rafu Shimpo*, March 27, 1936 (10513), 6; "Growers Accuse Reds; Charge Workers Group with Fomenting Issue Not Existing on Farms," *Rafu Shimpo*, March 29, 1936 (10515); "Japanese Farm Laborers Not Expected to Join in Farm Strike Despite Move; Agitation Blamed on Minor Group Affiliated with Communist Organizations of Other Nationalities; Spokesman for Growers Accuses Radicals," *Rafu Shimpo*, March 31, 1936.

57 "One Hundred Niseis at Work to Break Strike near Venice," *Kashu Mainichi*, April 28, 1936 (1571), 1; "Venice Japanese Rescued by Nisei Volunteers: To Continue Celery Packing," *Kashu Mainichi*, April 29, 1936 (1572), 1; "To Call Upon Nisei for Aid," *Rafu Shimpo*, April 25, 1936 (10542); "Valley Nisei Preparing to Meet Strikes," *Rafu Shimpo*, May 6, 1936 (10553), 7; "Mobile Units of Workers Organized to Pick Crops as L.A. Strike Prolonged," *Rafu Shimpo*, May 12, 1936 (10559), 6.

58 "Venice Japanese Rescued by Nisei Volunteers: To Continue Celery Packing," *Kashu Mainichi*, April 29, 1936 (15720).

59 "Co-Operation Pledged Growers by JACL Heads as Strike Menace Rises," *Kashu Mainichi*, April 27, 1936 (1570); "Nisei Aid Venice Celery Growers Harvest Crop as Strike Loses Ground," *Rafu Shimpo*, April 28, 1936 (10545), 8. See also "Near Riot in Berry Strike Frustrated by Police; Nisei Students Quit School to Aid Pickers," *Rafu Shimpo*, June 7, 1933 (9516).

60 "'Red' on the Farm Front," editorial, *Rafu Shimpo*, December 13, 1936, 4.

61 "Editorial," *Kashu Mainichi*, August 13, 1933, n.p.

62 "'Red' on the Farm Front," editorial, *Rafu Shimpo*, December 13, 1936, 4. Also see "Farm Federation in Appeal to City Nisei Volunteers to Pick Bean Crop in Palos Verdes Labor Shortage/American Groups in Support of Japanese Growers Stand in Strike," *Rafu Shimpo*, May 7, 1936 (10554). The newspapers were incorrect in their assertions that there were no Reds among the Issei. See Ichioka, *Issei*, 91–145.

63 "Fear Racial War as Farm Labor Strike Spreads in Santa Maria Valley Area," *Rafu Shimpo*, November 22, 1934 (10037), 6. *Rafu Shimpo* quotes Mexican labor leader Velardes: "The prolonging of this strike is bringing about race hatred between Mexican and Japanese." "Labor Leader Presents His Case in Strike," *Rafu Shimpo*, May 24, 1936 (10571).

64 "Three Hundred Rioters in Effort to Force Japanese Ranchers to Meet Demands; Rages On," *Kashu Mainichi*, April 25, 1936 (1568).

65 "New Strike in San Diego Is Squelched," *Rafu Shimpo*, June 29, 1934 (9898), 6. Other headlines include "Man Hunt Follows Gun Play"; "Violence Flames in Oxnard Beet Strike at Laborers Riot"; and "Riots Rage in Compton District; Nipponese in Emergency Conference." Many articles connect the strikers with violence, such as "Violence Breaks Loose in Lettuce Strike Area"; "Violence Looms as Laborers Routed from Harvest Field"; "Two Growers Knifed by Farm Hand as Agitators Incite Sacramento Strike"; "Police Probe Explosions in Lettuce Shed"; and "Nisei Driver Victim of Gas Attack." Jamieson notes that the conflict between Japanese growers and a largely Mexican and Filipino labor force in the 1933 El Monte strike was characterized by less violence than strikes aimed at white growers. Jamieson, *Labor Unionism*, 91.

66 "Filipino Bandits Rob Nisei Couple, Threaten to Kill Baby Daughter," *Rafu Shimpo*, Monday, February 22, 1937 (10836), 6. "Mexican Gunman Wounds Nipponese Woman in Robbery," *Kashu Mainichi*, April 24, 1933 (501); "Three Nisei Robbed in Super Market Hold-Up by Negroes," *Kashu Mainichi*, December 18, 1939 (2867); "Lil' Tokio Raids Confessed; Two Mexicans Jailed," *Kashu Mainichi*, November 6, 1933; "Filipino Trio Arrested in Police Drive to Protect Lil' Tokio," *Rafu Shimpo*, April 1, 1940 (11945).

67 Some articles directly referred to a crime wave. "Crime Wave Hits Lil' Tokio Stores," *Kashu Mainchi*, October 12, 1933 (670); "Robbery Wave Hits Japanese Town," *Rafu Shimpo*, October 19, 1935 (10359), 6.

68 "Police Seek Mexican Pair in Attack-Murder of Girl as Uncle Denies Charges," *Rafu Shimpo*, March 10, 1937, 6.

69 "Youth Near Death, Confesses Shooting Niece in 'Accident'; Autopsy Shows No Attack Made on Girl," *Rafu Shimpo*, March 11, 1937 (10853), 8; "Nisei Girl Kidnapped Killed; Youth Wounded," *Kashu Mainichi*, March 10, 1937 (1877); "Youth Confesses to Kidnap, Murder," *Kashu Mainichi*, March 11, 1937.

70 This should be seen in the context of the criminalization of youth that culminated in the Sleepy Lagoon murder trial just five years later.

71 "Succumbing to Domination Seen as Fate of Farms," *Kashu Mainichi*, November 26, 1939 (2845).

72 Suzuki, "Introduction." Mary Sato Nakamura and Isami Nakamura, "Hiroshi Namakura," in *Treadmill*.

73 Hayashi points out that for every individual at Tule Lake from Manzanar who answered

"No" on the loyalty oath, four were simply accompanying their parents. B. Hayashi, *Democratizing*, 156.

74   B. Hayashi, *Democratizing*, 20–21.

75   In reading *Treadmill* in relation to Roosevelt's Four Freedoms, I place the novel alongside work by Carlos Bulosan, Américo Paredes, and C. L. R. James. See Salvidar, *Borderlands of Culture*, 217–18. Celebrating Japan in contrast to US imperialism is problematic given Japan's war crimes and imperial ambitions, as José Limón points out. Limón, "Border Literary Histories."

76   Nakamura, *Treadmill*, 217.

77   Berlant, *Queen of America Goes to Washington DC*, 18.

78   Glenn, *Unequal Freedom*, 53; Berlant, *Queen of America*, 18.

79   Nakamura, *Treadmill*, 162.

80   Ibid., 161.

81   Ibid., 165.

82   Ibid., 174.

83   Ibid.

84   I am influenced here by Chu's contention that the absence or transformation of the marriage plot in Asian American fiction reflects the inability of an author to demonstrate "the individual's reconciliation with the social order." Chu, *Assimilating Asians*, 18.

85   Nakamura, *Treadmill*, 173.

86   Here I draw on Traise Yamamoto's assertion that interracial romance in US popular culture often masks subordination through romantic love. T. Yamamoto, *Masking Selves* 38.

87   Hunt, *Inventing Human Rights*, 38–50; Armstrong, *Desire and Domestic Fiction*.

88   Szalay, *New Deal Modernism*, 162–83.

89   Chu, *Assimilating Asians*, 3. On the Asian American bildungsroman, also see Ho, *In Her Mother's House*.

90   Nakamura, *Treadmill*, 219–20.

91   Ibid., 219.

4. "THE EARTH TREMBLED FOR DAYS"

1   Thank you to Routledge for allowing me to reprint sections of S. Wald, "Hisaye Yamamoto."

2   Crow, "MELUS Interview," 75.

3   Cheung, "Interview with Hisaye Yamamoto," 76.

4   Crow, "MELUS Interview," 75–76.

5   Ibid., 75–76.

6   Yamamoto briefly departed the camp to work as a cook in Springfield, Massachusetts, before the end of internment. However, when her brother Johnny was killed in Italy fighting as part of the 442nd Regimental Combat Team, she returned to Poston to be with her parents.

7   Briones, "Hardly 'Small Talk,'" 437.

8   Cheung, "Interview with Hisaye Yamamoto," 81.

9   Cheung, "Introduction," ix.

10 The stories included in Foley's list include "The High-Heeled Shoes" (1948), "The Brown House" (1951), and "Epithalamium" (1960). Cheung, "Introduction," 3–7.

11 Cheung, "Interview with Hisaye Yamamoto," 81.

12 According to Stafford, their conversations led to Yamamoto's move to a Catholic Worker farm. Yone U. Stafford, "Pacifist Conference at Peter Maurin Farm," *Catholic Worker* 20, no. 3 (October 1953): 2.

13 Crow, "MELUS Interview," 77.

14 Ibid.

15 Ibid.

16 Cornell, Ellsberg, and Forest, *Penny a Copy*, 3.

17 Robert Ludlow, "Christian Anarchism," *Catholic Worker* (September 1949): 4–5; Hennacy, *Autobiography*. The term "Christian Anarchism" was first used in the paper in 1949, and Ludlow's frequent columns on anarchism over the next several months make clear that some objected to its use. Day called herself a personalist rather than an anarchist, and by the 1950s Ludlow himself was also using "personalist," bickering over anarchism with Hennacy in the paper's pages. Ruth Ann Heaney insisted that Maurin identified himself to her in private conversation as an anarchist but chose not to use the label publicly because "people weren't ready" for it. Ruth Ann Heaney, "Dear Tom" *Catholic Worker* 17, no. 2 (July–Aug. 1950): 7.

18 Cheung, "Interview with Hisaye Yamamoto," 85. Many Catholic Workers believed small communities could empower the individual who had been disempowered through social injustice. Klejment and Roberts, *American Catholic Pacifism*, 5.

19 Piehl, *Breaking Bread*, 23; Day and Sicius, *Peter Maurin*, xiii, xxvii.

20 Cheung, "Interview with Hisaye Yamamoto," 85.

21 Collinge, "Peter Maurin's Ideal," 386.

22 Maurin's "green revolution" should not be confused with the term's later and quite separate use to endorse the distribution of synthetic fertilizers, industrial pesticides, and hybrid seed.

23 Day and Sicius, *Peter Maurin*, 105.

24 Collinge, "Peter Maurin's Ideal," 386.

25 Maurin, *Easy Essays*, 27.

26 Piehl, *Breaking Bread*, 97.

27 Day and Sicius, *Peter Maurin*, 81.

28 Piehl, *Breaking Bread*, 129; Marlett, "Down on the Farm," 408.

29 Thomas Campbell, "New Beginnings on the Land," *Catholic Worker* 19, no. 19 (May 1953): 5; William Guachat, "Reflections on the Green Revolution: The First Twenty Years Are the Hardest," *Catholic Worker* 19, no. 19 (May 1953): 5; Jack Thorton and Mary Thorton, "Five Years on the Land," *Catholic Worker* 18, no. 18 (February 1953): 1, 5.

30 Campbell, "New Beginnings," 5.

31 Stafford, "Pacifist Conference," 2.

32 Dorothy Day, "Peter Maurin Farm," *Catholic Worker* 20, no. 11 (June 1954): 2.

33 Rollande Potvin, "Visit to the Peter Maurin Farm," *Catholic Worker* 20, no. 5 (December 1953): 3.

34 Hisaye Yamamoto, "Seabrook Farms," *Catholic Worker* 20, no. 11 (June 1954): 3, 6.

35 Cheung, "Interview with Hisaye Yamamoto," 81.

36 Dorothy Day, "Peter Maurin Farm," *Catholic Worker* 20, no. 9 (April 1954): 5.

37 Day, "Peter Maurin Farm," 5.

38 Hisaye Yamamoto, "Peter Maurin Farm," *Catholic Worker* 21, no . 5 (December 1954): 3.

39 Hisaye Yamamoto, "Peter Maurin Farm," *Catholic Worker* 21, no. 6 (January 1955): 3.

40 Hisaye Yamamoto, "Peter Maurin Farm," *Catholic Worker* 22, no. 1 (July–August 1955): 6.

41 Crow, "MELUS Interview," 78.

42 Marlett, "Down on the Farm," 411.

43 Guachat, "Reflections," 5.

44 Cheung, "Interview with Hisaye Yamamoto," 85.

45 Crow, "MELUS Interview," 78.

46 Cheung, "Hisaye Yamamoto and Wakako Yamauchi," 365.

47 Cheung, "Interview with Hisaye Yamamoto," 85.

48 S. C. Wong, *Reading Asian American Literature*, 13–14.

49 H. Yamamoto, "Seventeen Syllables," 23.

50 Ibid., 32.

51 Ibid., 33.

52 Ibid., 35.

53 For example, Elaine Kim explains, "In 'Yoneko's Earthquake' and 'Seventeen Syllables,' the husbands are hard-working and serious but unable to tolerate their wives' efforts to create beauty and poetry. They ultimately crush their wives and shackle them to a life of endless toil behind them, not necessarily because they are evil, but because they cannot tolerate independence of any kind in their wives." Kim, "Hisaye Yamamoto," 115.

54 H. Yamamoto, "Seventeen Syllables," 23.

55 H. Yamamoto, "Yoneko's Earthquake," 44.

56 Ibid., 54.

57 Ibid., 55.

58 H. Yamamoto, "Seventeen Syllables," 33.

59 Ibid.

60 Hong, "Something Forgotten," 291.

61 Crow, "Issei Father," 119–20.

62 Higashida, "Re-Signed Subjects," 37.

63 Ibid., 38.

64 Hong, "Something Forgotten," 292, 295–96.

65 My interest in the politics of Yamamoto's domestic settings emerges from my reading of literary criticism by scholars such as Amy Kaplan, Claudia Tate, and Lora Romero. These scholars led me to perceive the domestic setting as ideologically significant in the Cold War context of the stories' production and that the family farm holds particular significance as a space that comingles the domestic and the economic in a time period where hegemonic representations of family relied on the separation of the two spheres.

66 Corber, *Homosexuality*; D'Emilio, *Making Trouble,* 57–73; Friedman, "Sadists and Sissies," 201–27; D. Johnson, *Lavender Scare*; Kozol, *Life's America*; May, *Homeward Bound*.

67   Dudziak, *Cold War Civil Rights*.

68   Kim, "Hisaye Yamamoto"; Yogi, "Legacies Revealed"; Mistri, "Seventeen Syllables"; Yogi, "Rebels and Heroines," 131. Asian American women, in particular, were seen as capable of seductive betrayal in the early Cold War due to a combination of orientalism, imperialism, and guilt over internment. Bow, *Betrayal*.

69   For momism, see May, *Homeward Bound*, 64–65, 84, 102–3, 128–29; Friedman, "Sadists and Sissies"; and Terry, "Momism."

70   H. Yamamoto, "Seventeen Syllables," 23.

71   Ibid., 24.

72   Eng, *Racial Castration*, 210.

73   For the crisis of masculinity, see Corber, *Homosexuality*; Cuordileone, "Politics"; Ehrenreich, *Hearts of Men*; D. Johnson, *Lavender Scare*; May, *Homeward Bound*; Kimmel, *Manhood in America*; Spiegel, *Make Room for TV*.

74   H. Yamamoto, "Seventeen Syllables," 37.

75   Ibid., 36.

76   Ibid., 23.

77   H. Yamamoto, "Yoneko's Earthquake," 52.

78   Ibid., 53.

79   Cheung, *Articulate Silences*.

80   McClintock, "Future Heaven," 100.

81   H. Yamamoto, "Seventeen Syllables," 24.

82   Ibid.

83   Ibid.

84   The inappropriateness of these choices is clear from the depictions of interracial romance in Japanese American ethnic newspapers, as discussed in chapter 3 and in Yoo, *Growing Up Nisei*, 83–85.

85   H. Yamamoto, "Seventeen Syllables," 27.

86   Ibid., 28.

87   Ibid.

88   Ibid., 38.

89   Ibid., 52.

90   H. Yamamoto, "Yoneko's Earthquake," 47.

91   Ibid.

92   Ibid., 48.

93   Kozol, *Life's America*, 107.

94   H. Yamamoto, "Yoneko's Earthquake," 50. Yoneko complains that her father refuses to let her make fudge because of the waste of sugar and because he "stuck his finger up his nose and pretended he was going to rub some snot off onto the dolls. Things like that." Ibid.

95   Ibid., 47.

96   Hong, "Something Forgotten," 292.

97   Yogi is among the few scholars to discuss the connection between Marpo and Christianity. Yogi, "Legacies Revealed," 150–51.

98   H. Yamamoto, "Yoneko's Earthquake," 46.

99 Ibid.

100 Ibid.

101 Ibid.

102 Literary critic Charles L. Crow recognizes this in his assertion that the earthquake, in shattering Yoneko's house, shatters her family. Crow, "Home and Transcendence," 201.

103 H. Yamamoto, "Yoneko's Earthquake," 49.

104 Ibid., 52.

105 Ibid., 53.

106 Ibid., 47.

107 For example, Sau-ling Cynthia Wong explains, "A writer like Monica Sone, intent on re-habilitating her group in accordance with white standards, may try to identify the forced marches of internment with mainstream mobility myths." Warren D. Hoffman even feels the need to situate his article "Home, Memory, and Narrative in Monica Sone's *Nisei Daughter*" in opposition to the "many" critics that "have quickly discounted the text as overly simplistic, as autobiography that quite consciously panders to a white audience." S. C. Wong, *Reading Asian American Literature*, 138; W. Hoffman, "Home, Memory, and Narrative," 230.

108 Sone, *Nisei Daughter*, 19.

109 In *No No Boy*, the narrator explains, "As things turned out, it wasn't all right to be Japa-nese and American. You had to be one or the other." In *Fifth Chinese Daughter*, the nar-rator perceives that she cannot be both American and Chinese: "She was now conscious that 'foreign' American ways were not only generally and vaguely different from their Chinese ways, but that they were specifically different, and the specific differences would involve a choice of action." In the final pages of the story, she gains success with her pottery (exploiting the white community's exotified fascination with her), and evinces an identity capable of encompassing both traditions. Okada, *No No Boy*, 91; J. S. Wong, *Fifth Chinese Daughter*, 21.

110 Du Bois, *Souls of Black Folk*.

111 Sone, *Nisei Daughter*, 100.

112 Ibid., 104.

113 Ibid., 236.

114 Ibid., 237.

115 Ibid., 124.

116 Cott, *Public Vows*.

117 H. Yamamoto, "Life Among the Oil Fields," 94.

118 Ibid.

119 Ibid., 95.

120 Ibid.

121 The memoir even opens with a quote from *The Great Gatsby*: "They missed collisions by inches, wavered on the edge of precipices, and skidded across tracks to the sound of the warning bell." H. Yamamoto, "Life Among the Oil Fields," 86.

122 Ibid., 95.

123 H. Yamamoto, "Yoneko's Earthquake," 48.

124 R. Lee, *Orientals*.

125 Nguyen, *Race and Resistance*, vi.
126 S. C. Wong, *Reading Asian American Literature*, 121.
127 Ibid., 122.

5. "THE AMERICAN EARTH"

1   Bulosan, *America Is in the Heart*, 326.
2   Gonzalez, *Guest Workers*.
3   Ngai, *Impossible Subjects*, 139; M. Garcia, *World of Its Own*, 175.
4   Ngai, *Impossible Subjects*, 96–126; San Juan Jr., *U.S. Imperialism*.
5   Evangelista, *Carlos Bulosan*, 2.
6   Bulosan, *Sound of Falling Light*; Evangelista, *Carlos Bulosan*, 2–66; Evangelista, "Carlos Bulosan," 10–18; San Juan, Jr., *Philippine Temptation*, 131–36; McWilliams, "Introduction," vii–xxiv.
7   San Juan Jr., *Philippine Temptation*, 144.
8   Ngai, *Impossible Subjects*; San Juan Jr., *U.S. Imperialism*, 4.
9   Ngai, *Impossible Subjects*, 103.
10   Ibid., 113–15.
11   Crouchett, *Filipinos in California*, 37–40; Ngai, *Impossible Subjects*, 119–26.
12   Crouchett, *Filipinos in California*, 40–44; Fujita-Rony, *American Workers*, 169–99; Friday, *Organizing Asian American Labor*.
13   McWilliams, "Introduction," vii.
14   Bulosan, *America Is in the Heart*, 3.
15   Ibid., 7.
16   Ibid., 4.
17   Ibid.
18   Vials, *Realism for the Masses*, 113, 140–44.
19   This claim aligns with the assertion of E. San Juan Jr., "The project of *America Is in the Heart*, then, is a reinscription of this inaugural moment of colonial dispossession in the hegemonic culture by a text which violates all generic expectations and foreground the earth, the soil, and the maternal psyche/habitus as the grounds of meaning and identity." San Juan Jr., *Philippine Temptation*, 144.
20   Chu, *Assimilating Asians*, 43.
21   Koshy, *Sexual Naturalization*, 127.
22   Bulosan, *Cry and the Dedication*.
23   Aparicio and Chavez-Silverman, *Tropicalizations*.
24   Keith, *Unbecoming Americans*, 37.
25   Ibid., 61.
26   Ibid.
27   Bulosan, *America Is in the Heart*, 10.
28   Ibid., 52.
29   Ibid., 189.
30   Ibid., 326.

31 Ibarra and Torres, *Man of Fire*, xiii–xxiii.

32 London and Anderson, *So Shall Ye Reap*, 44–45, 54–55, 84, 115–40; Loza, "Alianza de Braceros"; Pitti, "Ernesto Galarza"; Pitti, *Devil in Silicon Valley*, 136–45.

33 London and Anderson, *So Shall Ye Reap*, 115.

34 Ibid.

35 Ibarra and Torres correct previous discussions of Galarza's degrees. Ibarra and Torres, *Man of Fire*, xv, xxii.

36 London and Anderson, *So Shall Ye Reap*, 117.

37 Ibid., 118–28; Street, "Poverty." For more on the DiGiorgio grape strike and its relation to braceros, see Galarza, *Spiders in the House*; London and Anderson, *So Shall Ye Reap*, 40–45; Mitchell, *They Saved the Crops*, 123–25, 127; and Valdés, *Organized Agriculture*, 169–202.

38 Galarza, *Burning Light*, 34.

39 For more about the Bracero Program, see Anderson, *Bracero Program*; Calavita, *Inside the State*; D. Cohen, *Braceros*; Gamboa, *Mexican Labor*; J. R. Garcia, *Operation Wetback*; M. Garcia, *World of Its Own*, 172–88; Herrera-Sobek, *Bracero Experience*; Loza, "Braceros on the Boundaries"; D. Mitchell, *They Saved the Crops*; Ngai, *Impossible Subjects*, 127–66; Rosas, *Abrazando el Espíritu*; Scruggs, *Braceros*.

40 Ngai, *Impossible Subjects*, 139; M. Garcia, *World of Its Own*, 175.

41 Galarza explains this logic: "Standards set up for foreign workers in particular could easily become standards in general." Galarza, *Merchants of Labor*, 44.

42 M. Garcia, *World of Its Own*, 185.

43 Historians affirm this assessment of the program. M. Garcia, *World of Its Own*, 172–88; Vargas, *Labor Rights*, 278–79.

44 Schmidt Camacho, *Migrant Imaginaries*; Pitti, *Devil in Silicon Valley*, 136–47; Pitti, "Ernesto Galarza."

45 Loza, "Alianza de Braceros."

46 García y Griego, "Importation of Mexican Contract Laborers," 55.

47 J. R. Garcia, *Operation Wetback*.

48 Loza, "Alianza de Braceros"; Pitti, "Ernesto Galarza."

49 Letter from Edw. P. Hayes to Robert C. Goodwin, director, Bureau of Employment Security, September 20, 1956, Stanford University Libraries, Galarza Papers, MO224, Box 2, Folder 8; letter from Serafino Romaloili to president of International Unions, October 10, 1956, Stanford University Libraries, Galarza Papers, MO224, Box 2, Folder 8.

50 "Mexican Bracero Labor Proves Boon to California Farmers," *Christian Science Monitor* 12 (September 1956): 11, ProQuest Historical Newspapers, Christian Science Monitor (1908–1997); "Mexican Worker Group Abused, Union Charges," *Los Angeles Times*, July 29, 1956, 6, ProQuest Historical Newspapers, Los Angeles Times (1881–1987); G. W. Sherman, "Still Trampling Out the Vintage," *Frontier*, May 1957, 18–20, Stanford University Libraries, Galarza Papers, MO224, Box 3, Folder 3; Joseph P. Lyford, "An Army of Ill-Will Ambassadors," *New Republic*, 18, Stanford University Libraries, Galarza Papers, MO224, Box 3, Folder 3; "Book Reviews," *Catholic Worker*, 5, Stanford University Libraries, Galarza Papers, MO224, Box 3, Folder 3.

51 Street, *Photographing Farmworkers*, 173–74.

52 G. W. Sherman, "Still Trampling Out the Vintage," *Frontier*; letter to from Geo A.

Graham, president of the California Farm Labor Association, to James P. Mitchell September 11, 1956, Stanford University Library, Galarza Files, MO224, Box 2, Folder 8; "A Report on Strangers in Our Fields," Stanford University Library, Galarza Files, MO224, Box 2, Folder 8.

53 "Strangers in Our Fields, a Progress Report," April 15, 1957, Stanford University Libraries, MO224, Box 3, Folder 4.

54 As Mireya Loza and Bill Johnson González pointed out to me, Galarza may have selected this name because of the popular character Pito Perez in José Rubén Romero's picaresque novel *La vida inútil de Pito Pérez* (1938) and Míguel Contreras Torres's 1943 film.

55 Galarza, *Merchants of Labor*, 16.

56 I doubt Galarza came up with the chapter titles. They seem to have been produced when James O'Gara shortened Galarza's text from 250 pages to 80 and rearranged the material. Letter from James O'Gara to Mr. Edward Reed, May 11, 1955; letter from Edward Reed to Ernesto Galarza, May 14, 1956, Stanford University Libraries, Galarza Papers, MO224, Box 2, Folder 8.

57 The description of the Nadel files available on the website of the National Museum of American suggests that the photographs in *Strangers in Our Fields* were taken by Nadel. This seems questionable, as *Strangers in Our Fields* was published in 1956, and by most accounts Nadel began photographing braceros in 1958. According to Richard Steven Street, Nadel was inspired to document braceros after he read Galarza's report. Street, *Photographing Farmworkers*, 173; "Guide to the Leonard Nadel Photographs and Scrapbooks," Archives Center, National Museum of American History, accessed October 2, 2014, http://amhistory.si.edu/archives/AC1313.html.

58 Galarza, *Strangers*, 52.

59 Ibid., 54.

60 Ibid., 75.

61 Ibid. Historians counter this image of the helpless bracero by emphasizing the strikes and cultural activities in which braceros participated. Gamboa, *Mexican Labor*; Loza, "Alianza de Braceros," 215–36.

62 Galarza, *Strangers*, 76.

63 Ibid., 80.

64 Ishay, *History of Human Rights*; Hunt, *Inventing Human Rights*.

65 Galarza, *Burning Light*, 17.

66 Galarza, *Spiders*, 79, 179.

67 Bulosan, *America Is in the Heart*, 206.

68 Ibid., 313.

6. "ELIXIRS OF DEATH"

1 Rome, *Genius of Earth Day*, x.

2 Ibid.

3 Ibid., 209.

4 Gordon, "Poisons in the Fields," 51.

5   Price, *Flight Maps*, 175–78; Rome, *Genius of Earth Day*, 39, 46.

6   Sommers, "Interpreting Tomás Rivera," 99.

7   Sandoval, "La Raza," 225.

8   Hammerback and Jensen, *Rhetorical Career*, 39.

9   Ibid., 40.

10   Ibid., 25.

11   Jensen and Hammerback, *Words of Cesar Chavez*, 24.

12   Griswold del Castillo and Garcia, *Cesar Chavez*, 102.

13   Matthiessen, *Sal Si Puedes*.

14   Jenkins, "Introduction," xii.

15   Ibid.

16   Ehrlich, *Population Bomb*.

17   Matthiessen, *Sal Si Puedes*, 28.

18   Ibid.

19   Seymour, *Strange Natures*, vii; Sturgeon, *Environmentalism*, 104.

20   Matthiessen, *Sal Si Puedes*, 214.

21   Ibid., 32.

22   Joni Mitchell, "Big Yellow Taxi," *Ladies of the Canyon*, Reprise, 1970.

23   Matthiessen, *Sal Si Puedes*, 33.

24   Carson, *Silent Spring*, 18.

25   Rome, *Genus of Earth Day*, 22–23.

26   Steinbeck, *Grapes of Wrath*, 234.

27   Matthiessen, *Sal Si Puedes*, 37, 38.

28   Ibid., 6, 8, 12, 23, 27, 28, 39, 42, 48, 149, 154, 169, 189, 219, 236, 289, 296, 307, 322.

29   Ibid., 12.

30   Ibid., 42, 157.

31   Ibid., 10.

32   Ibid., 208.

33   Rome, *Genius of Earth Day*, 43, 190.

34   Matthiessen, *Sal Si Puedes*, 173.

35   Ibid., 357.

36   Rosier, "'Modern America,'" 711–35.

37   Ibid., 713–14, 719–20.

38   Ibid., 724.

39   Stavans, "Foreword," xvi; Matthiessen, *Sal Si Puedes*, 6.

40   Matthiessen, *Sal Si Puedes*, 362.

41   Ibid., 9.

42   Chicano nationalism in the 1960s and 1970s celebrated a *mestizaje* identity that emphasized indigenous Aztec roots. *Indigenismo* was central to *movimento* politics. Men in the Chicano nationalist movement often looked to an Aztec past to develop powerful masculine identities in response to the emasculating quality of dominant racial tropes and the socioeconomic oppression that Mexican Americans experienced. Gutiérrez, "Community, Patriarchy, and Individualism," 45; Rosales, *Chicano*, 56; Ruíz, "Morena/o, blanca/o," 345–46.

43 Matthiessen, *Sal Si Puedes*, 258.

44 Ibid., 359.

45 Ibid., 323.

46 Ibid.

47 Jensen and Hammerback, *Words of Cesar Chavez*, 44–45.

48 Ibid., 22.

49 Ibid., 31.

50 Matthiessen, *Sal Si Puedes*, 324.

51 Broyles-González, *Teatro Campesino*, xii.

52 Valdez, *Actos*, 20–34.

53 Broyles-González has critiqued academic discussions of *Los Actos* for prioritizing the involvement of Valdez in the production of the plays at the expense of the anonymous others who were just as involved in the productions. Broyles-González, *Teatro Campesino*, 130.

54 Bagby, "El Teatro Campesino," 78.

55 Valdez, *Actos*, 27.

56 Ibid., 28.

57 The overturning of the social order is a common trope in El Teatro Campesino. Broyles-González, *El Teatro Campesino*, 31.

58 Pulido, *Environmentalism*, 89–90.

59 Carson, *Silent Spring*, 17–36.

60 Alaimo, *Bodily Natures*, 95; Nash, *Inescapable Ecologies*, 216. While I borrow the term "trans-corporeal" from Alaimo, it is important that she differentiates Carson's work from "material memoirs" such as the writing of Sandra Steingraber, as Carson's text works to create an objective persona that removes the personal and the author's body from the discussion.

61 May, *Homeward Bound*, 1, 16.

62 Russell, *War and Nature*, 222.

63 Carson, *Silent Spring*, 178.

64 Ibid., 229, 174.

65 Edward R. Murrow, "Harvest of Shame," *CBS Reports*, CBS, November 26, 1960.

66 Holmes, *Fresh Fruit*; D. Mitchell, *Lie of the Land*; S. Wald, "Visible Farmers/Invisible Workers," 567–86.

67 Pulido, *Environmentalism*, 83.

68 Ibid., 95

69 Ibid., 103.

70 Gordon, "Poisons in the Fields," 61.

71 Ibid., 62–63.

72 While the UFW occasionally referenced chemical companies as part of the larger problem, they focused their public rhetoric on the inadequacies of state and grower regulations.

73 Jensen and Hammerback, *Words of Cesar Chavez*, 31. In another example of the UFW's scare tactics for consumers, *El Malcriado* accompanied an article on the dangers DDT posed to nursing mothers and their babies with a photo of the young white mothers protesting the use of pesticides on grapes. *El Malcriado* 3, no. 9 (August 1969): 3.

74 Pulido, *Environmentalism*, 105.

75 Ibid., 107.

76 "Ecology Action Plan," Box 10, Folder 5, New York Boycott, United Farm Workers Collection, Walter P. Reuther Library, Wayne State University (hereafter referred to as UFW Collection).

77 Gordon, "Poisons in the Fields," 52.

78 Ibid., 53.

79 Jensen and Hammerback, *Words of Cesar Chavez*, 44.

80 "The Poisons We Eat," pamphlet, Box 10, Folder 36, New York City Boycott, UFW Collection.

81 "Poisons," *El Malcriado* 3, no. 7 (July 1–15th, 1969): 11, UFW Collection.

82 "Pesticides Poison Farm Children," Box 10, Folder 36, New York City Boycott, UFW Collection.

83 "Chavez Tells of Pesticide Toll," Box 10, Folder 39, New York City Boycott, UFW Collection.

84 "Pesticides Poison Farm Children," Box 10, Folder 36, New York City Boycott, UFW Collection.

85 "Tulare Children Show Pesticide Poisoning Signs," Box 10, Folder 36, New York City Boycott, UFW Collection.

86 "Poisons," *El Malcriado* 3, no. 7 (July 1–15th, 1969): 11, UFW Collection.

87 Di Chiro, "Nature as Community," 315.

88 Cover, *El Malcriado* 2, no. 34 (February 16, 1969), UFW Collection.

89 Valdez, *Actos*, 115.

90 "Gristedes Promotes Poverty," Box 10, Folder 3, New York Boycott Collection, UFW Collection.

91 Valdez, *Actos*, 127.

92 Ibid., 129.

93 Ibid.

94 Ibid., 116.

95 "Gristedes Promotes Poverty," Box 10, Folder 3, New York Boycott Collection, UFW Collection.

96 Pamphlet, Box 10, Folder 35, New York Boycott, UFW Collection.

97 "Pesticide Use Snag Contract, Says Grape Boycott Head," Box 10, Folder 14, New York Boycott, UFW Collection.

98 Memo from Jerry Cohen, Box 10, Folder 38, New York City Boycott, UFW Collection.

99 Flyer, Box 11, Folder 12, New York Boycott, UFW Collection.

100 Nash, *Inescapable Ecologies*, 14.

101 Pulido, *Environmentalism*, 113.

102 Ibid., 112.

103 Ibid., 112–13.

104 Beck, *World at Risk*, 29–38.

105 Alaimo, *Bodily Natures*, 61–63. See the factsheets, handwritten notes on clippings, and memos from Jerry Cohen, Box 10, Folders 35, 36, and 37, New York City Boycott, UFW Collection.

106 "Pesticide Jungle: The Growing Menace," *El Malcriado* 3, no. 6 (July 1969): 7. In his public letter to the growers, Chavez explains, "We have recently become more aware of the prob-

lem [pesticides] through an increasing number of cases coming into our clinic." Letter from Cesar Chavez to Mike Bozick (January 14, 1969), Box 10, Folder 37, New York City Boycott, UFW Collection.

107 Pulido, *Environmentalism*, 116.

108 Harrison, *Pesticide Drift*.

109 Belasco, *Appetite for Change*, x.

110 Biltekoff, *Eating Right*, 82.

7. FIT CITIZENS AND POISONED FARMWORKERS

1   Allen, *Together at the Table*, 1.

2   Ibid.

3   Allen offers an excellent discussion of alternative food movement ideologies in the 1990s that help explain the visibility of the alternative food movement's ideological rifts in the twenty-first century. See Allen, *All at the Table*, 115–42.

4   Thanks to *Food, Culture, and Society* for allowing me to reprint portions of S. Wald, "Visible Farmers/Invisible Workers" in this chapter.

5   Berry, "Whole Horse"; Jackson, "Farming in Nature's Image"; Pollan, *Omnivore's Dilemma*, 123–29. See also Allen, *Together at the Table*, 137.

6   Pollan, *Omnivore's Dilemma*; Andrew Jenner, "How America's Most Famous Farmer Can Appeal to Left, Right, and Center," *Washington Post*, March 31, 2015, accessed May 25, 2015, https://www.washingtonpost.com/lifestyle/food/how-americas-most-famous -farmer-can-appeal-to-left-right-and-center/2015/03/31/77551480-d272-11e4-a62f -ee745911a4ff_story.html; Bryan Walsh, "This Land Is Your Land: Joel Salatin Wants to Lead America Back to the Farm," *Time*, October 24, 2011, accessed June 1, 2015, http:// content.time.com/time/magazine/article/0,9171,2096846,00.html; *Fresh*, directed by Ania Sofia Joanes (Ripple Effect Films, 2009), DVD; *Food, Inc.*, directed by Robert Kenner (Magnolia Pictures, 2008) , DVD.

7   Fiskio, "Unsettling Ecocriticism"; S. Wald, "Visible Farmers/Invisible Workers."

8   Pollan, *Omnivore's Dilemma*, 9.

9   Ibid., 231.

10   Ibid., 332.

11   Ibid., 166, 167.

12   Gray, *Labor and the Locavore*.

13   Allen, *Together at the Table*, 173.

14   Guthman, *Agrarian Dreams*, 174.

15   Schlosser, *Fast Food Nation*; *Food Chains*, directed by Sanjay Rawal (2015), DVD.

16   Mark Bittman, "Can We Finally Treat Food Workers Fairly?" *New York Times*, May 27, 2015, accessed May 28, 2015, http://www.nytimes.com/2015/05/27/opinion/can-we-finally -treat-food-workers-fairly.html?_r=0; Mark Bittman, "Homepage," MarkBittman.Com, accessed May 28, 2015, http://markbittman.com/.

17   "Food Chain Workers Alliance," Food Chain Workers Alliance, accessed May 28, 2015 http://foodchainworkers.org/ 2015.

18   S. Wald, "Visible Farmers/Invisible Workers."

19 Schlosser, *Fast Food Nation*, 270.

20 *Food, Inc.*, DVD.

21 Glickman, *Buying Power*, 61–114.

22 Deutsch, *Building a Housewife's Paradise*, 106–7; Weems, "African American Consumer Boycotts"; Glickman, *Buying Power*, 164–74.

23 "#BlackOut BlackFriday," accessed May 25, 2015, http://blackoutfriday.org/.

24 Glickman, *Buying Power*, 26.

25 Ibid., 126

26 Ibid., 179.

27 Ibid., 159.

28 Glickman, *Buying Power*, 178; L. Cohen, *Consumers' Republic*, 7.

29 Glickman, *Buying Power*, 160, 178–79.

30 Ibid., 190.

31 "About Us," Real Food Challenge, accessed May 25, 2015, http://www.realfoodchallenge .org/about-real-food-challenge.

32 "Campaign for Fair Food," Coalition of Immokalee Workers, accessed May 30, 2015, http://ciw-online.org/campaign-for-fair-food/; Estabrook, *Tomatoland*, 97–138.

33 "About Us," Slow Food USA, accessed May 31, 2015, https://www.slowfoodusa.org/about -us.

34 "Values Matters," Whole Foods Market, accessed May 31, 2015, http://www.whole foodsmarket.com/valuesmatter.

35 "Food with Integrity," Chipotle, accessed May 31, 2015, https://chipotle.com/food-with -integrity.

36 Glickman, *Buying Power*, 251.

37 Ibid., 250–51.

38 Biltekoff, *Eating Right*, 86–88.

39 On the problems with proclaiming an obesity epidemic, see Guthman, *Weighing In*, 24–45.

40 Alexandra Le Tellier, "Can Jamie Oliver's Food Revolution Solve Our Obesity Epidemic?" *Los Angeles Times*, May 21, 2012, accessed May 25, 2015, http://articles.latimes.com/2012 /may/21/news/la-ol-jamie-oliver-food-revolution-day-20120521.

41 Jones, *Green Collar Economy*, 53.

42 Biltekoff, *Eating Right*, 100–101.

43 Gottlieb and Joshi, *Food Justice*, 39–48.

44 Pollan, *Cooked*, 1–23.

45 Bowen, Elliott, and Brenton, "The Joy of Cooking?"

46 Biltekoff, *Eating Right*, 7

47 Ibid., 35

48 Ibid., 44.

49 Guthman, *Weighing In*, 46–65; Biltekoff, *Eating Right*, 125–30. On Neoliberalism, see Harvey, *A Brief History of Neoliberalism*.

50 Guthman, *Weighing In*, 55.

51 Biltekoff, *Eating Right*, 92–93, 125–29.

52 This resonates with Sarah Jaquette Ray's distinction between good ecological subjects and ecological others. Ray, *Ecological Others*, 2.

53 Biltekoff, *Eating Right*, 119.

54 Le Tellier, "Jamie Oliver's Food Revolution."

55 Biltekoff, *Eating Right*, 130.

56 *Fed Up*, directed by Stephanie Soechtig (2014), DVD.

57 Wendell Berry, "A Citizen's Response to the National Security Strategy," *Orion*, accessed June 17, 2017, https://orionmagazine.org/article/a-citizens-response-to-the-national -security-strategy/.

58 Michael Pollan, "Farmer-in-Chief," *New York Times Magazine*, October 12, 2008, accessed May 25, 2015, http://michaelpollan.com/articles-archive/farmer-in-chief/.

59 Ibid.

60 Glickman, *Buying Power*, 178.

61 Pollan, *Cooked*, 1–2.

62 Holmes, *Fresh Fruit*, 89.

63 Ibid., 156.

64 Ibid.

65 "$3 Million Study Aims to Boost Health of Immigrant Latino Farmworkers," News and Information, University of California Davis, May 12, 2014, accessed June 10, 2015, news. ucdavis.edu/search/news_detail.lasso?id=10920.

66 Moya, *Learning from Experience*, 202–9.

67 Viramontes, *Under the Feet of Jesus*, 49–50.

68 D. Mitchell, *Lie of the Land*, 1–2.

69 Viramontes, *Under the Feet of Jesus*, 53.

70 Ibid.

71 Historically "pastoral" refers to a type of poetry about shepherds conveying an escape or a retreat from urban life and often operating as a critique of city life. As Terry Gifford contends in *Pastoral*, the term is often used more broadly today, referring to any text focused on the country as a contrast to or critique of city life. For a more nuanced discussion of the term, see Gifford, *Pastoral*.

72 Pollan, *Omnivore's Dilemma*, 45, 83, 98, 113, 188.

73 Rothenberg, *With These Hands*, 6; Hansen and Donohoe, "Health Issues," 156.

74 Mobed et al., "Occupational Health Problems," 367; Hansen and Donohoe, "Health Issues," 155, 159.

EPILOGUE

1   Viramontes, *Under the Feet of Jesus*, 63.

2   I draw the term "denizenship" from Rachel Buff. Buff defines denizenship as "the ways in which inhabiting a place, as much as the officially defined boundaries of that place, lead people to make claims on that place." She extends this sense of denizenship to include what she calls "diasporan denizenship": "where im/migrants stake a claim to their homelands abroad and to their rights in the countries where, perforce, they live and work." Denizenship recognizes migrants' multiplicity of social ties and allegiances. Buff, *Immigration*, 4, 117, 173.

3   Viramontes, *Under the Feet of Jesus*, 148.

4   Park and Pellow, *Slums of Aspen*, 3–4.

5   LeMenager, *Living Oil*; Schneider-Mayerson, "Necrocracy in America."

6   Tuana, "Viscous Porosity"; Alaimo, "Trans-corporeal Feminisms," 238.

7   Tuana, "Viscous Porosity," 200–201.

8   Barad, *Meeting the Universe Halfway*.

9   This understanding of political belonging aligns with what Alicia Schmidt Camacho has called "migrant imaginaries." Schmidt Camacho, *Migrant Imaginaries*, 9.

10 Haraway, *Companion Species Manifesto*.

11 Eyder Peralta, "The Undocubus: In Charlotte, a Different Kind of Coming Out," *NPR*, September 3, 2012, http://www.npr.org/sections/itsallpolitics/2012/09/03/160508224/the -undocumented-bus-in-charlotte-a-different-kind-of-coming-out; "Undocubus," Tumblr, accessed September 10, 2013, http://www.tumblr.com/tagged/undocubus; Griselda Nevarez, "The Undocubus: Dream Activists Arrive in Charlotte to Make Their Voices Heard at the Democratic National Convention," VOXXI, *Huffington Post*, September 3, 2012, accessed October 22, 2014, http://www.huffingtonpost.com/2012/09/03/undocubus -dream-activists-democractic-convention_n_1852019.html; Latino Rebels, "10 Arrested at No Papers No Fears Protest at Democratic National Convention," *Latino Rebels*, September 4, 2012, accessed October 22, 2014, http://www.latinorebels.com/2012/09/04/ ten-arrested-at-no-papers-no-fear-protest-at-democratic-national-convention/.

12 No Papers, No Fear, "The Meaning of the Mariposa (Butterfly): A Symbol for All," No Papers, No Fear: Ride for Justice, September 20, 2012, accessed October 22, 2014, nopapersnofear .org/blog/post.php?s=2012-09-20-the-meaning-of-the-mariposa-butterfly-a-symbol -for-all; Voice of Art—Migration Is Beautiful, I AM OTHER network, YouTube, accessed October 22, 2014, https://www.youtube.com/watch?v=LWE2T8Bx5d8.

13 Samantha Leal, "Artist & Activist Favianna Rodriguez Talks Immigration, Rosario Dawson and Her New Web Series Episode," *Latina*, January 18, 2013, accessed September 15, 2013, http://www.latina.com/entertainment/artist-activist-favianna-rodriguez-talks- immigration-migrant-issues-documentary.

14 Favianna Rodriguez, "Migration Is Natural: Butterfly Stickers," Favianna.com, accessed September 10, 2013, http://favianna.flyingcart.com/?p=detail&pid=147&cat_id= Web.

15 "Migration Is Natural," Favianna Rodriguez, offset poster, 2013.

16 Scott Gold, "The Artist behind the Infamous 'Running Immigrants' Image," *Los Angeles Times*, April 4, 2008, accessed June 13, 2015, http://www.latimes.com/local/la-me -outthere4apr04-story.html.

17 "Migration Is Natural 4 x 4 Vinyl Stickers," accessed October 22, 2014, favianarodriguez .com.

18 Fleishman and Murphy, "Realistic Assessment."

19 This paragraph results from a conversation with Mireya Loza on differences between butterflies and braceros.

20 Schappert, *Last Monarch*, 6.

21 Ibid., 17–18.

22 Ibid., 81.

23 Monarch Watch, accessed September 5, 2013, www.monarchwatch.org.

24 Sturgeon, *Environmentalism*, 25.

25 Ibid., 20.

26 "Queer Butterfly," Julio Salgado, accessed September 11, 2015, http://juliosalgadoart
    .bigcartel.com/product/queer-butterfly.

27 Costanza-Chock, *Out of the Shadows*, 135–36.

28 This analysis draws from Mortimer-Sandilands and Erickson, *Queer Ecologies*, 1–51.

29 Schappert, *Last Monarch*, 55–72.

30 For eco-cosmopolitanism, see Heise, *Sense of Place*, 10.

31 No Papers, No Fear, "The Meaning of the Mariposa."

32 Loosey, Rayor, and Carter, "Transgenic Pollen." Biologists continue to debate the impact
    of Bt corn on monarch populations. Phil Schappert states that subsequent studies show
    that Bt corn would have a negligent impact on monarch butterflies, while Michelle So-
    lensky and Karen Oberhauser's edited collection suggests the possibility of continued
    risk. Schappert, *Last Monarch*, 69; Solensky and Oberhauser, *Monarch Butterfly*, 69–75.

33 Fitting, *Struggle for Maize*, 1.

34 Ibid., 4.

35 M. Sophia Newman, "Catastrophe and Optimism: South Asia at the UN Climate
    Summit," *Diplomat*, September 30, 2014, accessed April 27, 2015, http://thediplomat
    .com/2014/09/catastrophe-and-optimism-south-asia-at-the-un-climate-summit/;
    "South Asians Demand Climate Justice at People's Climate March in New York," Asian
    Americans for Civil Rights and Equality, accessed April 27, 2015, http://aacre.org/south
    -asians-demand-climate-justice-peoples-climate-march-new-york/; Amy Goodman and
    Aaron Maté, "Voices from the People's Climate March: Indigenous Groups Lead Historic
    400,000-Strong NYC Protest," *Democracy Now*, September 22, 2014, accessed April 27,
    2015, http://www.democracynow.org/2014/9/22/voices_from_the_peoples_climate
    _march.

36 Carolyn Kormann, "The Three Hundred Thousand," *New Yorker*, September 25, 2014,
    accessed October 22, 2014, http://www.newyorker.com/tech/elements/three-hundred
    -thousand-climate-march.

37 Kormann, "Three Hundred Thousand."

38 Ben Pomeroy, "Art and Warning and Protest at the People's Climate March," *Hyperal-
    lergic*, September 21, 2014, accessed April 27, 2015, http://hyperallergic.com/150491/art
    -as-warning-and-protest-at-the-peoples-climate-march/.

Bibliography

Adamson, Joni. *American Indian Literature, Environmental Justice, and Ecocriticism: The Middle Place*. Tucson: University of Arizona Press, 2000.

Adamson, Joni, Mei Mei Evans, and Rachel Stein, eds. *The Environmental Justice Reader: Politics, Poetics, and Pedagogy*. Tucson: University of Arizona Press, 2002.

Adamson, Joni, and Scott Slovic. "Guest Editors' Introduction: The Shoulders We Stand On: An Introduction to Ethnicity and Ecocriticism." *MELUS* 34, no. 2 (2009): 5–24.

Alaimo, Stacy. *Bodily Natures: Science, Environment, and the Material Self*. Bloomington: University of Indiana, 2010.

———. "Trans-corporeal Feminisms and the Ethical Space of Nature." In *Material Feminisms*, edited by Stacy Alaimo and Susan Hekman, 237–63. Bloomington: Indiana University Press, 2008.

———. *Undomesticated Ground: Recasting Nature as Feminist Space*. Ithaca: Cornell University Press, 2000.

Allen, Patricia. *Together at the Table: Sustainability and Sustenance in the American Agrifood System*. University Park: Pennsylvania State University Press, 2004.

Allmendinger, Blake. *Imagining the African American West*. Lincoln: University of Nebraska Press, 2005.

Almaguer, Tomás. *Racial Fault Lines: The Historical Origins of White Supremacy in California*. Berkeley: University of California Press, 2009.

Almanzar, Nelson A. Pichardo, and Brian W. Kulik. *American Fascism and the New Deal: The Associated Farmers of California and the Pro-Industrial Movement*. Lanham, MD: Lexington Books, 2013.

Anderson, Henry P. *The Bracero Program in California*. New York: Arno Press, 1976.

Aparicio, Frances R., and Susana Chavez-Silverman. *Tropicalizations: Transcultural Representations of Latinidad*. Hanover, NH: University Press of New England, 1997.

Arax, Mark. "A Lost Tribe's Journey to a Land of Broken Promises." *Los Angeles Times*, August 25, 2002.

Armbruster, Karla, and Kathleen R. Wallace. *Beyond Nature Writing: Expanding the Boundaries of Ecocriticism*. Charlottesville: University of Virginia Press, 2001.

Armstrong, Nancy. *Desire and Domestic Fiction*. New York: Oxford University Press, 1987.

Arnold, Jean, Lawrence Buell, Michael P. Cohen, Terrell Dixon, Elizabeth Dodd, Simon C.

Estok, Ursula K. Heise, Jonathan Levin, Patrick D. Murphy, Andrea Parra, William Slay-maker, Scott Slovic, Timothy Sweet, and Louise Westling. "Forum on Literatures of the Environment." *PMLA* 114, no. 5 (October 1999): 1089–104.

Azuma, Eiichiro. *Between Two Empires: Race, History, and Transnationalism in Japanese America*. New York: Oxford University Press, 2005.

Babb, Sanora. *Whose Names Are Unknown*. Norman: University of Oklahoma Press, 2004.

Bagby, Beth. "El Teatro Campesino: Interviews with Luis Valdez." *Tulane Drama Review* 11, no. 4 (1967): 70–80.

Bacon, David. *Illegal People: How Globalization Creates Migration and Criminalizes Immigrants*. Boston: Beacon Press, 2008.

Balderrama, Franscico E., and Raymond Rodriguez. *Decade of Betrayal: Mexican Repatriation in the 1930s*. Albuquerque: University of New Mexico Press, 1995.

Barad, Karen. *Meeting the Universe Halfway: Quantum Physics and the Entanglement of Matter and Meaning*. Durham, NC: Duke University Press, 2007.

Bardacke, Frank. *Trampling Out the Vintage: Cesar Chavez and the Two Souls of the United Farm Workers*. New York: Verso, 2012.

Battat, Erin Royston. *Ain't Got No Home: America's Great Migrations and the Making of an Interracial Left*. Chapel Hill: University of North Carolina Press, 2014.

———. "Okie Outlaws and Dust Bowl Fugitives: Steinbeck's *The Grapes of Wrath* and Discourses of Ethnicity and Race." In *The Grapes of Wrath: A Reconsideration*, vol. 2, edited by Michael J. Meyer, 453–80. New York: Rodopi, 2009.

Beck, Ulrich. *World at Risk*. Translated by Ciaran Cronin. Malden, MA: Polity Press, 2009.

Bederman, Gail. *Manliness and Civilization: A Cultural History of Gender and Race in the United States, 1880–1917*. Chicago: University of Chicago Press, 1996.

Beegel, Susan F., Susan Shillinglaw, and Wesley N. Tiffney, Jr., eds. *Steinbeck and the Environment: Interdisciplinary Approaches*. Tuscaloosa: University of Alabama Press, 1997.

Belasco, Warren. *Appetite for Change: How the Counterculture Took on the Food Industry*. Ithaca: Cornell University Press, 2006.

Bennett, Michael, and David Teague. *The Nature of Cities: Ecocriticism and Urban Environments*. Tucson: University of Arizona Press, 1999.

Benson, Jackson. *The True Adventures of John Steinbeck, Writer*. New York: Viking, 1984.

Benson, Jackson, and Anne Loftis. "John Steinbeck and Farm Labor Unionization: The Background of *In Dubious Battle*." *American Literature* 52 (1980): 194–223.

Berlant, Lauren. *The Queen of America Goes to Washington City: Essays on Sex and Citizenship*. Durham, NC: Duke University Press, 1997.

Berry, Wendell. "The Whole Horse: The Preservation of the Agrarian Mind." In *The Fatal Harvest Reader: The Tragedy of Industrial Agriculture*, edited by Andrew Kimbrell, 39–48. Washington, DC: Island Press, 2002.

Biltekoff, Charlotte. *Eating Right in America: The Cultural Politics of Food and Health*. Durham, NC: Duke University Press, 2013.

Bonus, Rick. *Locating Filipino Americans: Ethnicity and the Cultural Politics of Space*. Philadelphia: Temple University Press, 2000.

Bosniak, Linda. *The Citizen and the Alien: Dilemmas of Contemporary Membership*. Princeton, NJ: Princeton University Press, 2006.

Bow, Leslie. *Betrayal and Other Acts of Subversion: Feminism, Sexual Politics, Asian American Women's Literature*. Princeton, NJ: Princeton University Press, 2001.

Bowen, Sarah, Sinikka Elliott, and Joslyn Brenton. "The Joy of Cooking?" *Contexts* 13, no. 3 (2014): 20–25.

Boyle, T. C. *The Tortilla Curtain*. New York: Penguin, 1996.

Briones, Matthew M. "Hardly 'Small Talk': Discussing Race in the Writing of Hisaye Yamamoto." *Prospects* 29 (2005): 435–71.

Brodkin, Karen. *How Jews Became White Folks and What That Says about Race in America*. New Brunswick, NJ: Rutgers University Press, 1998.

Broussard, Albert S. *Black San Francisco: The Struggle for Racial Equality in the West, 1900–1954*. Lawrence: University Press of Kansas, 1993.

Brown, Kathleen M. *Good Wives, Nasty Wenches, and Anxious Patriarchs: Gender, Race, and Power in Colonial Virginia*. Chapel Hill: University of North Carolina Press, 1996.

Brown, Sandy, and Christy Getz. "Farmworker Food Insecurity and the Production of Hunger in California." In *Cultivating Food Justice: Race, Class, and Sustainability*, edited by Alison Hope Alkon and Julian Agyeman, 121–46. Cambridge, MA: MIT Press, 2011.

Broyles-González, Yolanda. *El Teatro Campesino: Theater in the Chicano Movement*. Austin: University of Texas Press, 1994.

Buell, Lawrence. *The Future of Ecocriticism: Environmental Crisis and Literary Imagination*. Oxford: Blackwell, 2005.

Buff, Rachel. *Immigration and the Political Economy of Home: West Indian Brooklyn and American Indian Minneapolis, 1945–1992*. Berkeley: University of California Press, 2001.

Bullard, Robert. "Environmental Justice in the Twenty-First Century." In *The Quest for Environmental Justice: Human Rights and the Politics of Pollution*, edited by Robert Bullard, 19–42. San Francisco: Sierra Club Books, 2005.

Bulosan, Carlos. *America Is in the Heart: A Personal History*. Seattle: University of Washington Press, 1991.

———. *The Cry and the Dedication*. Philadelphia: Temple University Press, 1995.

———. *Sound of Falling Light: Letters in Exile*. Edited by Dolores S. Feria. Quezon City: University of the Philippines Press, 1960.

Calavita, Kitty. *Inside the State: The Bracero Program, Immigration, and the I.N.S.* New York: Routledge, 1992.

Caminero-Santangelo, Byron. *Different Shades of Green: African Literature, Environmental Justice, and Political Ecology*. Charlottesville: University of Virginia Press, 2014.

Canelo, Maria José. "Carey McWilliams and the Question of Cultural Citizenship in the 1940s." PhD diss., New York University, 2003.

Carson, Rachel. *Silent Spring*. New York: Houghton Mifflin Harcourt, 1994.

Chan, Sucheng. *This Bittersweet Soil: The Chinese in California Agriculture, 1860–1910*. Berkeley: University of California Press, 1986.

Cheung, King-Kok. *Articulate Silences: Hisaye Yamamoto, Maxine Hong Kingston, Joy Kogawa*. Ithaca: Cornell University Press, 1993.

———. "Hisaye Yamamoto and Wakako Yamauchi." In *Words Matter: Conversations with Asian American Writers*, edited by King-Kok Cheung, 343–82. Honolulu: University of Hawai'i Press, 2000.

———. "Interview with Hisaye Yamamoto." In *"Seventeen Syllables": Hisaye Yamamoto*, edited by King-Kok Cheung, 71–88. New Brunswick, NJ: Rutgers University Press, 1994.

———. Introduction to *"Seventeen Syllables": Hisaye Yamamoto*, edited King-Kok Cheung, 3–7. New Brunswick, NJ: Rutgers University Press, 1994.

———. Introduction to *"Seventeen Syllables" and Other Stories*, by Hisaye Yamamoto, xi–xxc. Latham: Kitchen Table, 1988.

Chiang, Connie Y. "Imprisoned Nature: Toward an Environmental History of the World War II Japanese American Incarceration." *Environmental History* 15 (April 2010): 236–67.

Chu, Patricia. *Assimilating Asians: Gendered Strategies of Authorship in Asian America.* Durham, NC: Duke University Press, 2000.

Coates, Peter. *American Perceptions of Immigrant and Invasive Species: Strangers on the Land.* Berkeley: University of California Press, 2006.

Cohen, Deborah. *Braceros: Migrant Citizens and Transnational Subjects in Postwar United States and Mexico.* Chapel Hill: University of North Carolina Press, 2013.

Cohen, Lizabeth. *A Consumers' Republic: The Politics of Mass Consumption in Postwar America.* New York: Knopf, 2003.

Collinge, William J. "Peter Maurin's Ideal of Farming Communes." In *Dorothy Day and the Catholic Worker Movement: Centenary Essays*, edited by William J. Thorn, Philip M. Runkel, and Susan Mourtin, 385–99. Milwaukee, WI: Marquette University Press, 2001.

Conlogue, William. *Working the Garden: American Writers and the Industrialization of Agriculture.* Chapel Hill: University of North Carolina Press, 2001.

Consumers League of New York. *The Joads in New York.* New York: Consumers League, 1945.

Coontz, Stephanie. *The Way We Never Were; American Families and the Nostalgia Trap.* New York: Basic, 1992.

Corber, Robert J. *Homosexuality in Cold War America: Resistance and the Crisis of Masculinity.* Durham, NC: Duke University Press, 1997.

Corman, Catherine A. "Teaching—and Learning from—Carey McWilliams." *California History* 80 (2001–2): 204–24.

Cornell, Thomas C., Robert Ellsberg, and Jim Forest, eds. *A Penny a Copy: Readings from The Catholic Worker.* Maryknoll, NY: Orbis Books, 1995.

Costanza-Chock, Sasha. *Out of the Shadows, into the Streets! Transmedia Organizing and the Immigrant Rights Movement.* Boston: MIT Press, 2014.

Cott, Nancy. *Public Vows: A History of Marriage and the Nation.* Cambridge, MA: Harvard University Press, 2000.

Creef, Elena Tajima. *Imagining Japanese America: The Visual Construction of Citizenship, Nation, and Body.* New York: New York University Press, 2004.

Crévecoeur, J. Hector St. John D. *Letters from an American Farmer.* New York: Oxford University Press, 1997.

Critser, Greg. "The Making of a Cultural Rebel: Carey McWilliams, 1924–1930." *Pacific Historical Review* 55 (1986): 226–55.

———. "The Political Rebellion of Carey McWilliams." *UCLA Historical Journal* 4 (1983): 34–65.

Cronon, William. *Changes in the Land: Indians, Colonists, and the Ecology of New England.* New York: Hill and Wang, 1983.

———. "The Trouble with Wilderness." In *Uncommon Ground: Rethinking the Human Place in Nature*, edited by William Cronon, 69–90. New York: Norton, 1995.

Crouchett, Lorraine Jacobs. *Filipinos in California: From the Days of the Galleons to the Present*. El Cerrito, CA: Downey, 1988.

Crow, Charles L. "Home and Transcendence in Los Angeles Fiction." In *Los Angeles in Fiction*, edited by David Fine, 189–205. Albuquerque: University of New Mexico Press, 1984.

———. "The Issei Father in the Fiction of Hisaye Yamamoto." In *"Seventeen Syllables": Hisaye Yamamoto*, edited by King-Kok Cheung, 119–28. New Brunswick, NJ: Rutgers University Press, 1994.

———. "A MELUS Interview: Hisaye Yamamoto." *MELUS* 14.1 (1987): 73–84.

Cunningham, Charles. "Rethinking the Politics of *The Grapes of Wrath*." *Cultural Logic: An Electronic Journal of Marxist Theory and Practice* 2 (2002), http://clogic.eserver.org/2002/cunningham.html.

Cuordileone, K. A. "Politics in the Age of Anxiety: Cold War Political Culture and the Crisis in American Masculinity, 1949–1960." *Journal of American History* 87 (2000): 515–45.

Daniel, Cletus E. *Bitter Harvest: A History of California Farmworkers, 1870–1941*. Ithaca, NY: Cornell University Press, 1981.

Daniels, Roger. *Asian America: Chinese and Japanese in the United States since 1850*. Seattle: University of Washington Press, 1988.

———. *The Politics of Prejudice: The Anti-Japanese Movement in California and the Struggle for Japanese Exclusion*. Berkeley: University of California Press, 1962.

Davis, Mike. "Optimism of the Will." *Nation*, September 19, 2005, 25–27.

Day, Dorothy, and Francis J. Sicius. *Peter Maurin: Apostle to the World*. Maryknoll, NY: Orbis Books, 2004.

De Graf, Lawrence B., Kevin Mulroy, and Quintard Taylor, eds. *Seeking El Dorado: African Americans in California*. Seattle: University of Washington Press, 2001.

Deloria, Philip J. *Playing Indian*. New Haven, CT: Yale University Press, 1998.

DeLoughrey, Elizabeth, and George B. Handley, eds. *Postcolonial Ecologies: Literature of the Environment*. Oxford: Oxford University Press, 2011.

D'Emilio, John. *Making Trouble: Essays on Gay History, Politics, and the University*. New York: Routledge, 1992.

Deming, Alison Hawthorne, and Lauret E. Savoy, eds. *The Colors of Nature: Culture, Identity, and the Natural World*. Minneapolis: Milkweed, 2002.

Denning, Michael. *The Cultural Front: The Laboring of American Culture in the Twentieth Century*. New York: Verso, 1997.

Deutsch, Tracey. *Building a Housewife's Paradise: Gender, Politics, and American Grocery Stores in the Twentieth Century*. Chapel Hill: University of North Carolina Press, 2010.

Di Chiro, Giovanna. "Nature as Community: The Convergence of Environment and Social Justice." In *Uncommon Ground: Rethinking the Human Place in Nature*, edited by William Cronon, 298–320. New York: Norton, 1996.

Ditsky, John. "The Ending of *The Grapes of Wrath*: A Further Commentary." In *Critical Essays on Steinbeck's "The Grapes of Wrath*,*" edited by John Ditsky, 116–24. Boston: Hall, 1989.

Drinnon, Richard. *Keeper of Concentration Camps: Dillon S. Myer and American Racism*. Berkeley: University of California Press, 1987.

Du Bois, W. E. B. *The Souls of Black Folk*. New York: Dover Thrift Editions, 1994.

Dudziak, Mary. *Cold War Civil Rights: Race and the Image of American Democracy*. Princeton, NJ: Princeton University Press, 2000.

Dunaway, Finis. *Natural Visions: The Power of Images in American Environmental Reform*. Chicago: University of Chicago Press, 2005.

Ehrenreich, Barbara. *The Hearts of Men: American Dreams and the Flight from Commitment*. Garden City, NY: Doubleday, 1983.

Ehrlich, Paul. *The Population Bomb*. New York: Buccaneer Books, 1971.

Eisinger, Chester E. "Jeffersonian Agrarianism in *The Grapes of Wrath*." In *A Casebook on The Grapes of Wrath*, edited by Agnes McNeil Donohue, 143–50. New York: Thomas Crowell, 1968.

Eng, David L. *Racial Castration: Managing Masculinity in Asian America*. Durham, NC: Duke University Press, 2001.

Estabrook, Barry. *Tomatoland: How Modern Industrial Agriculture Destroyed Our Most Alluring Fruit*. Kansas City: Andrews McMeel Publishing, 2011.

Evangelista, Susan. "Carlos Bulosan." In *Dictionary of Literary Biography*, vol. 312, *Asian American Writers*, edited by Deborah Madsen, 10–18. New York: Thomson Gale, 2005.

———. *Carlos Bulosan and His Poetry*. Seattle: University of Washington Press, 1985.

Finney, Carolyn. *Black Faces, White Spaces: Reimagining the Relationship of African Americans to the Great Outdoors*. Chapel Hill: University of North Carolina Press, 2014.

Finseth, Ian Frederick. *Shades of Green: Visions of Nature in the Literature of American Slavery, 1770–1860*. Athens: University of Georgia Press, 2009.

Fiskio, Janet. "Unsettling Ecocriticism: Rethinking Agrarianism, Place, and Citizenship." *American Literature* 84, no. 2 (2012): 301–25.

Fitting, Elizabeth. *The Struggle for Maize: Campesinos, Workers, and Transgenic Corn in the Mexican Countryside*. Durham, NC: Duke University Press, 2011.

Flamming, Douglas. *Bound for Freedom: Black Los Angeles in Jim Crow America*. Berkeley: University of California Press, 2005.

Fleishman, Erica, and Dennis D. Murphy. "A Realistic Assessment of the Indicator Potential of Butterflies and Other Charismatic Taxonomic Groups." *Conservation Biology* 23, no. 5 (October 2009): 1109–16.

Foley, Neil. *The White Scourge: Mexicans, Blacks, and Poor Whites in Texas Cotton Culture*. Berkeley: University of California Press, 1997.

French, Warren. "The Education of the Heart in *The Grapes of Wrath*." In *Twentieth Century Interpretations: "The Grapes of Wrath,"* edited by Robert Con Davis, 24–35. Englewood Cliffs, NJ: Prentice Hall, 1982.

Friday, Chris. *Organizing Asian American Labor: The Pacific Coast Canned-Salmon Industry, 1870–1942*. Philadelphia: Temple University Press, 1994.

Friedman, Andrea. "Sadists and Sissies: Anti-Pornography Campaigns in Cold War America." *Gender and History* 15, no. 2 (2003): 201–27.

Fujita-Rony, Dorothy. *American Workers, Colonial Power: Philippine Seattle and the Transpacific West, 1919–1941*. Berkeley: University of California Press, 2003.

———. "A Shared Pacific Arena: Empire, Agriculture, and the Life Narratives of Mary Paik Lee, Angeles Monrayo, and Mary Tomita." *Frontiers* 34, no. 2 (2013): 25–51.

Galarza, Ernesto. *Barrio Boy*. Notre Dame, IN: University of Notre Dame Press, 1971.

———. *The Burning Light, Action, and Organizing in the Mexican Community in California: Oral History Transcript and Related Material, 1977–1992*. Berkeley: University of California Bancroft Library, 1982.

———. *Farm Workers and Agri-business in California, 1947–1960*. Notre Dame, IN: University of Notre Dame Press, 1977.

———. *Merchants of Labor: The Mexican Bracero Story*. Charlotte, NC: McNally and Loftin, 1964.

———. *Spiders in the House and Workers in the Field*. Notre Dame, IN: University of Notre Dame Press, 1970.

———. *Strangers in Our Fields*. Washington, DC: U.S. Section, Joint United States–Mexico Trade Commission, 1956.

Gamber, John. *Positive Pollutions and Cultural Toxins: Waste and Contamination in Contemporary U.S. Ethnic Literatures*. Lincoln: University of Nebraska Press, 2012.

Gamboa, Erasmo. *Mexican Labor and World War II: Braceros in the Pacific Northwest, 1942–1947*. Seattle: University of Washington Press, 2000.

Gantner, Donald Christopher. "Regional Imagination and Radical Conscience: Carey McWilliams in the West." PhD diss., University of California, Los Angeles, 2001.

Ganz, Marshall. *Why David Sometimes Wins: Leadership, Organization, and Strategy in the California Farm Worker Movement*. New York: Oxford University Press, 2010.

Garcia, Matthew. *From the Jaws of Victory: The Triumph and Tragedy of Cesar Chavez and the Farm Worker Movement*. Berkeley: University of California Press, 2012.

———. *A World of Its Own: Race, Labor, and Citrus in the Making of Greater Los Angeles, 1900–1970*. Chapel Hill: University of North Carolina Press, 2001.

Garciá, Juan Ramon. *Operation Wetback: The Mass Deportation of Mexican Undocumented Workers in 1954*. Westport, CT: Greenwood, 1980.

García y Griego, Manuel. "The Importation of Mexican Contract Laborers to the United States, 1942–1964." In *Between Two Worlds: Mexican Immigrants in the United States*, edited by David G. Gutiérrez, 45–85. Wilmington, DE: Scholarly Resources, 1996.

Geary, Daniel. "Carey McWilliams and Antifascism, 1934–1943." *Journal of American History* 90, no. 3 (2003): 912–34.

Gifford, Terry. *Pastoral*. New York: Routledge, 1999.

Glenn, Evelyn Nakano. *Unequal Freedom: How Race and Gender Shaped American Citizenship and Labor*. Cambridge, MA: Harvard University Press, 2002.

Glickman, Lawrence B. *Buying Power: A History of Consumer Activism in America*. Chicago: University of Chicago Press, 2009.

Gonzalez, Gilbert G. *Guest Workers or Colonized Labor? Mexican Labor Migration to the United States*. Boulder, CO: Paradigm, 2006.

———. *Labor and Community: Mexican Citrus Worker Villages in a Southern California County, 1900–1950*. Chicago: University of Illinois Press, 1994.

Gordon, Robert. "Poisons in the Fields: The United Farm Workers, Pesticides, and Environmental Politics." *Pacific Historical Review* 68, no. 1 (February 1999): 51–77.

Gottlieb, Robert. *Forcing the Spring: The Transformation of the American Environmental Movement*. Revised edition. Washington, DC: Island Press, 2005.

Gottlieb, Robert, and Anupama Joshi. *Food Justice*. Cambridge, MA: MIT Press, 2010.

Gray, Margaret. *Labor and the Locavore*. Berkeley: University of California Press, 2013.

Gregory, James N. *American Exodus: The Dustbowl Migration and Okie Culture in California*. New York: Oxford University Press, 1989.

Griswold del Castillo, Richard, and Richard A. Garcia. *Cesar Chavez: A Triumph of the Spirit*. Norman: University of Oklahoma Press, 1995.

Grodzins, Mortin. *Americans Betrayed: Politics and the Japanese Evacuation*. Chicago: University of Chicago Press, 1949.

Guerin-Gonzales, Camille. *Mexican Workers and American Dreams: Immigration, Repatriation, and California Farm Labor, 1900–1939*. New Brunswick, NJ: Rutgers University Press, 1994.

Guthman, Julie. *Agrarian Dreams: The Paradox of Organic Farming in California*. Berkeley: University of California Press, 2004.

———. *Weighing In: Obesity, Food Justice, and the Limits of Capitalism*. Berkeley: University of California Press, 2011.

Gutiérrez, Ramón A. "Community, Patriarchy, and Individualism: The Politics of Chicano History and the Dream of Equality." *American Quarterly* 45, no. 1 (March 1993): 44–72.

Hagenstein, Edwin C., Sara M. Gregg, and Brian Donahue, eds. *American Georgics: Writings on Farming, Culture, and the Land*. New Haven, CT: Yale University Press, 2011.

Hammerback, John C., and Richard J. Jensen. *The Rhetorical Career of César Chávez*. College Station: Texas A&M Press, 1998.

Hansen, Eric, and Martin Donohoe. "Health Issues of Migrant and Seasonal Farmworkers." *Journal of Health Care for the Poor and Underserved* 14, no. 2 (May 2003): 153–64.

Haraway, Donna. *The Companion Species Manifesto: Dogs, Species, and Significant Otherness*. Chicago: Prickly Paradigm Press, 2003.

———. *Primate Visions*. New York: Routledge, 1989.

Harris, Cheryl L. "Whiteness as Property." *Harvard Law Review* 106, no. 8 (1993): 1707–91.

Harrison, Jill. *Pesticide Drift and the Pursuit of Environmental Justice*. Boston: MIT Press, 2011.

Hartranft, Marshall V. *The Grapes of Gladness: California's Refreshing and Inspiring Answer to "The Grapes of Wrath."* Los Angeles: DeVorss, 1939.

Harvey, David. *A Brief History of Neoliberalism*. Oxford: Oxford University Press, 2007.

Hayashi, Brian Masura. *Democratizing the Enemy: The Japanese American Internment*. Princeton, NJ: Princeton University Press, 2004.

Hayashi, Robert T. "Beyond Walden Pond: Asian American Literature and the Limits of Ecocriticism." In *Coming into Contact: Explorations in Ecocritical Theory and Practice*, edited by Annie Merrill Ingram, Ian Marshall, Daniel J. Philippon, and Adam W. Sweeting, 58–79. Athens: University of Georgia Press, 2007.

———. *Haunted by Waters: A Journey through Race and Place in the American West*. Iowa City: University of Iowa Press, 2011.

Heise, Ursula K. *Sense of Place and Sense of Planet: The Environmental Imagination of the Global*. Oxford: Oxford University Press, 2008.

Henderson, George L. *California and the Fictions of Capital*. New York: Oxford University Press, 1999.

Hennacy, Ammon. *The Autobiography of a Catholic Anarchist*. New York: Catholic Worker Books, 1954.

Herrera-Sobek, María. *The Bracero Experience: Elitelore versus Folklore.* Los Angeles: UCLA Latin American Center Publications, University of California, 1979.

Higashida, Cheryl. "Re-Signed Subjects: Women, Work, and World in the Fiction of Carlos Bulosan and Hisaye Yamamoto." *Studies in the Literary Imagination* 34, no. 1 (2004): 35–60.

Higham, John. *Strangers in the Land: Patterns of American Nativism, 1860–1925.* New Brunswick, NJ: Rutgers University Press, 1983.

Ho, Wendy. *In Her Mother's House: The Politics of Asian American Mother-Daughter Writing.* Walnut Creek, CA: Alta Mira, 1999.

Hoffman, Abraham. *Unwanted Mexican Americans in the Great Depression: Repatriation Pressures, 1929–1939.* Tucson: University of Arizona Press, 1974.

Hoffman, Warren D. "Home, Memory, and Narrative in Monica Sone's *Nisei Daughter.*" In *Recovered Legacies: Authority and Identity in Early Asian American Literature*, edited by Keith Lawrence and Floyd Cheung, 229–48. Philadelphia: Temple University Press, 2005.

Holmes, Seth. *Fresh Fruit, Broken Bodies: Migrant Farmworkers in the United States.* Berkeley: University of California Press, 2013.

Hong, Grace Kyungwon. "'Something Forgotten Which Should Have Been Remembered': Private Property and Cross-Racial Solidarity in the Work of Hisaye Yamamoto." *American Literature* 71, no. 2 (1999): 291–310.

Huggan, Graham, and Helen Tiffin. *Postcolonial Ecocritism: Literature, Animals, Environment.* New York: Routledge, 2010.

Hughes, Langston. "Harvest." In *The Political Plays of Langston Hughes*, edited by Susan Duffy, 68–137. Carbondale: Southern Illinois University Press, 2000.

Huhndorf, Shari M. *Going Native: Indians in the American Cultural Imagination.* New York: Cornell University Press, 2001.

Hunt, Lynn. *Inventing Human Rights: A History.* New York: Norton, 2007.

Ibarra, Armando, and Rodolfo D. Torres, eds. *Man of Fire: Selected Writings by Ernesto Galarza.* Urbana: University of Illinois Press, 2013.

Ichioka, Yuji. *The Issei: The World of the First Generation Japanese Immigrants, 1885–1924.* New York: Macmillian, 1988.

———. "Japanese Immigrant Response to the 1920 California Alien Land Law." *Agricultural History* 58, no. 2 (1984): 157–78.

Igler, David. *Industrial Cowboys: Miller and Lux and the Transformation of the Far West, 1850–1920.* Berkeley: University of California Press, 2005.

Ignatiev, Noel. *How the Irish Became White.* New York: Routledge, 1996.

Ishay, Micheline. *The History of Human Rights: From Ancient Times to the Globalization Era.* Berkeley: University of California Press, 2008.

Iwata, Masakazu. "The Japanese Immigrants in California Agriculture." *Agricultural History* 36, no. 1 (1962): 25–37.

Jackson, Wes. "Farming in Nature's Image: Natural Systems Agriculture." In *The Fatal Harvest Reader: The Tragedy of Industrial Agriculture*, edited by Andrew Kimbrell, 65–76. Washington, DC: Island Press, 2002.

Jacoby, Karl. *Crimes Against Nature: Squatters, Poachers, Thieves, and the Hidden History of American Conservation.* Berkeley: University of California Press, 2001.

Jamieson, Stuart. *Labor Unionism in American Agriculture.* New York: Arno, 1976.

Jefferson, Thomas. *Notes on the State of Virginia*. Chapel Hill: University of North Carolina Press, 1954.

Jenkins, McKay. Introduction to *The Peter Matthiessen Reader*, by Peter Matthiessen, xi–xxxvi. Edited by McKay Jenkins. New York: Vintage, 2000.

Jensen, Richard J., and John C. Hammerback. *The Words of Cesar Chavez*. College Station: Texas A&M Press, 2002.

Johnson, David K. *The Lavender Scare: Cold War Persecution of Gays and Lesbians in the Federal Government*. Chicago: University Chicago Press, 2004.

Johnson, Michael K. *Black Masculinity and the Frontier Myth in American Literature*. Norman: University of Oklahoma Press, 2002.

Jones, Van. *The Green Collar Economy: How One Solution Can Fix Our Two Biggest Problems*. New York: Harper, 2008.

Kaplan, Amy. "Manifest Domesticity." *American Literature* 70 No. 3 (September 1998): 581–606.

Keith, Joseph. *Unbecoming Americans: Writing Race and Nation from the Shadows of Citizenship, 1945–1960*. New Brunswick, NJ: Rutgers University Press, 2012.

Kim, Elaine. "Hisaye Yamamoto: A Woman's View." In *"Seventeen Syllables": Hisaye Yamamoto*, edited by King-Kok Cheung, 109–17. New Brunswick, NJ: Rutgers University Press, 1994.

Kimmel, Michael. *Manhood in America: A Cultural History*. New York: Oxford University Press, 2005.

Kingsolver, Barbara. *Flight Behavior*. New York: Harper, 2012.

Klein, Kerwin Lee. *Apocalypse Noir: Carey McWilliams and Posthistorical California*. Berkeley: University of California Press, 1997.

Klejment, Anne, and Nancy L. Roberts. *American Catholic Pacifism: The Influence of Dorothy Day and the Catholic Worker Movement*. Westport, CT: Praeger, 1996.

Kolodny, Annette. *The Lay of the Land: Metaphor as Experience and History in American Life and Letters*. Chapel Hill: University of North Carolina Press, 1975.

Kosek, Jake. *Understories: The Political Life of Forests in Northern New Mexico*. Durham, NC: Duke University Press, 2006.

Koshy, Susan. *Sexual Naturalization: Asian Americans and Miscegenation*. Stanford, CA: Stanford University Press, 2004.

Kozol, Wendy. *Life's America: Family and Nation in Post-War Photojournalism*. Philadelphia: Temple University Press, 1994.

Kristeva, Julia. *Powers of Horror: An Essay on Abjection*. New York: Columbia University Press, 1982.

Lancaster, Ashley Craig. "Subverting Eugenic Discourse: Making the Weak Strong in John Steinbeck's *Their Blood Is Strong* and *The Grapes of Wrath*." In *The Grapes of Wrath: A Reconsideration*, vol. 2, edited by Michael J. Meyer, 421–48. New York: Rodopi, 2009.

Lange, Dorothea, and Paul Schuster Taylor. *An American Exodus: A Record of Human Erosion*. New York: Reynal and Hitchcock, 1939.

Lee, Erika. *At America's Gate: Chinese Immigration during the Exclusion Era, 1882–1943*. Chapel Hill: University of North Carolina Press, 2003.

Lee, Robert G. *Orientals: Asian Americans in Popular Culture*. Philadelphia: Temple University Press, 1999.

LeMenager, Stephanie. *Living Oil: Petroleum Culture in the American Century*. Oxford: Oxford University Press, 2014.

LeSeur, Geta J. *Not All Okies Are White: The Lives of Black Cotton Pickers in Arizona*. Columbia: University of Missouri Press, 2000.

Limón, José. "Border Literary Histories, Globalization, and Critical Regionalism." *American Literary History* 20, no. 1 (2008): 160–82.

Lipsitz, George. *The Possessive Investment in Whiteness: How White People Profit from Identity Politics*. Philadelphia: Temple University Press, 1998.

Lisca, Peter. "The Dynamics of Community in *The Grapes of Wrath*." In *Critical Essays on Steinbeck's "The Grapes of Wrath,"* edited by John Ditsky, 87–96. Boston: Hall, 1989.

———. "*Editors' Introduction*" In *"The Grapes of Wrath": Text and Criticism* by John Steinbeck, edited by Peter Lisca, 547–61. New York: Penguin, 1997.

Liu, Yvonne Yen, and Dominique Apollon. "The Color of Food." Applied Research Center, 2011.

Loftis, Anne. *Witness to the Struggle*. Reno: University of Nevada Press, 1998.

London, Joan, and Henry Anderson. *So Shall Ye Reap*. New York: Crowell, 1970.

Losey, John E., Linda S. Rayor, and Maureen E. Carter. "Transgenic Pollen Harms Monarch Larvae." *Nature* 399 (May 20, 1999): 214.

Lopez, Ian Haney. *White by Law: The Legal Construction of Race*. New York: New York University Press, 2006.

Loza, Mireya. "Alianza de Braceros Nacionales de Mexico en los Estados Unidos, 1943–1964." In *Que Fronteras? Mexican Braceros and a Re-Examination of the Legacy of Migration*, edited by Paul Lopez, 215–36. Dubuque, IA: Kendall Hunt Publishing, 2011.

———. "Braceros on the Boundaries." PhD diss., Brown University, 2011.

Lye, Colleen. *America's Asia: Racial Form and American Literature, 1893–1945*. Princeton, NJ: Princeton University Press, 2005.

Marlett, Jeffrey D. "Down on the Farm and Up to Heaven: Catholic Worker Farm Communes and the Spiritual Virtues of Farming." In *Dorothy Day and the Catholic Worker Movement: Centenary Essays*, edited by William J. Thorn, Philip M. Runkel, and Susan Mourtin, 406–17. Milwaukee, WI: Marquette University Press, 2001.

Matsumoto, Valerie. *Farming the Home Place: A Japanese American Community in California, 1919–1982*. Ithaca, NY: Cornell University Press, 1993.

Matthiessen, Peter. *Sal Si Puedes: Cesar Chavez and the New American Revolution*. Berkeley: University of California Press, 2000.

Maurin, Peter. *Easy Essays*. Eugene, OR: WIPF & Stock, 2003.

May, Elaine Tyler. *Homeward Bound: American Families in the Cold War Era*. New York: Basic, 1999.

McBroome, Delores Nason. "Harvests of Gold: African American Boosterism, Agriculture, and Investment in Allensworth and Little Liberia." In *Seeking El Dorado: African Americans in California*, edited by Lawrence B. De Graf, Kevin Mulroy, and Quintard Taylor, 149–80. Seattle: University of Washington Press, 2001.

McClintock, Anne. "No Longer in a Future Heaven." In *Dangerous Liaisons: Gender, Nation, and Postcolonial Perspectives*, edited by Anne McClintock, Aamir Mufti, and Ella Shohat, 89–112. Minneapolis: University of Minnesota Press, 1997.

———. *Imperial Leather: Race, Gender, and Sexuality in the Colonial Context*. New York: Routledge, 1995.

McWilliams, Carey. *California: The Great Exception*. Berkeley: University of California Press, 1999.

———. *The Education of Carey McWilliams*. New York: Simon and Schuster, 1979.

———. "Exit the Filipino." *Nation*, September, 4, 1935, 265.

———. *Factories in the Field: The Story of Migratory Farm Labor in California*. Boston: Little, Brown, 1939.

———. "Getting Rid of the Mexican." *American Mercury* (March 1933): 322–29.

———. *Honorable in All Things*. Interviewed by Joel Gardner. Los Angeles. Oral History Program, University of California Regents, 1982.

———. *Ill Fares the Land: Migrants and Migratory Labor in the United States*. Boston: Little, Brown, 1942.

———. Introduction to *American Is in the Heart: A Personal History*, by Carlos Bulosan, vii–xxiv. Seattle: University of Washington Press, 1991.

———. "Is Your Name Gonzales?" *Nation*, March 15, 1947, 302–3.

———. "Nervous LA." *Nation*, June 10, 1950, 570–71.

———. "Poverty Follows the Crops." *Nation*, March 23, 1946, 343.

———. *Prejudice: Japanese-Americans, Symbol of Racial Intolerance*. Boston: Little, Brown, 1944.

Meyer, Lee Ann. "Great Exception: Carey McWilliams' Path to Activism." PhD diss., Claremont Graduate School, Claremont, CA, 1996.

Miller, Sally, ed. *The Ethnic Press in the United States: A Historical Analysis and Handbook*. New York: Greenwood, 1987.

Mistri, Zenobia Baxter. "'Seventeen Syllables': A Symbolic Haiku." In *"Seventeen Syllables": Hisaye Yamamoto*, edited by King-Kok Cheung, 195–202. New Brunswick, NJ: Rutgers University Press, 1994.

Mitchell, Don. *The Lie of the Land: Migrant Workers and the California Landscape*. Minneapolis: University of Minnesota Press, 1996.

———. *They Saved the Crops: Labor, Landscape, and the Struggle over Industrial Farming in Bracero-Era California*. Athens: University of Georgia Press, 2012.

Mitchell, Ruth Comfort. *Of Human Kindness*. New York: AMS, 1976.

Mobed, Ketty, Ellen B. Gold, and Marc B. Schenker. "Occupational Health Problems among Migrant and Seasonal Farm Workers." *Western Journal of Medicine*. (September 1992): 367–73

Modell, John. *The Economics and Politics of Racial Accommodation: The Japanese of Los Angeles, 1900–1942*. Urbana: University of Illinois Press, 1977.

Molina, Natalia. *How Race Is Made in America*. Berkeley: University of California Press, 2014.

Moore, Shirley Ann Wilson. *To Place Our Deeds: The African American Community in Richmond, California, 1910–1963*. Berkeley: University of California Press, 2000.

Morrison, Toni. *Playing in the Dark: Whiteness and the Literary Imagination*. Cambridge, MA: Harvard University Press, 1992.

Mortimer-Sandilands, Catriona, and Bruce Erickson, eds. *Queer Ecologies: Sex, Nature, Politics, Desire*. Bloomington: University of Indiana Press, 2010.

Moya, Paula. *Learning from Experience: Minority Identities, Multicultural Struggles*. Berkeley: University of California Press, 2002.

Murphy, Patrick D. *Farther Afield in the Study of Nature-Oriented Literature*. Charlottesville: University of Virginia Press, 2000.

Myers, Jeffrey. *Converging Stories: Race, Ecology, and Environmental Justice in American Litera-*
ture. Athens: University of Georgia Press, 2005.

Nakamura, Hiroshi. *Treadmill*. New York: Mosaic, 1996.

Nakamura, Mary Sato, and Isami Nakamura. "Hiroshi Nakamura, 1915–1973." *Treadmill* by
Hiroshi Nakamura. New York: Mosaic, 1996.

Nash, Linda. *Inescapable Ecologies: A History of Environment, Disease, and Knowledge*. Berkeley:
University of California Press, 2007.

Navarro, Joseph R. "The Contributions of Carey McWilliams to American Ethnic History."
Journal of Mexican-American History 2, no. 1 (Fall): 1–21.

Neiwert, David. *Strawberry Days: How Internment Destroyed a Japanese American Community*.
New York: Palgrave Macmillian, 2005.

Ngai, Mae. *Impossible Subjects: Illegal Aliens and the Making of Modern America*. Princeton, NJ:
Princeton University Press, 2004.

Nguyen, Viet Thanh. *Race and Resistance: Literature and Politics in Asian America*. New York:
Oxford University Press, 2002.

Nixon, Rob. *Slow Violence and the Environmentalism of the Poor*. Cambridge, MA: Harvard
University Press, 2013.

Okada, John. *No No Boy*. Seattle: University of Washington Press, 1979.

Okihiro, Gary Y. "Fallow Field: The Rural Dimension of Asian American Studies." In *Frontiers*
of Asian American Studies, edited by Gail M. Nomura, Russell Endo, Stephen H. Sumida,
and Russell C. Leong, 6–13. Pullman: Washington State University Press, 1989.

Outka, Paul. *Race and Nature from Transcendentalism to the Harlem Renaissance*. New York:
Palgrave Macmillan, 2008.

Owens, Louis. *Trouble in the Promised Land*. Boston: Twayne, 1989.

———. "The Culpable Joads: Desentimentalizing *The Grapes of Wrath*." In *Critical Essays on*
Steinbeck's The Grapes of Wrath, edited by John Ditsky, 108–16. Boston: Hall, 1989.

Pagan, Eduardo Obregon. *Murder at the Sleepy Lagoon: Zoot Suits, Race, and Riot in Wartime*
L.A. Chapel Hill: University of North Carolina Press, 2003.

Parini, Jay. *John Steinbeck: A Biography*. New York: Holt, 1995.

Park, Lisa, and David Pellow. *The Slums of Aspen: Immigrants vs. the Environment in America's*
Eden. New York: New York University Press, 2011.

Park, Robert. *The Immigrant Press and Its Control*. New York: Classic, 1922.

Pawel, Miriam. *The Union of Their Dreams: Power, Hope, and Struggle in Cesar Chavez's Farm-*
worker Movement. New York: Bloomsbury Press, 2010.

Peña, Devon G. *Mexican Americans and the Environment: Tierra y Vida*. Tucson: University of
Arizona Press, 2005.

Piehl, Mel. *Breaking Bread: The Catholic Worker and the Origin of Catholic Radicalism in America*.
Tuscaloosa: University of Alabama Press, 2006.

Pitti, Stephen J. *The Devil in Silicon Valley: Northern California, Race, and Mexican Americans*.
Princeton, NJ: Princeton University Press, 2003.

———. "Ernesto Galarza, Mexican Immigration, and Farm Labor Organizing in Postwar
California." In *The Countryside in the Age of the Modern State: Political Histories of Rural*
America, edited by Catherine McNicol Stock and Robert D. Johnston, 161–88. Ithaca NY:
Cornell UP, 2001.

Pollan, Michael. *Cooked: A Natural History of Transformation*. New York: Penguin, 2013.

———. *Omnivore's Dilemma: A Natural History of Four Meals*. New York: Penguin, 2006.

Price, Jennifer. *Flight Maps: Adventures with Nature in Modern America*. New York: Basic Books, 2000.

Pulido, Laura. *Environmentalism and Economic Justice: Two Chicano Struggles in the Southwest*. Tucson: University of Arizona Press, 1996.

Ray, Sarah Jaquette. *The Ecological Other: Environmental Exclusion in American Culture*. Tucson: University of Arizona Press, 2013.

Reed, T. V. "Toward an Environmental Justice Ecocriticism." In *The Environmental Justice Reader: Politics, Poetics, and Pedagogy*, edited by Joni Adamson, Mei Mei Evans, and Rachel Stein, 145–62. Tucson: University of Arizona Press, 2002.

Richardson, Peter. *American Prophet: The Life and Work of Carey McWilliams*. Ann Arbor: University of Michigan Press, 2005.

Robinson, Forrest G. "Remembering Carey McWilliams." *Western American Literature* 34, no. 4 (Winter 2000): 411–34.

Rodgers, Lawrence R. Foreword to *Whose Names Are Unknown*, by Sanora Babb, vii–xii. Norman: University of Oklahoma Press, 2004.

Roediger, David R. *The Wages of Whiteness: Race and the Making of the American Working Class*. New York: Verso, 1991.

Rome, Adam. *The Bulldozer in the Countryside: Suburban Sprawl and the Rise of American Environmentalism*. Cambridge: Cambridge University Press, 2001.

———. *The Genius of Earth Day: How a 1970 Teach-In Unexpectedly Made the First Green Generation*. New York: Hill and Wang, 2013.

Romero, Lora. *Home Fronts: Domesticity and Its Critics in the Antebellum United States*. Durham, NC: Duke University Press, 1997.

Roos, Bonnie, and Alex Hunt eds. *Postcolonial Green: Environmental Politics and World Narratives*. Charlottesville: University of Virginia, 2010.

Rosales, F. Arturo. *Chicano! The History of the Mexican American Civil Rights Movement*. Houston: Arte Publico, 1997.

Rosas, Ana Elizabeth. *Abrazando el Espíritu: Bracero Families Confront the US-Mexico Border*. Berkeley: University of California Press, 2014.

Rosier, Paul C. "'Modern America Desperately Needs to Listen': The Emerging Indian in the Age of Environmental Crisis." *Journal of American History* 100, no. 3 (December 2013): 711–35.

Ross, Andrew. "The Social Claim on Urban Ecology" (interviewed by Michael Bennet). In *The Nature of Cities: Ecocriticism and Urban Environments*, edited by Michael Bennett and David W. Teague, 15–30. Tucson: University of Arizona Press, 1999.

Rothenberg, Daniel. *With These Hands: The Hidden World of Migrant Farmworkers Today*. New York: Harcourt Brace & Company, 1998.

Ruffin, Kimberly N. *Black on Earth: African American Ecoliterary Traditions*. Athens: University of Georgia Press, 2010.

Ruíz, Vicki. *Cannery Women, Cannery Lives: Mexican Women, Unionization, and the California Food Processing Industry, 1930–1950*. Albuquerque: University of New Mexico Press, 1987.

———. "Morena/o, Blanca/o y Café con Leche: Racial Constructions in Chicana/o Historiography." *Mexican Studies/ Estudios Mexicanos* 20, no. 2 (Summer 2004): 343–60.

Russell, Edmund. *War and Nature: Fighting Humans and Insects with Chemicals from World War I to Silent Spring.* New York: Cambridge University Press, 2001.

Sachs, Aaron. "Civil Rights in the Field." *Pacific Historical Review* 73, no. 2 (2004): 215–48.

Sackman, Douglas Cazaux. *Orange Empire: California and the Fruits of Eden.* Berkeley: University of California Press, 2005.

Salvidar, Ramon. *The Borderlands of Culture: Americo Paredes and the Transnational Imaginary.* Durham, NC: Duke University Press, 2006.

Sanchez, George. *Becoming Mexican American: Ethnicity, Culture, and Identity in Chicano Los Angeles, 1900–1945.* New York: Oxford University Press, 1993.

Sandoval, Arturo. "La Raza." In *Earth Day—The Beginning: A Guide for Survival*, edited by National Staff of Environmental Action, 224–25. New York: Arno Press, 1970.

San Juan, E. Jr., *The Philippine Temptation: Dialectics of Philippines-U.S. Literary Relations.* Philadelphia: Temple University Press, 1996.

———. *U.S. Imperialism and Revolution in the Philippines.* New York: Palgrave Macmillan, 2007.

Sarver, Stephanie L. *Uneven Land: Nature and Agriculture in American Writing.* Lincoln: University of Nebraska Press, 1999.

Saxton, Alexander. "In Dubious Battle: Looking Backward." *Pacific Historical Review* 73, no. 2 (2004): 249–62.

———. *The Indispensable Enemy: Labor and the Anti-Chinese Movement in California.* Berkeley: University of California Press, 1971.

Schappert, Phil. *The Last Monarch Butterfly: Conserving the Monarch Butterfly in a Brave New World.* Buffalo, NY: Firefly Books, 2004.

Schlosser, Eric. *Fast Food Nation: The Dark Side of the All American Meal.* New York: Harper, 2005.

Schmidt Camacho, Alicia. *Migrant Imaginaries: Latino Cultural Politics in the U.S.-Mexico Borderlands.* New York: New York University Press, 2008.

Schneider-Mayerson, Matthew. "Necrocracy in America: American Studies Begins to Address Fossil Fuels and Climate Change." *American Quarterly* 67, no. 2 (June 2015): 529–40.

Schweninger, Lee. *Listening to the Land: Native American Literary Responses to the Landscape.* Athens: University of Georgia Press, 2008.

Scruggs, Otey M. *Braceros, "Wetbacks," and the Farm Labor Problem: Mexican Agricultural Labor in the United States, 1942–1954.* New York: Garland Publishing, 1988.

Seymour, Nicole. *Strange Natures: Futurity, Empathy, and the Queer Ecological Imagination.* Bloomington: University of Indiana Press, 2013.

Shillinglaw, Susan. "California Answers *The Grapes of Wrath*." In *The Critical Response to John Steinbeck's "The Grapes of Wrath*," edited by Barbara Heavilin, 183–201. Westport, CT: Greenwood, 2000.

———. *On Reading "The Grapes of Wrath."* New York: Penguin, 2014.

Shinozuka, Jeannie. "Deadly Perils: Japanese Beetles and the Pestilent Immigrant, 1920s–1930s." *American Quarterly* 65, no. 4 (December 2013): 831–52.

Sides, Josh. *L.A. City Limits: African American Los Angeles from the Great Depression to the Present.* Berkeley: University of California Press, 2003.

Slotkin, Richard. *The Fatal Environment: The Myth of the Frontier in the Age of Industrialization*. Norman: University of Oklahoma Press, 1998.

———. *Gunfighter Nation: The Myth of the Frontier in Twentieth Century America*. New York: Atheneum, 1992.

———. *Regeneration through Violence: The Mythology of the American Frontier, 1600–1860*. Norman: University of Oklahoma Press, 2000.

Smith, Henry Nash. *The Virgin Land: The American West as Symbol and Myth*. Cambridge, MA: Harvard University Press, 1970.

Smith, Kimberly K. *African American Environmental Thought: Foundations*. Lawrence: University Press of Kansas, 2007.

Smith, Page. *Democracy on Trial: The Japanese American Evacuation and Relocation in World War II*. New York: Simon and Schuster, 1995.

Solensky, Michelle J., and Karen S. Oberhauser. *The Monarch Butterfly: Biology and Conservation*. Ithaca, NY: Comstock Publishing, 2004.

Sommers, Joseph. "Interpreting Tomás Rivera." In *Modern Chicano Writers: A Collection of Critical Essays*, edited by Joseph Sommers and Tomás Ybarra-Frausto, 94–107. Edgewood Cliffs, NJ: Prentice Hall, 1979.

Sone, Monica. *Nisei Daughter*. Seattle: University of Washington Press, 1979.

Spence, Mark David. *Dispossessing the Wilderness: Indian Removal and the Making of the National Parks*. New York: Oxford University Press, 1999.

Spigel, Lynn. *Make Room for TV: Television and the Family Ideal in Postwar America*. Chicago: University of Chicago Press, 1992.

Stanley, Amy Dru. *From Bondage to Contract: Wage Labor, Marriage, and the Market in the Age of Slave Emancipation*. New York: Cambridge University Press, 1998.

Starr, Kevin. *Endangered Dreams: The Great Depression in California*. New York: Oxford University Press, 1996.

———. "The Light and the Dark." In *Reading California: Art, Image, and Identity, 1900–2000*, edited by Stephanie Barron, Sheri Berstein, and Ilene Susan Fort, 14–29. Berkeley: Los Angeles Museum of Art / University of California Press, 2000.

Stavans, Ilan Stavans. Foreword to *Sal Si Puedes: Cesar Chavez and the Next American Revolution*, by Peter Matthiessen, vii–xxii. Berkeley: University of California Press, 2000.

Stein, Rachel, ed. *New Perspectives on Environmental Justice: Gender, Sexuality, and Activism*. New Brunswick, NJ: Rutgers University Press, 2004.

———. *Shifting the Ground: American Women Writers' Revisions of Nature, Gender, and Race*. Charlottesville: University Press of Virginia, 1997.

Stein, Walter J. *California and the Dustbowl Migration*. Westport, CT: Greenwood, 1973.

Steinbeck, John. *"The Grapes of Wrath": Text and Criticism*. Edited by Peter Lisca. New York: Penguin, 1997.

———. *The Harvest Gypsies: On the Road to "The Grapes of Wrath."* Berkeley: Heyday Books, 1988.

———. *In Dubious Battle*. New York: Penguin, 2006.

Stern, Alexandra Minna. *Eugenic Nation: Faults and Frontiers of Better Breeding in Modern America*. Berkeley: University of California Press, 2005.

Street, Richard Steven. *Beasts of the Field: A Narrative History of California Farmworkers*,

1769–1913. Stanford: Stanford University Press, 2004.

———. *Photographing Farmworkers in California*. Stanford, CA: Stanford University Press, 2004.

———. "Poverty in the Valley of Plenty: The National Farm Labor Union, DiGiorgio Farms, and Suppression of Documentary Photography in California, 1947–66." *Labor History* 48, no. 1 (2007): 25–48.

Sturgeon, Noël. *Environmentalism in Popular Culture: Gender, Race, Sexuality, and the Politics of the Natural*. Tucson: University of Arizona Press, 2008.

Suzuki, Peter. Introduction to *Treadmill*, by Hiroshi Nakamura. New York: Mosaic, 1996.

Szalay, Michael. *New Deal Modernism: American Literature and the Invention of the Welfare State*. Durham, NC: Duke University Press, 2000.

Sze, Julie. "From Environmental Justice Literature to the Literature of Environmental Justice." In *The Environmental Justice Reader: Politics, Poetics, and Pedagogy*, edited by Joni Adamson, Mei Mei Evans, and Rachel Stein, 163–80. Tucson: University of Arizona Press, 2002.

Takaki, Ronald T. *Iron Cages: Race and Culture in Nineteenth-Century America*. Seattle: University of Washington Press, 1979.

Tate, Claudia. *Domestic Allegories of Political Desire: The Black Heroine's Text at the Turn of the Century*. New York: Oxford University Press, 1992.

Taylor, Paul. *On the Ground in the Thirties*. Salt Lake City: Peregrine, 1983.

tenBroek, Jacobus, Edward N. Barnhart, and Floyd W. Matson. *Prejudice, War, and the Constitution: Causes and Consequences of the Evacuation of the Japanese Americans in World War II*. Berkeley: University of California Press, 1975.

Terry, Jennifer. "'Momism' and the Making of Treasonous Homosexuals." In *"Bad" Mothers: The Politics of Blame in Twentieth-Century America*, edited by Molly Ladd-Taylor and Lauri Umansky, 169–90. New York: New York University Press, 1998.

Thomas, Dorothy Swaine, and Richard Nishimoto. *The Spoilage: Japanese American Evacuation and Resettlement during World War II*. Berkeley: University of California Press, 1946.

Timmerman, John. "The Squatter's Circle in *The Grapes of Wrath*." *The Critical Response to John Steinbeck's The Grapes of Wrath*, edited by Barbara Heavilin, 134–47. Westport,CT: Greenwood, 2000.

Tsu, Cecila M. *Garden of the World: Asian Immigrants and the Making of Agriculture in California's Santa Clara Valley*. Oxford: Oxford University Press, 2013.

Tuana, Nancy. "Viscous Porosity: Witnessing Katrina." In *Material Feminisms*, edited by Stacy Alaimo and Susan Hekman, 188–213. Bloomington: Indiana University Press, 2008.

Turner, Frederick Jackson. *The Frontier in American History*. New York: Holt, 1920.

Turner, James Morton. *The Promise of Wilderness: American Environmental Politics since 1964*. Seattle: University of Washington Press, 2013.

Valdés, Dionicio Nodín. *Organized Agriculture and the Labor Movement before the UFW*. Austin: University of Texas Press, 2011.

Valdez, Luis. *Actos: El Teatro Campesino*. San Juan Bautista, CA: Cucaracha Publications, 1971.

Vargas, Zaragosa. *Labor Rights Are Civil Rights: Mexican American Workers in Twentieth-*

Century America. Princeton, NJ: Princeton University Press, 2005.

Vaught, David. *Cultivating California: Growers, Specialty Crops, and Labor, 1875–1920*. Baltimore: John Hopkins University Press, 1999.

———. "Factories in the Field Revisited." *Pacific Historical Review* 66 (May 1997): 149–84.

Vázquez, David. "'They Don't Understand Their Own Oppression': Theorizing an Alternative Ethos of Preservation in John Rechy's *The Miraculous Day of Amalia Gómez*." Imagining Latino/a Studies: Past, Present & Future, Chicago, July 2014.

Vera Cruz, Philip. *A Personal History of Filipino Immigrants and the Farmworkers Movement*. Seattle: University of Washington Press, 2000.

Vials, Chris. *Realism for the Masses: Aesthetics, Popular Front Pluralism, and U.S. Culture, 1935–1947*. Jackson: University of Mississippi Press, 2009.

Viramontes, Helena María. *Under the Feet of Jesus*. New York: Plume, 1996.

Wald, Alan M. Introduction to *Cry of the Tinamou*, by Sanora Babb. Lincoln: University of Nebraska Press, 1997.

Wald, Priscilla. "Naturalization." In *Keywords in American Cultural Studies*, edited by Bruce Burgett and Glenn Hendler, 170–74. New York: New York University Press, 2007.

Wald, Sarah D. "Hisaye Yamamoto as Radical Agrarian." In *Asian American Literature and the Environment*, edited by Lorna Fitzsimmons, Youngsuk Chae, and Bella Adams, 149–66. New York: Routledge Press, 2014.

———. "Visible Farmers/Invisible Workers: Locating Immigrant Labor in Food Studies." *Food, Culture, and Society* 14, no. 4 (2011): 567–86.

———. "'We Ain't Foreign': Constructing the Joads' White Citizenship." In *The Grapes of Wrath: A Reconsideration*, vol. 2, edited by Michael J. Meyer, 481–505. Atlanta: Rodopi Press, 2009.

Walz, Eric. "From Kumamoto to Idaho: The Influence of Japanese Immigrants on the Agricultural Development of the Interior West." *Agricultural History* 74, no. 2 (2000): 404–18.

Weber, Devra. *Dark Sweat, White Gold: California Farm Workers Cotton and the New Deal*. Berkeley: University of California Press, 1994.

Weems, Robert. "African American Consumer Boycotts during the Civil Rights Era." *Western Journal of Black Studies* 19, no. 1 (1995): 72–79.

Weglyn, Michi. *The Years of Infamy: The Untold Story of America's Concentration Camps*. Seattle: University of Washington Press, 1996.

Weiss, Richard. "Ethnicity and Reform: Minorities and the Ambience of the Depression Era." *Journal of American History* 66, no. 3 (1979): 566–85.

White, Richard. "Are You an Environmentalist or Do You Work for a Living?" In *Uncommon Ground: Rethinking the Human Place in Nature*, edited by William Cronon, 171–85. New York: W. W. Norton, 1996.

Wixson, Douglas, ed. *On the Dirty Plate Trail: Remembering the Dust Bowl Refugee Camps*, by Sanora Babb and Dorothy Babb. Austin: University of Texas Press, 2007.

Wong, Jade Snow. *Fifth Chinese Daughter*. Seattle: University of Washington Press, 1989.

Wong, Sau-ling Cynthia. *Reading Asian American Literature: From Necessity to Extravagance*. Princeton, NJ: Princeton University Press, 1993.

Wright, Laura. *Wilderness into Civilized Shapes: Reading the Postcolonial Environment*. Athens: University of Georgia Press, 2010.

Yamamoto, Hisaye. "Life Among the Oil Fields: A Memoir." In *"Seventeen Syllables" and Other Stories*, 86–95. New Brunswick, NJ: Rutgers University Press, 2003.

———. "Seventeen Syllables." In *"Seventeen Syllables": Hisaye Yamamoto*, edited by King-Kok Cheung, 21–40. New Brunswick, NJ: Rutgers University Press, 1994.

———. "Yoneko's Earthquake." In *"Seventeen Syllables": Hisaye Yamamoto*, edited by King-Kok Cheung, 41–58. New Brunswick, NJ: Rutgers University Press, 1994.

Yamamoto, Traise. *Masking Selves, Making Others: Japanese American Women, Identity, and the Body*. Berkeley: University of California Press, 1999.

Ybarra, Priscilla Solis. "Erasure by U.S. Legislation: Ruiz de Burton's Nineteenth-Century Novels and the Lost Archive of Mexican American Environmental Knowledge." In *Environmental Criticism for the Twenty-First Century*, edited by Stephanie LeMenager, Ken Hiltner, and Teresa Shewry, 135–47. New York: Routledge, 2012.

Yogi, Stan. "Legacies Revealed: Uncovering Buried Plots in the Stories of Hisaye Yamamoto." In *"Seventeen Syllables": Hisaye Yamamoto*, edited by King-Kok Cheung, 143–60. New Brunswick, NJ: Rutgers University Press, 1994.

———. "Rebels and Heroines: Subversive Narratives in the Stories of Wakako Yamauchi and Hisaye Yamamoto." In *Reading the Literatures of Asian America*, edited by Shirley Geok-lin Lim and Amy Ling, 131–50. Philadelphia: Temple University Press, 1992.

Yoo, David K. *Growing Up Nisei: Race, Generation, and Culture among Japanese Americans of California*. Chicago: University of Illinois Press, 1999.

Index

Note: Page numbers followed by *fig.* indicate illustrations.

Abbey, Edward, 12–13
abject aliens: concept, 221n4; constructed in agrarianism, 53, 131–33; consumer citizenship as reinforcing status of, 24; deterritorialized workers cast as, 78–80; farmworkers as, 5–6, 191, 201; racial construction of, 17–18, 19–20, 76, 104; understanding process of rendering, 207–8. *See also* alien citizens; aliens; farmworkers
abstract personhood, 94–95, 97–100, 101, 177
Adam and Eve narrative (Genesis), 49–50, 53–54, 121. *See also* pastoral literatures
Adams, Ansel, 79, 80
Adamson, Joni, 13, 17
Adventures of Huckleberry Finn (Twain), 58
advertisements: anti-immigrant ideologies in, 16–17; for chemicals, 175; food politics in, 195–96; on pesticides, 160; Sun-Maid raisin girl in, 202, 203, 204; white male farmer ideal in, 3, 4, 6
African Americans: citizenship categories unsettled by, 37, 227n46; Jefferson's view of land and, 221–22n9; newspaper of (see *Los Angeles Tribune*). *See also* black Dust Bowl migrants; blackness; blacks
agency: of Asian American texts, 98–100; of butterflies, 218; denied to nonwhite workers, 39–41; of earth (land), 53, 68; of Japanese, 89–90; of transnational migrants, 218; of women, 53
agrarianism: alternative food movement as

reviving ideal of, 18, 200; California as Eden of, 53–54; Chavez linked to ideal, 160, 169; collective land ownership vs., 32–33; communism as threat to, 27, 42–43, 48–50, 225n2; consumers' republic as replacing ideal of, 194; critique of land owners based in, 60–61; dual versions of, 3–6; failure of, 39–40, 52–53; farming as transformative act in, 8; farmworker advocates' invocation of, 157–58; as imperial venture, 131–33; Jefferson's version of, 6–7, 10, 12, 73; Joads as heirs of, 61–62; multiracial industrial unionism as key to rebuilding, 53, 65–66, 69–74; racist foundations of, 17–18, 30–31, 40–41, 76, 130. *See also* agriculture; anarchist agrarianism; Bracero Program; Catholic Worker agrarianism; democracy; land owners and land ownership; national belonging; naturalization; pastoral literatures; racialization; white male farmer
agrarian partisans, 28, 29, 54, 224n69, 225n6
agricultural labor. *See* farmers; farmworkers; migrant farm labor
"Agricultural Pest No. 1," 29–30, 225n6
Agricultural Workers Organizing Committee (AWOC), 23, 156–57
agriculture: as business, 82–83; capital investments necessary in, 32–33; equitable production in, 70–71; genetically modified (GM) corn in, 218–19, 253n32; hopes for new system in, 72–73; as key to national security, 199–200; number of US citizens working in, 3;